D0364029

Royal Horticultural Society

LIBRARIES NI
WITHDRAWN FROM STOCK

GROWING VEGETABLES & HERBS

MITCHELL BEAZLEY

RHS GROWING VEGETABLES & HERBS

First published in Great Britain in 2011 by Mitchell Beazley,
an imprint of Octopus Publishing Group Ltd, Endeavour House,
189 Shaftesbury Avenue, London WC2H 8JY
www.octopusbooks.co.uk

An Hachette UK Company
www.hachette.co.uk

Published in association with The Royal Horticultural Society

Reprinted 2012

This edition published 2013

Design and layout copyright © Octopus Publishing Group Ltd 2011, 2013
Text copyright © The Royal Horticultural Society 2011, 2013

All rights reserved. No part of this work may be reproduced or utilised in any form or by any means, electronic or mechanical, including photocopying, recording or by any information storage and retrieval system, without the prior written permission of the publishers.

The publishers will be grateful for any information that will assist them in keeping future editions up to date. Although all reasonable care has been taken in the preparation of this book, neither the publishers nor the authors can accept any liability for any consequence arising from the use thereof, or the information contained therein.

ISBN: 978 1 84533 782 7

A CIP record for this book is available from the British Library

Set in Gill Sans and Minion
Printed and bound in China

Author Guy Barter
Publisher Lorraine Dickey
Commissioning Editor Helen Griffin
Senior Editor Leanne Bryan
Copy-editors Helen Griffin, Joanna Chisholm
Proofreader Helen Ridge
Indexer Helen Snaith
Art Directors Jonathan Christie, Pene Parker
Senior Art Editor Juliette Norsworthy
Designer Two Associates
Picture Research Manager Giulia Hetherington
Production Manager Peter Hunt
RHS Commissioning Editor Rae Spencer-Jones

CONTENTS

WHY GROW YOUR OWN?

Inexpensive food, available all year round, has become everyone's birthright, or so it seems. Fortunately, home-grown vegetables and, especially, herbs can be astonishingly cheap to grow. A packet of lettuce, for example, fertilised with home-made compost can provide summer salads for very little money. That said, costs can soon rise when nets, fleece and slug controls are bought – this book tells growers how to minimise these costs.

There is a great deal of exercise, pleasure and satisfaction to be had from growing your own. Although the physical effort of vegetable growing peaks in summer, there is much that can be done in winter to prepare for the summer scramble. This book also tries to help the grower with ideas about how to spread the work through the year.

Being outside and working with plants also seems to touch a human need and brings great satisfaction to many people. It is sociable, too: swapping tips and plants, and sharing seeds builds bridges between people.

Freshness and flavour decline very quickly after harvesting crops, so where time and space are limited, gardeners get most satisfaction from growing vegetables, whose freshness is highly valued. Growing your own herbs is also especially satisfying, as the enjoyment of herbs is all about flavour.

Home production also assures consumers that the produce has been grown in ways that they are happy with. Examples of this include low pesticide use, lack of excessive packaging, and no exploitation of labour.

For many people, the cost of commercial food production to the environment – the large amounts of water, fuel and non-renewable resources involved – is too high. However, produce grown by organic and other 'natural' growing methods, such as biodynamic, commands a premium price.

Fortunately, organic produce is by definition especially easy to grow at home, where the non-chemical methods of pest and disease control and plant nutrition are so much easier to follow than on a commercial scale. Natural growing systems do not put plants under pressure, and the care lavished on them when grown on a small scale leads to healthy plants that are troubled little by pests and diseases. In fact, as long as

A well-stocked plot like this one will not only provide an abundance of fresh and tasty produce but is also an opportunity for exercise and getting closer to the natural world.

the problems do not actually kill the plant or damage the usable portion, they can usually be tolerated.

Natural assistance

Unbeknown to many gardeners, nature works to help them almost all the time. Natural predators, parasites and diseases suppress pests, and diseases require quite specific conditions in order to infect. While in the soil, natural processes work to provide a limited but significant natural increase in fertility, if given a chance. For these reasons, modern vegetable and herb growers intervene much less frequently with synthetic materials than was once the case. Indeed, many of the powerful chemicals that were once thought essential are no longer available to home gardeners, while others with less obvious effects are now offered. Although this is for the most part good, it does leave gardeners at the mercy of remedies that actually have no proven effect. This book tries to help growers avoid these, while suggesting the best of the newer materials and methods on offer. However, from time to time growers will be obliged to accept that a certain percentage of their crops might sometimes be lost, or even that some crops cannot be grown in their garden. This is a small price to pay to garden in a way that benefits our environment rather than degrades it.

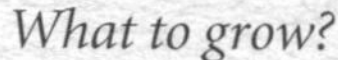

What to grow?

Salads, peas and beans are popular candidates, and in winter fresh leeks, crisp crinkly savoys and kale sprouts are flavoursome alternatives to white cabbages and root vegetables.

Seasonality is an important facet of growing your own. Learning to anticipate and relish seasonal treats is especially noteworthy when you have grown them yourself.

With all these good reasons to grow, what holds people back? All too often it is a lack of skill, confidence and access to land. This book aims to address the first two issues, but access to land is not so straightforward.

It was once the case that most people would have been familiar with at least some aspects of gardening, but this faded until, relatively recently, gardening in schools became much more

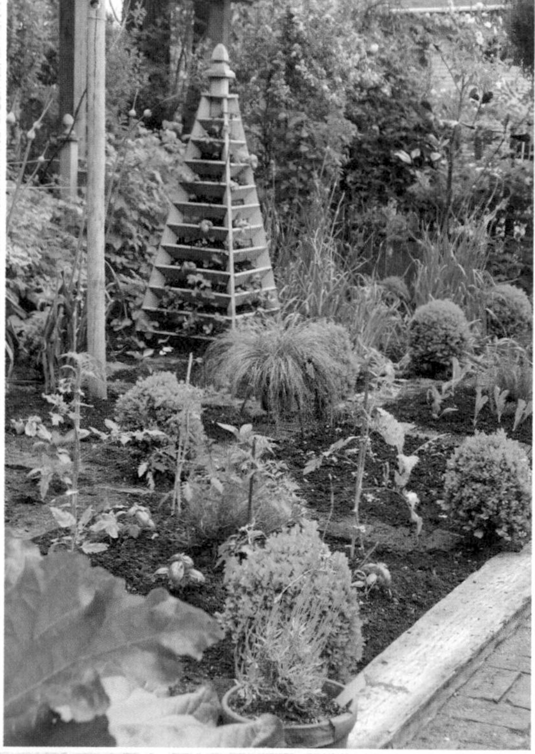

A great deal can be grown in small, easy-to-access beds.

Green tomatoes can be made into chutney or ripened indoors.

information on offer confuses people – which information is best and who should be believed? This book accepts that there is usually more than one way to achieve a desired end. While suggesting alternatives, it also offers at least one reasonably certain technique in sufficient detail so that informed choices can be made.

Despite national initiatives to share land with gardeners and make more

widespread. There is evidence that the skills acquired by children at school are taken home and passed on to parents and other adults.

Another factor is that books, videos and web-based information have made access to the knowledge needed to grow vegetables much more widespread. It could be that the very quantity of the

allotments available to a wider group of people, shrinking garden sizes and the development of back gardens mean that access to land is still a major issue. In the meantime, there is much that can be done on quite small areas of ground, or even in containers, that will make a difference to both your diet and your lifestyle.

RULES & TOOLS

• CLIMATE & LOCAL WEATHER CONDITIONS •

Commercial growers are extremely picky about the soil and site in which they choose to grow their crops – it is the difference between profit and failure. Home gardeners usually have to work with what they have and choose crops to suit. To make the best of a garden, it has to be 'read' to see the possibilities and the drawbacks.

CLIMATE

Weather is what is going on at any given time and this builds up to a longer-term climate. Weather is very variable and hard to predict, but that does not matter. It is the pattern of the seasons and the average weather that influences how we garden. This pattern is reasonably stable so that gardeners know the range of

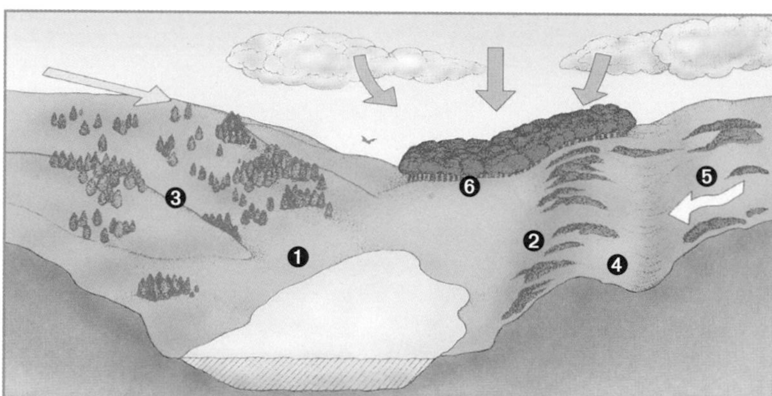

MIXED CLIMATE CAUSED BY LOCAL CONDITIONS

In this localised climate, the lake shore ❶ has a mild climate due to the water's influence. Slope ❷ gets more sun than north-facing slope ❸. Frost pockets ❹ form as cold air is trapped by the ridge. The hilltop ❺ is cooler due to the effect of altitude and wind. The woodland shelters the field ❻ from the prevailing wind.

Wind protection is as important as temperature, and even a modest hedge can speed up the maturity of early crops by up to two weeks.

what can happen in individual seasons in terms of sunlight, temperatures, rainfall and windiness and, therefore, can plan accordingly.

LOCATION

Climate is significantly modified by location. Near the sea, the summer peaks in temperature are reduced by the time it takes for water to warm up in summer, and as the water loses heat slowly in winter, this reduces the severity of winter cold. Inland, far from the sea, the opposite occurs: summer peaks are higher and winter chills colder.

MICROCLIMATE

On a smaller scale, more sunlight and warmth are trapped by south-facing slopes than by north-facing ones, so growth begins and ends earlier in the year, and growth rates are higher, especially in winter when sunlight is limited. In addition, cold air drains

MICROCLIMATE

A typical west-facing back garden shows many variations in microclimate that can all be exploited by the gardener. Here there are two sunny, sheltered walls: one at the back of the house ❶, which is ideal for tender plants in pots; and another alongside the garage ❷, which is home to a wall-trained apricot tree. The sunniest spots away from the walls are reserved for the patio, lawn, glasshouse, vegetable patch and small wildlife pond. The tree ❸ at the front of the house casts a lot of early morning shade, while the alleyway ❹ at the side of the house acts as a wind tunnel, affecting the bed on the right of the garden. The fence on this side casts shade most of the day, so the border ❺ is filled with shade-lovers. The compost heap ❻ is in a cool, shaded position.

from slopes as it is heavier than warm air. Slopes are, therefore, usually better for growing than valley bottoms, where frosts are more frequent and more severe.

Altitude is another factor. With every 300m (1,000ft) rise in altitude, there is a fall in average temperature of 0.5°C (1°F), so that gardens in hilly regions are not only windier but colder, too. Plant growth is directly related to temperature, so slower growth can be expected.

Most British gardens are sheltered by hedges and fences, which is useful as wind is the most damaging aspect of our weather. If there is no shelter, erect windbreaks to protect crops (see p56).

SUN & SHADE

In smaller gardens, shade influences what you grow and how. Vegetables do not flourish in shade, and herbs usually require full sun to produce their fullest flavours. However, where there is more than six hours of sun per day in midsummer, most crops will do fairly well.

Trees not only cast shade but their roots can extend for up to three times the height of the tree. These roots are concentrated within the top 90cm (2¾ft) of soil and are most dense wherever the soil is fertile, moist and free of competing grass, which robs tree roots of rain.

MODIFYING THE MICROCLIMATE

Gardeners can modify the growing conditions within a garden. On a grand scale, walled gardens with sunny walls, shaded areas and offering year-round shelter were traditionally used. Although few gardeners will build walled gardens now, sunny sheltered borders or patio areas for potted crops can be used. Raised beds with the soil mounded and raked so that the surface gently slopes to the south will catch more light and warmth in spring. Shallow trenches roofed with cloches, fleece or polythene can make economical temporary 'glasshouses' for tender and early crops. In fact, polythene spread on the surface will warm the soil and trap moisture in it. Clear polythene is best, but black is also effective if stretched taut with close contact to level soil and will also suppress weeds. A sandwich of clear or black plastic is best. Tricks like these are especially practical in small gardens and can greatly increase their productivity.

Well-spaced crops need room to grow, and wigwams should be strategically set where they won't cast undue shade.

OVERWET SOILS

After wind damage, lack of drainage is the commonest factor reducing vegetable and, especially, herb growth. In winter, wet soil cannot be worked, causing delays in spring planting and sowing. In summer, overwet soils can quickly kill plants, and even short periods of this can reduce growth, increase root disease and lead to high slug populations. In autumn, root vegetables will be hard to harvest without damage, and crops will rot if left in the wet ground, to gather in winter.

One solution is pipe drainage, where perforated pipes are laid 40–50cm (16–20in) below ground and covered with gravel or a geotextile, to avoid silting up the drains. Where pipe drainage cannot be undertaken, building raised beds, 15–45cm (6–18in) high, depending on the degree of drainage required, is a very effective remedy.

SEASONS

More than most plants, vegetables and herbs are intensely seasonal. Light levels and warmth peak in early and midsummer. Fair light and plenty of warmth occur in late summer, but by early autumn growth slows markedly, and in mid-autumn, light levels and warmth decline and growth is negligible until early next spring. In spring, cold nights and limited light slow growth, but it is vital to establish the year's crops in the ground, seedbeds or pots in the glasshouse during this period.

Many gardeners find it more economical and convenient to buy their plants from nurseries and, for example, use onion sets rather than seed – all this gets the ground covered for that vital summer period. It follows also that winter and, indeed, spring supplies of vegetables and herbs need to be sown the preceding spring and summer respectively, and do most of their growing before winter.

Spring crops such as purple sprouting broccoli need to be big enough to respond to rising warmth and light levels in mid- to late spring. There are usually 'windows' of about two to three weeks for many gardening tasks, after which, results will be disappointing. If this sounds a daunting situation, the calendar on pp180–184 will help you plan ahead, so that windows of good weather can be optimised.

• UNDERSTANDING YOUR SOIL •

Soil can be simply managed to ensure it is well supplied with water and nutrients that are essential for good crops.

Soil is made up of mineral granules, which vary in texture: coarse, as in sand; very fine, as in clay; or intermediate in size, as in silt. The character of the soil is determined by which size of particle dominates.

TYPES OF SOIL

Water and nutrients quickly drain through sandy soils, which dry out in summer and need heavy and repeated feeding during the growing season.

Clay soils retain water and nutrients but drain slowly. Although they require little watering and feeding, it is often hard to get plants established in clay soils ready for the peak summer growing season.

Silt soils hold water and nutrients nearly as well as clays but they drain much more readily. However, silt is unstable and the soil will be damaged if it is worked when wet.

The ideal soil – loam – consists of enough sand and silt to keep it open and free-draining, but also enough clay to retain nutrients and water. Loam is rare in gardens or allotments. Soils where sand predominates are called light; where clay predominates, heavy.

Soil has, for practical purposes, two layers: topsoil, which is dark, rich in nutrients and soil organisms, friable and ramified with plant roots; and subsoil, which is usually pale, has few roots and soil organisms and lacks nutrients, tends to be airless and will not support good crops. Topsoil is usually 15–30cm (6–12in) deep and vegetables require 25cm (10in) of reasonable soil for good growth, although herbs are less demanding. The subsoil may be a few centimetres deep to over a metre and often rests on bedrock.

Organic matter is present in modest amounts in most cultivated soils, about two percent, but has a disproportionate effect on the soil. It binds the soil particles into lumps, officially called peds, which make even solid, impenetrable clay more open. Even where clay does not dominate, organic matter binds what clay and silt there is into these valuable lumps through which roots and water can move. Much of the manuring and digging done by gardeners is to make and preserve these soil particles. A common feature of gardens is that the process of house building can damage soil.

Acid or alkaline?

Soil can be acid or alkaline and this is measured with pH test kits or meters. The pH scale goes from 1–14, with pH1 being intensely acid and pH14 very alkaline. Most soils fall in the range of pH5 to pH8. Some nutrients are unavailable in alkaline soils. At low pH levels, nutrients are available but aluminium and other ions are soluble in acid soils and these harm plants. Soil has a natural tendency to become more acid under the influence of rain.

There is no realistic remedy for most alkaline soils, but acid soils can cheaply and easily be modified by adding lime. More lime is needed to neutralise acid clay soils than sandy soils due to the buffering effect of the clays. Test kits are often sufficiently accurate for use by gardeners, but a laboratory test will give precise results and guidance for how much lime to add. Liming materials must be finely ground and take at least a year to have their full effect, even if they are mixed into the soil.

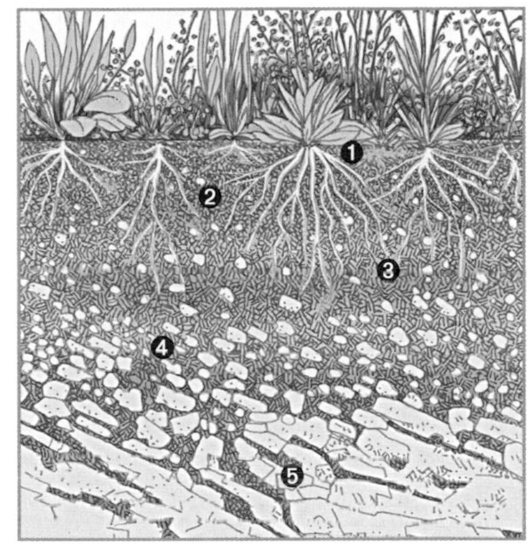

A TYPICAL SOIL PROFILE

❶ *humus layer* ❷ *topsoil* ❸ *subsoil* ❹ *bedrock fragments* ❺ *bedrock*

ASSESSING YOUR SOIL

Looking at soil is the first step. Digging a pit 60cm (24in) deep, or until impenetrable subsoil is encountered, and about 60cm (24in) square will reveal the depth of the topsoil and the nature of the subsoil. If hard, solid-looking areas without plant roots are found, then there is a compaction problem and this hard region must be disrupted, usually by digging to a suitable depth. Another indicator of a hard area, known as a pan, is horizontal root growth.

The soil particles in the extracted soil can also be revealing. If friable and crumb-like, they should support good root growth and allow roots to extract water and nutrients from within the particles. If large, hard lumps, blocks or flakes are found, much of the water and nutrients will be unavailable to plants, so digging, adding organic matter and leaving dug soil exposed to frosts and drying will be necessary to improve the particle structure.

Drainage

Sour smells and grey soil colour can indicate poor drainage. To confirm this, fill the hole with water, cover against rain and leave to soak away overnight. If the water has not drained within 24 hours, poor drainage must be remedied.

Numbers of earthworms exposed in digging the hole are also revealing. Few worms present suggest a poor soil that will require generous manuring and cultivation. Abundant worms (80–120 per square metre/yard) indicate a soil rich in organic matter.

Soil nutrient status and pH only change slowly in response to use by plants and it is worth having soil analysed every four years for the main nutrients: nitrogen, phosphorus and potassium and magnesium. A pH test is also a good idea.

COMMON SOIL TYPES

Clay soils are made up of very small particles that stick together, making drainage and air penetration slow.

Sandy soils consist of relatively large particles. Water drains easily and there is plenty of air for plant roots.

Silty soils contain medium-sized particles that can be sticky and heavy but are quite nutrient-rich.

WATER AND WATERING

In theory, there is sufficient rain to grow good crops in Britain without watering. In practice, drought at sowing or planting time can devastate plants, and dry spells at certain stages, when peas are in flower, for example, can do irreparable damage to yields. Timely watering at these periods can make all the difference. Conversely, watering at other times will often not give benefits that match the cost and effort of doing so. Crops on sandy soils are much more vulnerable than those on clay soils.

ANALYSING YOUR SOIL

Sampling is the first and most vital step in soil analysis of a new and unknown plot. Take a sample before any fertiliser or manure is applied to the ground.

Collect soil to a depth of 15cm (6in) with a trowel and place it in a bucket while walking in a 'w' shaped path across the plot. Since garden soil can vary markedly within a short distance, at least 25 samples may be required, especially if there are obvious differences in soil appearance or a known history of differences in the area.

Mix the bucket of soil very carefully and bag up a representative sample and send it for analysis.

Laboratories that analyse soil samples for amateur gardeners will provide an interpretation of the results.

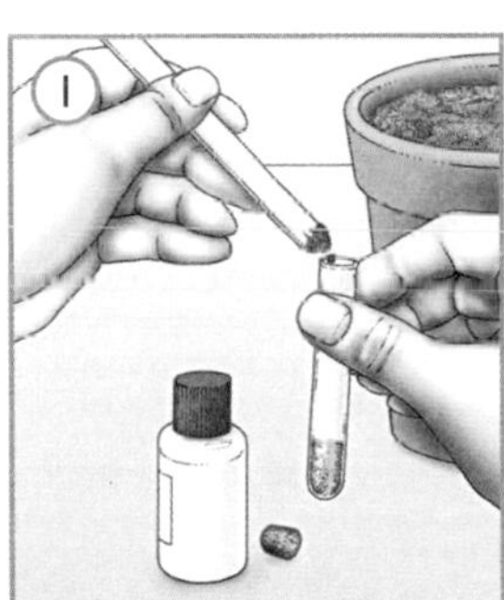

Place a small, random sample of soil from different parts of your garden in the receptacle.

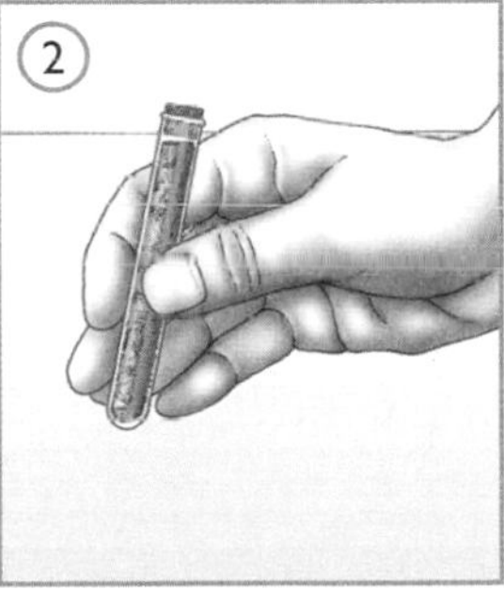

Shake the sample in the solution provided. The solution will change colour according to the soil's pH.

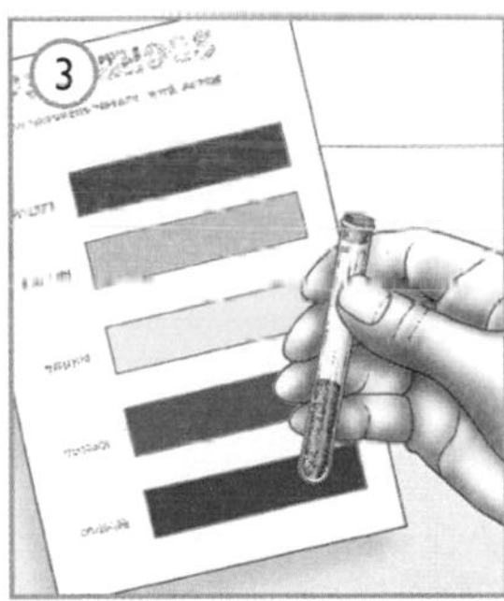

Plants grow best when the soil is slightly acid (pH6.5), while very acid soil (pH5.5) often limits growth.

• PLANNING YOUR PLOT •

Because of the very seasonal nature of vegetable and herb culture, it is well to have a plan of what you want to grow, how much you will need and when certain key stages are reached: sowing dates, planting dates, harvesting and so on. Everyone has their own methods but an annual 'cropping plan' of the plot on squared paper, marked up with what is to go where and when, is easy to arrange and can be taken into the garden for reference. A written plan helps avoid growing the same crop in the same place, which can encourage the build-up of soilborne pests and diseases.

For larger plots, more than 20 square metres (yards), a crop rotation is worth carrying out. Crops are grown in rotation so that any piece of the plot only bears crops prone to soilborne troubles once every three or more years. For small plots, rotation is more trouble than it is worth and growing things where most convenient should be satisfactory.

CROP ROTATION

Rotations are a tool with which to plan and maintain your garden and help manage pests and diseases – they can be adapted to fit individual needs, local climate and soil types.

Three-year crop rotation plan

A common crop rotation is a three-course one with the plot divided into three equal parts, with each part grouped in rotation with:

- Year one – cabbage family crops
- Year two – potatoes and tomatoes
- Year three – everything else, including parsnips, carrots and other root crops, celery, salads, the onion family including leeks and garlic, peas and beans.

Four-year crop rotation plan

A four-year rotation, when fewer potatoes are needed, involves dividing the plot into four areas:

- Year 1 – potatoes and tomatoes
- Year 2 – parsnips, carrots and other root crops, celery, salads, onion family including leeks and garlic
- Year 3 – peas, beans of all sorts
- Year 4 – cabbage family crops.

- Courgettes, pumpkins, squash, sweet corn are largely free of soilborne ailments and can be fitted in anywhere.

The important point is that certain crops – especially potatoes and tomatoes, which get potato cyst nematode; the cabbage family, which suffers from the fungal disease club root; and the onion family, which gets fungal white rot – are grown with at least two years between them. Although this helps slow down the development of problems and can aid in management to keep losses to an acceptable level, the resting cysts or spores of these troubles can survive in the soil for 10 years or more. So rotation should be viewed as a partial remedy and is best backed up by growing resistant cultivars and following strict crop hygiene, with the destruction of all infected plants and roots. In gardens, crop rotations are ineffective against airborne diseases and pests that fly.

Crop rotations have other advantages: it is easier to fit in cultivation and organise manuring if similar crops with similar requirements are grown close together. It is also possible that crops use different nutrients, and varying the cropping will avoid undue depletion of a particular nutrient.

THREE-YEAR CROP ROTATION PLAN

	AREA 1	AREA 2	AREA 3
YEAR 1	Cabbage family crops	Potatoes and tomatoes	Roots, peas and beans, and everything else
YEAR 2	Potatoes and tomatoes	Roots, peas and beans, and everything else	Cabbage family crops
YEAR 3	Roots, peas and beans, and everything else	Cabbage family crops	Potatoes and tomatoes

• PLANNING YOUR CROPS •

Another advantage of a well-planned crop rotation system is that bare, unused ground can be identified and used to grow a quick-growing, early-maturing crop, such as rocket salad leaves in spring or Chinese leaves for autumn cutting. This is known as catch cropping.

Another ruse is to use the gaps between widely spaced slow-growing plants, such as Brussels sprouts, to grow some radishes or turnips that will be gathered before the Brussels sprouts shade them.

COMPANION PLANTING

Certain combinations of plants are believed to assist each other by repelling or deterring pests, helping each other acquire nutrients, attract pollinators and other beneficial insects, and providing other mutual benefits. Although there is evidence to support these practices, the benefits are not easily predictable and often cannot be reproduced. An example is the practice of planting onions and carrots, with five rows of onions to one row of carrots. This is reported to be sometimes effective in reducing carrot root fly damage.

Organic gardening guides give a wide range of plants and companions, and, as long as companion plants do not compete with crops, there is no drawback to trying these methods, other than the cost and work involved.

INTERPLANTING VEGETABLE CROPS

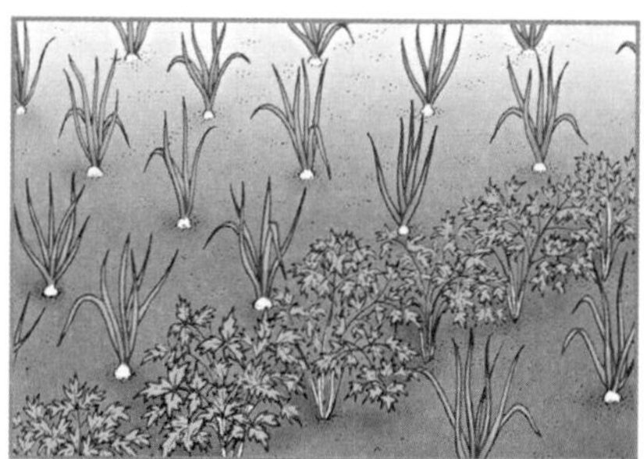

Carrot root fly is thought to be deterred by the smell of onions, so one row of carrots is often planted to every four rows of onions.

To reduce aphid and root fly damage, alternate rows of cabbages and French beans are planted. Both crops are planted at the same size so that one does not dominate.

INTERCROPPING

The gaps between slow-growing crops can be planted with fast-maturing crops that are harvested before they present any competition. Slow-growing leeks and speedy spinach are ideal partners, as are parsnips and radishes.

Clover deters pests from attacking cauliflowers.

Companion plants are effective when they cover the bare soil around crops, as pests are less able to find crop plants against a green background. Clover, when trimmed and managed, is a good plant to grow around brassicas to help prevent cabbage root fly damage, for example.

• TOOLS & EQUIPMENT •

High-quality handmade tools with forged steel heads and strong wooden handles are a pleasure to work with and will last a lifetime. Cheap ones made of thin pressed steel will do the job, but they are likely to wear out and may break at a critical time.

A spade of stainless steel is generally the most useful tool, and taller gardeners will appreciate long-handled ones, while slightly built gardeners could try lightweight spades with fibreglass shafts.

Garden forks are nearly as useful as spades, especially for clay soils, while hand forks might be convenient for working between and around herbs.

A seed rake is ideal for drawing and covering grooves (drills) in the soil when sowing seeds, while a broad hay, or landscapers' rake, is better for levelling large areas.

The Dutch push hoe, or variations such as push–pull hoes, are the best weed control method on most soils, but the swan-necked draw hoe with a chopping action comes into its own on stiff or stony soils and for tasks such as seed sowing and earthing up potatoes. Wide hoes for quick work and narrow ones for closely spaced crops are good investments.

Trowels are essential for planting and weeding around plants.

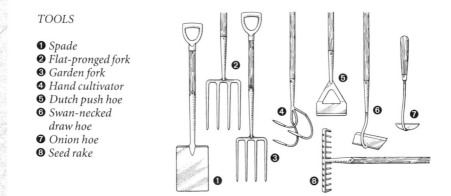

TOOLS

❶ *Spade*
❷ *Flat-pronged fork*
❸ *Garden fork*
❹ *Hand cultivator*
❺ *Dutch push hoe*
❻ *Swan-necked draw hoe*
❼ *Onion hoe*
❽ *Seed rake*

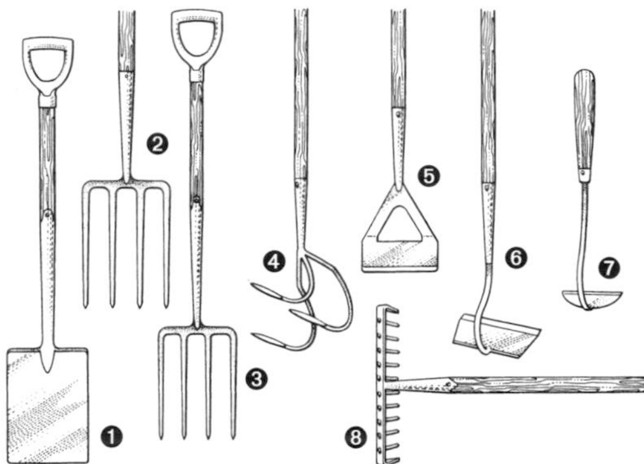

A wheelbarrow is essential: robust, lightweight garden ones rival the heavier, clumsier, but cheaper, builders' barrows for efficiency.

Watering equipment usually consists of hosepipes – brass snap-fittings and braided pipes will save a lot of frustration – and if sprinklers are to be used, choose ones with a spike that can be trodden into the ground. Fine and coarse roses will be needed for both pipes and watering cans, and an extension lance for the hosepipe will help where watering at height is needed.

Some forms of protection to get seeds and seedlings off to a good start and help heat-loving crops in summer are invaluable – horticultural fleece is now the most widely used material for this purpose. Other options for plant protection include glasshouses, cold frames and cloches (see p55).

A small 3-litre (2/3-gallon) sprayer is sufficient for most gardeners – a powerful jet of water can hinder many pests. To avoid accidents, a separate, well-labelled, sprayer is a wise precaution for gardeners who use weedkillers.

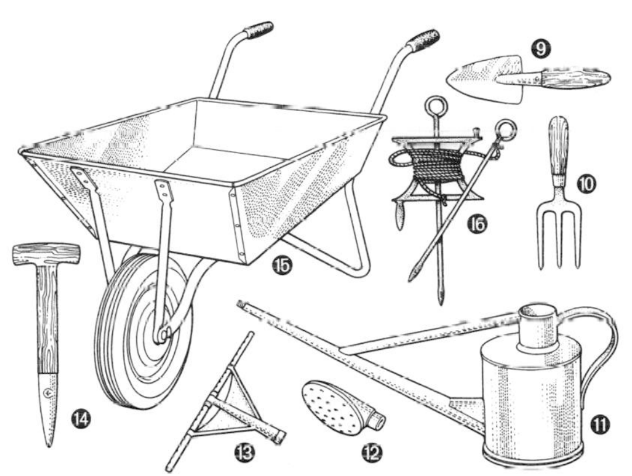

9 *Trowel*
10 *Hand fork*
11 *Watering can*
12 *Brass rose*
13 *Dribble bar*
14 *Dibber*
15 *Wheelbarrow*
16 *Garden line*

Finally, a shed of some description to hold equipment and store produce will be needed. However, if you have little room, space-saving stackable boxes with plenty of ventilation are readily available.

BASIC
TECHNIQUES

• PREPARING THE GROUND •

Digging is mainly done to kill weeds and, to a certain extent, to remove compaction, which impedes drainage and root penetration. It is also used to incorporate lime and manure, so they work quickly and effectively, and to loosen the soil to aid sowing and planting. Complete digging by mid-spring to avoid soil moisture loss.

DIGGING TECHNIQUES

For the initial digging, mark the ground into two equal halves using string and pegs. Then dig a 30cm (12in) wide trench, a spade deep, across the end of one of the halves. Place the excavated soil beside the same end of the other half. Dig down the first half and back up the second until the original soil is reached. Use this to fill the trench.

There should be a clear area of about 30cm (12in) between the dug soil and the upturned soil so the spade is not moving already dug ground and there is room to bury manure and debris. Insert the spade at a slight angle to lift a slice of earth and invert it so the original surface is buried. The slice can get ragged and burial of weeds and manure incomplete, so an initial cut, 5cm (2in) deep, can be made on one or both sides of the slice to ensure it comes away cleanly.

When there is too much debris or too many weeds to handle, remove these with a hoe and compost separately. Lift any turf with a spade and bury it upside down in the digging trench or remove it, stack it upside down, cover in black plastic and leave it to rot down into friable loam.

Although weeds can be cleared by digging, it is often more effective to kill

A fork is more suited to digging sticky soil than a spade.

GETTING THE SOIL READY FOR CULTIVATION

Cultivate the soil in spring using a hand cultivator or rake to break up any large clods. Work to a depth of about 15–20cm (6–8in) using a backwards and forwards motion. Remove weeds and debris as you do so.

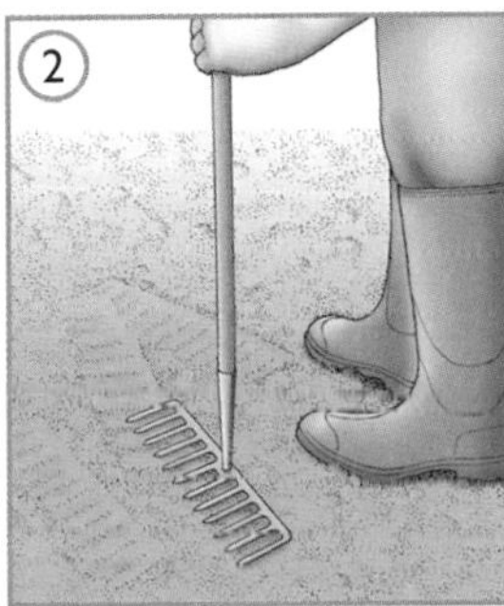

Consolidate the soil by breaking up any clods with the head of a rake. Use the rake to fill any depressions with soil, but do not overwork the soil. Where possible, do not tread on the soil unless it is light and 'fluffy'.

Apply a general-purpose fertiliser by spreading a base dressing evenly over the newly cultivated soil. Work the fertiliser into the top 10–15cm (4–6in) of the soil using a hand cultivator or rake.

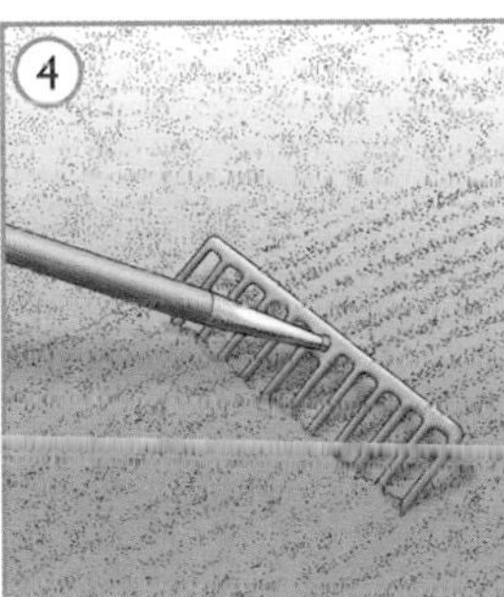

Level the surface with the rake to produce a final, level tilth. Move the rake backwards and forwards with as little movement as possible, keeping the teeth of the rake only just in the soil surface.

them with glyphosate-based weedkillers or by covering the soil with opaque material, such as black plastic, for a growing season.

If weeds are dead or absent and there is no requirement to incorporate manure or lime into your plot, then digging can be dispensed with. Compaction can be eliminated by loosening the soil with a fork, and the necessary loose surface needed for sowing or planting can be achieved with a hoe or cultivator. This is often lighter work than normal digging yet it still prepares the soil to support good crop growth.

Digging deeper than 25cm (10in), using double digging for example, is not essential and may be impossible if there is a rocky or solid clay subsoil. However, where possible, it may be worth attempting to extend the rooting zone and, therefore, access to soil moisture in light soils. Other situations where deeper digging is helpful include

Mulches of organic matter feed crops and can control weeds along with digging and hoeing.

before planting long-lived crowns of asparagus, which root to a great depth and need rich deep soil, making raised beds, and before no-dig regimes, where the improved soil will remain uncompacted indefinitely because trampling is avoided.

In double digging, a trench is excavated (as for ordinary digging) after marking out the plot with string and pegs as before, but this time the trench is 60cm (24in) wide and the base of the trench is broken up with a fork and, ideally, enriched with organic matter. Another 60cm (24in) trench is then excavated and placed over the newly enriched subsoil. The base of the new trench is now treated as before, and so on, until the plot is entirely dug.

Rotavators are also capable of replacing digging where efficient burial of weeds or materials is not required.

NO-DIG GARDENING

No-digging methods, also called no-plough or no-till cultivation, are common in farming and have been found to improve root growth, although there is limited uptake of the method due to weed problems. No-digging works best on heavy clay soils. Light sandy soils tend to slump without annual digging. Weeds can be removed by hand or by weedkiller, or, better, prevented by mulching. This is done, ideally, every year, with plenty of well-rotted organic matter, although opaque weed control membranes can sometimes be used.

The full benefits of this powerful cultural technique might not become apparent for several years. By then. surface weed seeds should gradually have died out, no dormant weed seeds will have been brought to the surface, and the organic matter will have been carried down to enrich the earth at depth by soil organisms, including worms, whose burrowing maintains the soil's porosity.

• GROWING IN RAISED BEDS •

Modern small-scale vegetable gardens can often be most easily managed by bed systems where 1–1.5m (3–5ft) wide beds are separated by 40–50cm (16–20in) wide paths. The paths allow easy access to the whole bed from both sides, and the short rows are highly convenient when sowing small blocks or rows of crops. Because all traffic is kept to the paths, there is no soil compaction and less need to dig or loosen the soil. Plants can be spaced slightly closer (about 10 percent) than usual because extra light will reach them from the paths.

Raising the beds enhances drainage and eases management, but at the price of a greater need for watering in dry spells – especially if the beds are raised to 15cm (6in) or more. However, raised beds are most useful for clay soils, where drought stress is less common than with other soils and where there is a greater need for drainage, and for avoiding the heavy labour of digging.

Vegetables and especially herbs can also be grown in containers. Indeed, many vegetables such as French beans, peppers and tomatoes are sufficiently decorative to earn a place on the patio. As long as sufficient depth and adequate drainage are present, the actual shape of the container does not matter. A minimum container depth of 40cm (16in) is ideal to avoid severe difficulties in watering, but smaller soil volumes, as in growing bags for example, are feasible where careful and frequent watering is possible. Depths greater than 60cm (2ft) are unlikely to be vital so use lightweight

CONTAINERS FOR CROPS

Growing bags

Cheap and effective but shallow, so they might need watering twice or more each day during spells of hot weather.

Tubs, planters and large pots

Easy to water and manage but costly to fill with a good-quality growing medium.

Fish boxes

The polystyrene boxes used by fishmongers and grocers to supply chilled food make good planters for salads and other small crops.

Planting a different crop in each square neatly allows small spaces to be used effectively.

broken-up polystyrene as a free-draining filler in very deep containers.

The results from peat-free potting media are usually acceptable, and most gardeners wish to support the peat-free media industry as it strives to find a substitute for endangered peat.

Soil-based potting media such as John Innes No 3 would be perfect if they were all made to the original recipe, but as good loam is scarce, these media can no longer be relied on. Home-made soil-based potting media (of two parts garden soil and one part well-rotted organic matter, with added fertiliser) can give good results but the garden soil may contain diseases and weed seeds.

Containers will need much more watering than crops in the ground, not least because they can be planted more densely due to light reaching them from around the pot. Liquid feeding with soluble fertiliser is also likely to be necessary. Organic liquid fertilisers are usually too weak to be fully effective, so organic growers should add well-rotted manure to containers.

Just one potato tuber planted in a used compost sack yields a very useful crop.

• SOIL MANAGEMENT •

Managing soil is one of the most interesting and rewarding aspects of vegetable growing. Carbon dioxide in the air and water in the soil are the raw materials from which plants are made. The soil must also provide nutrients, especially nitrogen, phosphorus and potassium, and nearly as much sulphur, calcium and magnesium, and small, trace amounts of boron, copper, iron, manganese, molybdenum and zinc. Some vegetables, such as beetroot and carrots, need sodium as well. Fortunately, soil, especially if well supplied with additions of bulky organic matter, usually supplies enough trace elements and calcium and sulphur, and a very large proportion of the nitrogen, phosphorus and potassium required by mosts vegetable crops.

Nutrients move very slowly through the soil, and roots usually have to seek them out. Although fertilisers can be added near the plant, this is expensive and, in fact, not a feasible option for organic growers.

HOW TO IMPROVE THE SOIL

Although it is possible to grow vegetables without adding organic matter to any soils bar very sandy ones, it is much harder. Traditionally, this has been done at a convenient part of the rotation (see pp22–23) every three to four years. While this might be enough for fertile soils and long-established, well-manured gardens, many new vegetable gardens need organic matter additions every other year or even annually if the content is to be significantly raised. Most cultivated soils have about two percent organic matter – a bare minimum. Double this is ideal.

The catch is that organic matter rots down in the soil, but little of it is retained to improve the soil structure in the long term. As it decomposes, the added organic matter supplies nutrients and enhances the soil's water capacity – a good manure dressing (two bucketfuls per square metre/yard) will store the equivalent of about 50mm (2in) of rain. However, it is difficult to get the best results from crops that need heavy feeding without using fertilisers. These are more concentrated than organic matter and are especially valuable in spring, when organic matter decomposes slowly in the cold soil, and when surplus nitrogen and, to a lesser extent, other nutrients have been washed away by winter rain.

GREEN MANURES

Green manures are crops that are grown to be dug into the soil. Quick-growing

ORGANIC MATTER

Garden compost
Cheap, very effective but hard to make in sufficient quantities

Mushroom compost
Cheap, if you live close to a mushroom farm

Farmyard manure
Available in livestock-farming areas but can contain weed seeds

Straw
Compost with nitrogen fertiliser

Municipal compost
Composted green waste good if not twiggy or riddled with plastics

green manures, such as mustard and fodder radish, are sown and used in a short period, about eight weeks, between mid-spring and early autumn They capture and retain plant nutrients otherwise washed out of the soil by winter rains, releasing them as the plants rot the following spring to feed new crops.

LEAFMOULD

Fallen leaves are a free and often abundant resource that can be stacked for several years to rot into leafmould or added in moderation to compost bins, where they will rot down more quickly. For growing vegetables, composted leaves are as good as leafmould proper.

GROWING A GREEN MANURE CROP

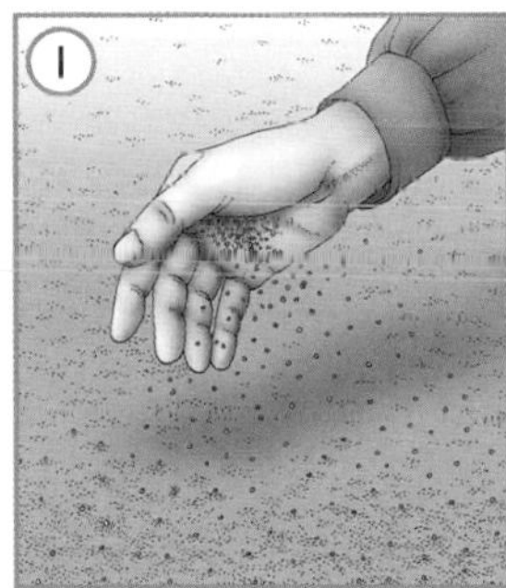

Sow seeds in rows or scatter over the ground. They will grow quickly to cover the soil.

Chop the foliage down when the land is needed or when the green manure is beginning to mature.

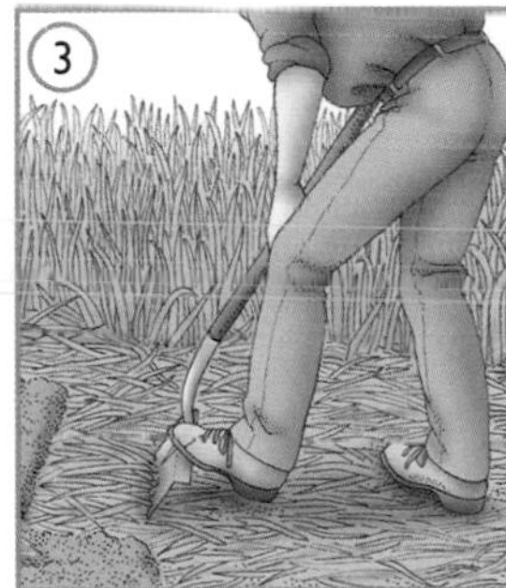

Leave the clippings to wilt, then dig them into the soil. As they rot, they will release nutrients.

TURNING THE COMPOST HEAP

Plant remains decay naturally – without our help. Micro-organisms help this process in the heap, and as their numbers grow, so does the rate of decomposition. Assist the process by turning the heap to let the air penetrate.

When adding new material, break up large clumps with a fork. Introduce more oxygen months later by removing the material from the heap and mixing it with a fork.

FERTILISERS

Fertiliser nutrient content is usually printed on the packet as percentages of nitrogen (N), phosphorus oxide (P) and potassium oxide (K). Avoid fertilisers sold without a stated nutrient content. Organic fertilisers often have a low nutrient content, as the essence of organic growing is that the soil is fed, not the plants. If done well, the reduced yield of organic crops

MAKING LEAFMOULD

Collect leaves after rain when they are moist. Rake them up or shred them with a lawnmower.

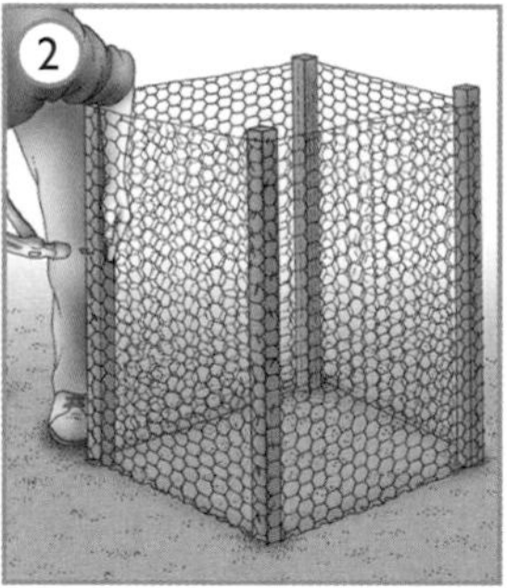

Make a container for the leaves. Hammer four posts into the ground and staple wire netting to them.

Fill the container with leaves, watering if dry. Leaves decay slowly by fungal action over 1–2 years.

FERTILISER TERMS EXPLAINED

Balanced fertiliser contains more or less equal amounts of nutrients

Base dressing solid fertilisers mixed into the soil before sowing and planting to feed crops as they grow

Compound or general fertiliser contains two or more nutrients

Controlled-release fertiliser releases nutrients over a pre-determined period

Foliar feeds fertiliser applied to the leaves and absorbed into the plants; stimulates growth where roots or soil are in poor condition

Liquid fertiliser nutrients dissolved in water and poured onto the plants' roots; ideal for containers and good for emergency feeding

Topdressing fertilisers sprinkled around crops to boost growth

compared to that of heavily fertilised crops need not be pronounced. Light use of low-nutrient-content organic fertilisers to supplement bulky organic manures and compost is an effective alternative to reliance on concentrated fertilisers that may disrupt natural soil processes.

SPECIFIC NUTRIENTS

Nitrogen (N) is required for stem and leaf production. These are needed if the plant is to grow roots and thrive.

Phosphorus (P) is important for rapid growth and for roots and vegetables.

Potassium (K) aids water uptake and photosynthesis. It also prevents soft weak growth and enhances flowering.

Magnesium may be deficient in alkaline soils and where potassium fertiliser has been overused. Organic matter should supply necessary magnesium; in case of deficiency, spray Epsom salts on the foliage.

Once any soil deficiencies have been remedied, apply a balanced fertiliser, such as chicken manure pellets or the compound fertiliser growmore. Raking dry, granular, pelleted or powdered fertilisers into the soil before planting is effective. Hungry crops may need so much fertiliser that to apply enough to satisfy their needs at sowing or planting could inhibit germination or seedling growth; in these instances, give half the fertiliser later as topdressing.

• SOWING & PLANTING •

It is crucial that crops get off to a good start. The first step is to ensure the soil is firm but not hard underneath and loose and friable in the top 5cm (2in) of soil. This is usually accomplished by digging and raking (see pp30–31).

Sown seeds are buried in the moist soil where they are protected from drying out as well as from birds. They are buried just deep enough to achieve these aims but not too deep so that their reserves are used up in trying (and failing) to reach the surface. Therefore, although big bean seeds may be sown 2–3cm (¾–1in) deep, smaller seeds are sown as shallowly as possible – usually 1.5–2cm (½–¾in) deep.

Seeds also require warmth. Most hardy crops need 6–7°C (43–45°F), and tender plants such as tomatoes need at least 18°C (64°F). This means that the seed of most hardy crops cannot be sown until mid-spring, although sowings one or two months earlier are feasible with the help of cloches or fleece. Seed of tender crops cannot be relied upon until late spring or even early summer.

As early summer is too late for plants to give a good crop before autumn, it is usual to raise many of these, especially those with small seeds such as tomatoes and peppers, in warm, well-lit places such as greenhouses and plant out (transplant) after cold weather has passed. Big vigorous seeds such as sweet corn or runner beans can give good results if sown outdoors.

SOWING SEEDS OUTDOORS

Once weeds start germinating, it is safe to sow seeds. To get plants off to a flying start, warm the soil with cloches, clear plastic or fleece for six weeks prior to sowing. This not only warms the soil but also excludes rain so that the soil is dry enough to draw out the shallow grooves in the soil (called drills) into which seeds are placed. Seeds also need moisture, so the day before sowing, water the soil well. Alternatively, trickle water into the drill and then sow the seeds on the wet soil at the base of the drill.

Watering after sowing can pack down the soil, forming a hard surface that seeds struggle to break through. Where soil frequently slumps in this way, seeds can be covered with multipurpose potting media.

Seeds are vulnerable to birds and mice, and, later, as the seedlings emerge, to attack from slugs and pests.

TRANSPLANTS

Bare root

Some plants, such as leeks and cabbages, can be grown in the soil or in seedtrays and, after watering, gently removed, and planted bare-root in the soil without harm.

Celltrays

Trays of mini-cells allow many plants to be grown economically in a small space and removed and planted with minimal root damage.

Plug plants

Transplants can be bought as rooted seedlings in very small celltrays so that the roots are contained in a thumb-sized plug of potting media.

Pots

Pots are ideal for larger plants but take up more space and use more potting media. Pots 7–9cm (3–4in) in diameter are especially economical and useful.

DRILL SOWING

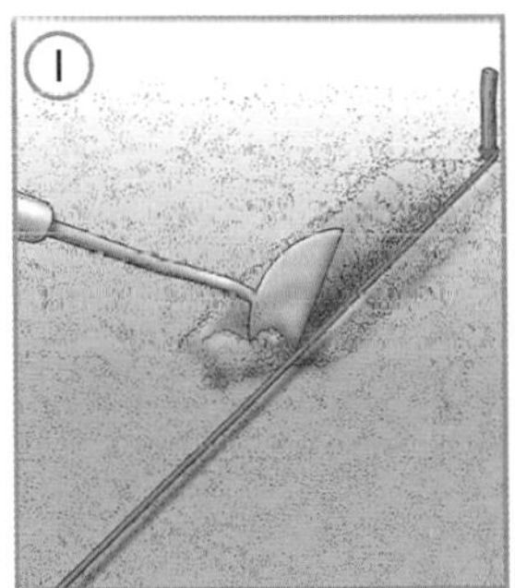

Stretch string between pegs at each end of the row at ground level. Draw out a drill with one of the hoe edges.

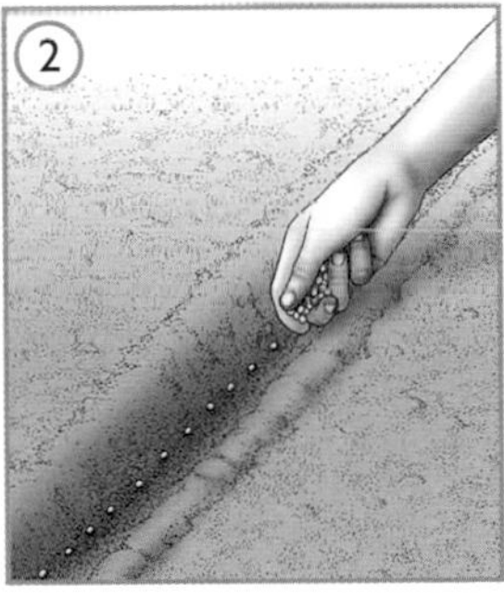

Water the bottom of the drill. Sprinkle seeds thinly and evenly, cover with soil, and firm in.

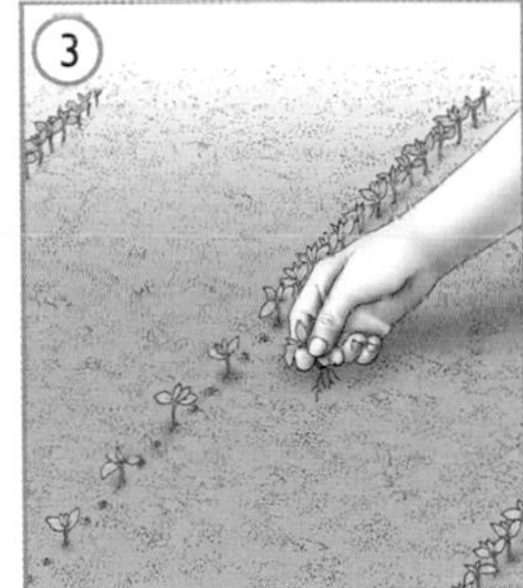

Thin excess seedlings as soon as possible. Leave the strongest to grow: you may thin a row several times.

SPECIAL SEEDS

Primed seeds

Primed seeds are given enough water to bring them to the brink of germination, which they do quickly when sown in moist soil.

Seed mats and tapes

To aid sowing, seeds can be bought set in tapes to sow in rows, or mats to place in seedtrays, which will germinate and grow when watered. They depend on being used fresh, containing the best-quality seeds and being carefully stored before use. Consequently, they can be rather costly.

Pelleted seeds

Pelleting is used to make odd-shaped seeds suitable for sowing by machine, but offer no great advantage for home gardeners.

Seed dressing

These seeds are treated to protect against pests and diseases; handle them with gloved hands, and scrub hands after sowing.

SOWING SEEDS INDOORS

Indoors, scatter seeds thinly on the surface of pots or seedtrays filled with suitable potting media, and then sprinkle with a fine material such as vermiculite or sieved potting media. Alternatively, sow individual seeds in pots or celltrays. This is quick and convenient, but with some small seeds it is necessry to sow two or three seeds per container to avoid 'blanks'; later, discard surplus seedlings.

After watering, leave the seeds to germinate in a warm, bright place. Heated propagators are ideal for this and a good investment. As soon as they can be handled by their leaves (never by their stems), 'prick out' the seedlings into individual pots, cells in celltrays or, indeed, suitably spaced, in seedtrays. This is a little laborious but is ideal when relatively few plants are needed.

Transplants allow a wide range of food to be grown over a long period of time.

VARIATIONS ON SEED SOWING

Station sowing is ideal for large seeds. Sow 3–5 seeds per station at their final spacing, and thin later.

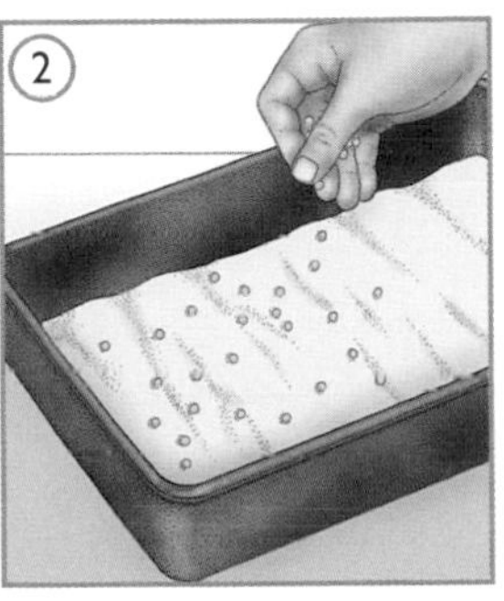

Pre-germinate seed on damp paper in an airtight box at 18–22°C (64–72°F) until roots are visible. Sow at once.

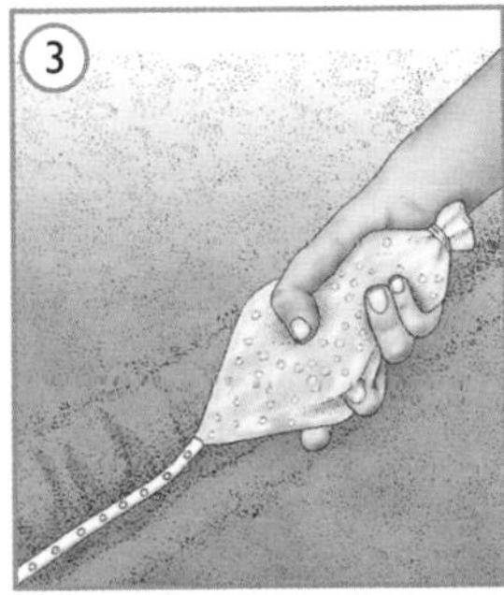

Stir small or fine seeds into a non-fungicidal wallpaper paste and squeeze from a bag with a hole.

TRANSPLANTING SEEDLINGS

With care, watering and speed, young plants that are large enough to handle can be planted in their final positions after being raised in a seedbed or taken from elsewhere in the row to fill in gaps.

PLANTING OUT

Before planting out, seedlings grown indoors are often 'hardened off' by a two-week period in conditions intermediate between indoors and outside, such as a cold frame, which is gradually opened fully, or under a double layer of fleece, with one layer removed after a week.

Both soil and transplants must be moist for good planting. Place each plant in a hole made with a trowel and then fill it with water. When it drains, firm the damp soil well around the plant, making sure the plant is not buried too deeply. Set out cabbage-family plants with the lowest leaves at soil level – the foliage should tear when tugged before the plant moves.

Puddling-in is invaluable in dry spells. Water the hole repeatedly until the transplant sits in a mass of wet soil that will sustain it possibly until fully established.

BRINGING ON TRANSPLANTED SEEDLINGS

Every day each transplant needs about 150ml (5fl oz) of water until it is fully established, so water regularly. Use a coarse rose, and water at the base of the plant in the morning or evening, to minimise evaporation.

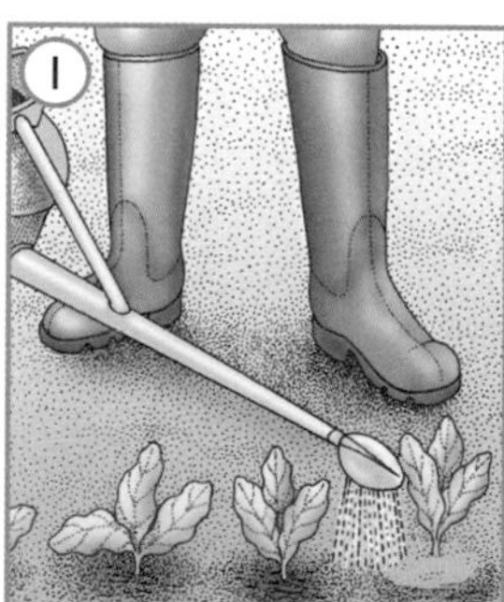

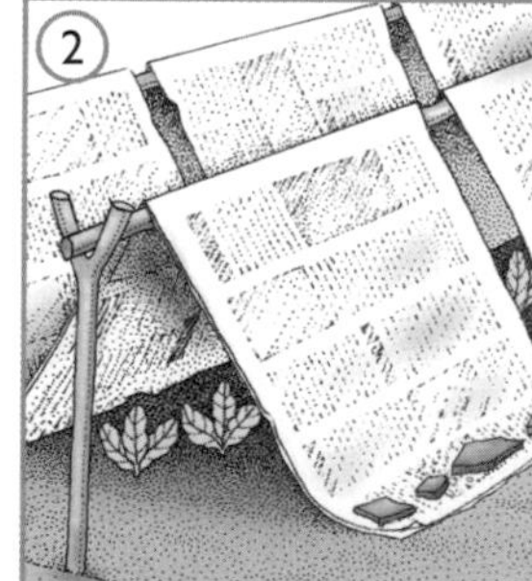

Protect newly transplanted seedlings on cold spring nights with makeshift tents made from newspaper and canes. Hold the paper in place with stones and remove the covers during the day.

• WATERING •

When water falls on the soil, it travels down into the soil until all the spaces and pores have been filled, and then continues until all the water is absorbed by the soil. Watering, therefore, fills soil with water to a certain depth and does not just dampen it. It is important to add enough water to wet the soil at the depth of the roots.

Water evaporates within plant leaves creating a 'suction' that (to simplify) is transmitted to the roots through the stem, drawing water up into the plant from the roots. This is easy at first as water held in the bigger pores in the soil is extracted, but in smaller pores the plants have to overcome surface tension and it becomes increasingly hard for them to extract water and they begin to wilt. Plants, however, are adapted to lack of water and save moisture by closing the pores (stomata) in their leaves. Stomata allow carbon dioxide into the plant so that photosynthesis can occur. When stomata close, growth slows and harvests are delayed and reduced.

In Britain, on a bright summer day, plants lose the equivalent of 25mm (¾in) of rain every 10–14 days. In hot, windy conditions, up to 5mm (¼in) per day can be lost, and in cool, dull, still weather virtually no water is lost. Therefore, the maximum irrigation used by gardeners, assuming no rain falls, is 20 litres (4⅓ gallons) per square metre/yard every 10 days, around three 9-litre (2 gallon) watering cans per square metre/yard.

Clay soils can look moist even though plants are unable to extract water, and sandy soils can look dry but still contain moisture, so checking the moistness of soil is the best way to know when to water. Water your garden with a can or hosepipe, directing water in as gentle a flow as possible to the base of plants. Aim to soak the top 25cm (10in) of soil, as lesser watering does not meet plants' needs.

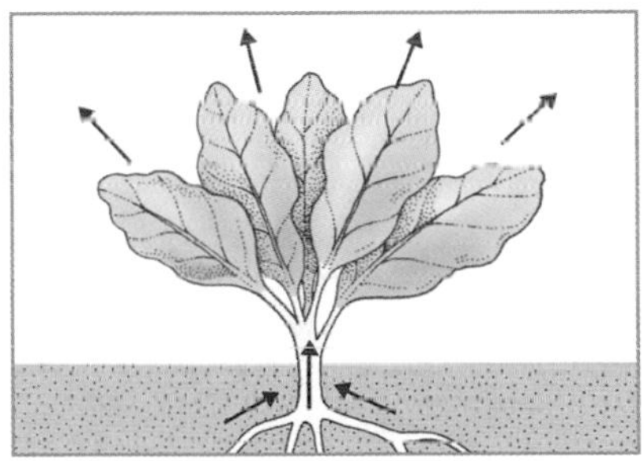

WATER TRANSPORT

The water absorbed from the soil by roots is pulled up through the plant, carrying nutrients and fuelling chemical processes, and is lost through transpiration from the leaves.

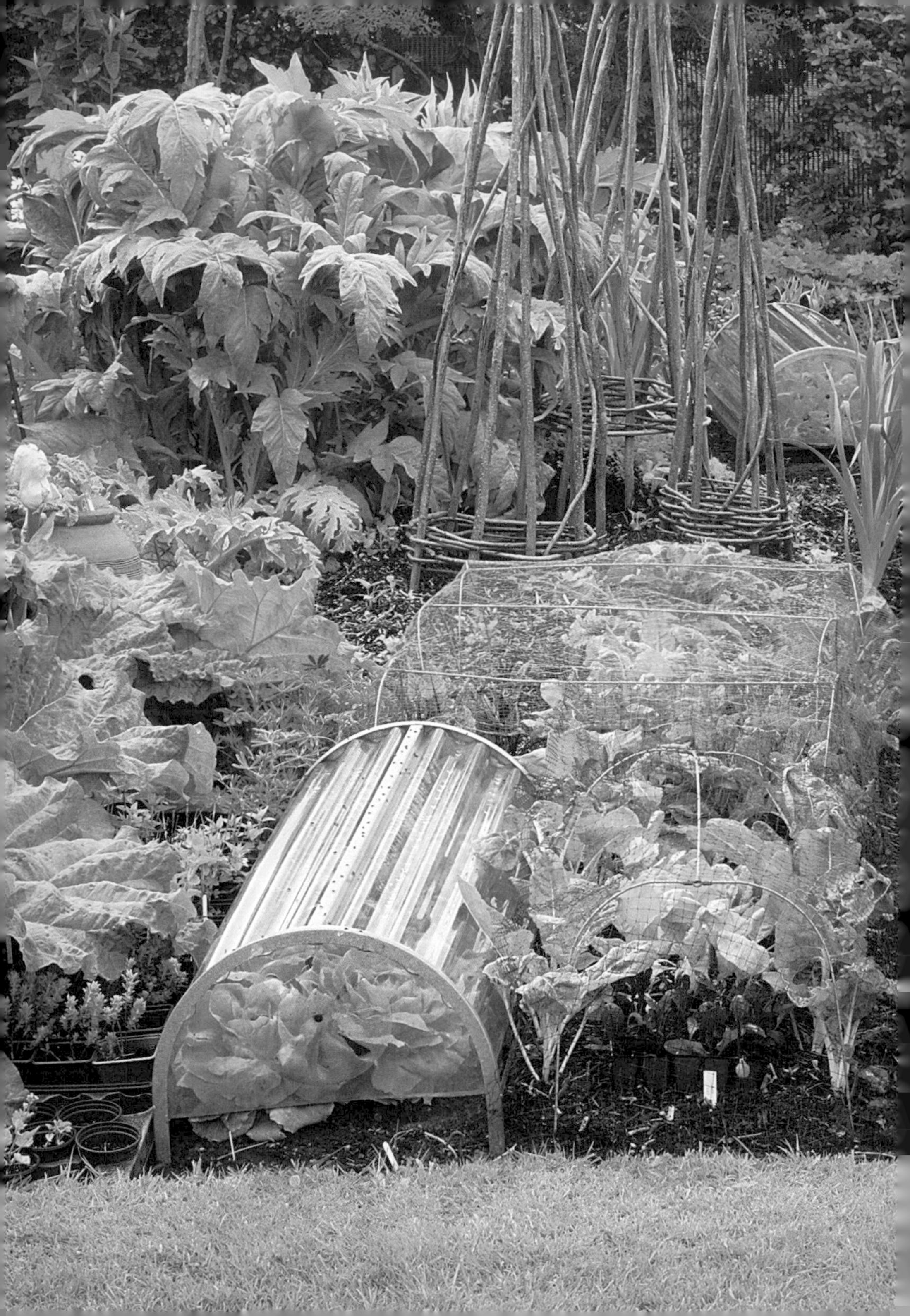

CROP
PROTECTION

• WEEDS •

Weeds, like crops, also thrive on fertile soil. They are great survivors but, fortunately, they have their weeknesses, too. Exploiting these can greatly reduce the chore of weeding.

HOW WEEDS SURVIVE

Weeds have two survival strategies. The first is to produce enormous numbers of seeds that lurk buried in the soil, only germinating when they 'sense' that conditions are right. The reservoir of weed seeds buried in the soil is called the 'weed seed bank'. Conditions that trigger germination include light, nitrates in the soil (indicating fertility) and fluctuating temperatures (indicating that the seed is close to the soil surface).

The weeds that adopt this strategy have life cycles that mimic those of vegetable crops, taking advantage of periods of clear fertile soil in order to grow quickly, and shedding seeds at an early age in order to avoid being destroyed. These weed plants may be annuals (completing their life cycle in one year) or ephemerals (completing several life cycles in a year). They are particularly abundant where the soil is light and easily worked.

The second strategy adopted by certain weeds is to have highly persistent roots that resist being dug up either by being very deep or easily fragmenting into sections, each of which can produce a new plant. These plants are perennials. They are especially damaging where the soil is rich in clay and, therefore, heavy and stiff. Root fragments can lurk in clods, safe from picking out or drying. The weed fragments in waiting in the soil are called the 'weed bud bank'.

WEED CONTROL

Annual weeds

Annual and ephemeral weeds include groundsel, annual meadow grass, shepherd's purse, annual nettles, chickweed and fat hen. Do not allow these weeds to produce seeds, as they can lurk in the soil for years. Canny gardeners can exploit the need for weed seeds to sense the environment by preparing seedbeds or land for transplants and leaving them for the weeds to grow. Once the weeds have germinated they can be killed by shallow hoeing or with weedkiller to leave the soil weed-free. If the soil is not disturbed and no weed seeds are brought to the surface, there will be fewer weeds in the subsequent crop. This is called a 'sterile seedbed'. In very weedy gardens, it is worth raising plants in pots and celltrays and taking time to eradicate weeds by using a sterile seedbed before planting.

Annual weeds have limited resources and if uprooted by hoeing or other shallow cultivation, they find it hard to recover. Similarly, if the soil around plants is covered with a mulch of opaque material or at least 5cm (2in) of weed-free organic matter, such as mushroom compost, annual weeds will be prevented.

Annual weeds are also very vulnerable to weedkillers, including contact ones, which damage any plant tissue that they touch, or the systemic weedkiller glyphosate, which is taken up by the treated weed, killing it, but not taken up from the soil by other plants. However, there is not much opportunity to use pesticides in vegetable or herb gardens as the chemicals are not selective and are likely to damage crops.

Annual weeds must not be added to the compost bin or dug into the soil, as their seeds will survive domestic composting and burial. Instead, they should be burnt or consigned to your local council for industrial composting, which generates high enough temperatures to kill weed seeds. Annual weed seeds do not survive on the soil surface for long – no-digging regimes aim to exploit this fact to control annual weeds (see p33).

PERENNIAL WEED ROOT SYSTEMS

The carrot-like taproots of thistles (above), dandelions and docks grow straight down into the soil.

With care, the roots of bindweed, ground elder and couch grass (above) can be picked out and destroyed.

The tiny bulbils that develop around the roots of oxalis break off easily and grow into new plants.

Perennial weeds

Perennial weeds include field bindweed, couch grass and horsetail. They are vulnerable to digging where they are deeply buried and the more obvious roots picked out. However, they usually survive hoeing. Since vegetable plots are dug frequently, perennial weeds are seldom a serious problem and they can be kept in check by being winkled out with a fork or trowel. Also very effective is spot treatment with a glyphosate weedkiller, but take great care not to get the weedkiller on valued edible plants, as it harms all plants it touches.

Perennial weeds are able to overwhelm permanent crops such as asparagus and herbs where there is no opportunity for digging, and these should be eradicated by cultivation or weedkiller before planting, while the bed is still unplanted. Any subsequent interlopers should be quickly destroyed because if they become established, the planting will soon have to be replaced and the bed painstakingly weeded.

WEED CONTROL METHODS

Hand-weeding and pulling

These are slow and laborious methods but there is no other way for gardeners to remove weeds from within rows and at the base of plants. With straight rows and evenly spaced plants, achieved by

KEEPING WEEDS AT BAY

Annual weeds and vegetables have similar life cycles – they grow and set seed in one year. Consequently, annual weeds grow when crops grow and are shielded by the crops' foliage. They then set seed while the crop is still in place so that the seeding weeds are often overlooked by the gardener. Annual weed seeds tend to build up in vegetable garden soils.

Dig out perennial weeds in winter. Remove every fragment of root or they will regenerate.

Mulch plants with well-rotted compost after rain or watering to conserve water and suppress weeds.

careful sowing and planting, you will be able to kill most weeds simply by hoeing, reducing the need to hand-weed.

Hoeing

Slicing weeds off at soil level with a sharp hoe is rather slow and fiddly, but it can be highly effective in dry weather. In wet weather, hoeing becomes ineffective, and after prolonged wet spells, hand-weeding is needed. In extreme cases, crops might have to be abandoned. It is important to work shallowly to avoid damaging crop roots and bringing up more weed seeds. When hoeing perennial weeds, it might be necessary to remove roots. In dry weather, young hoed weeds can be left to die, but in unsettled weather, they should be removed and destroyed as they can reroot under rain.

Weedkillers

Selective and preventative weedkillers are not available to home gardeners and, like all weedkillers, are incompatible with organic gardening. Contact weedkillers, such as those based on pelargonic acid, can be used to treat weeds on bare soil or, with great care and a hooded sprayer, around widely spaced plants. Systemic translocated glyphosate-based weedkillers are very useful in clearing ground when making new gardens

On dry, warm days, slice weed stems with a sharp hoe, keeping the blade level and just below the soil surface.

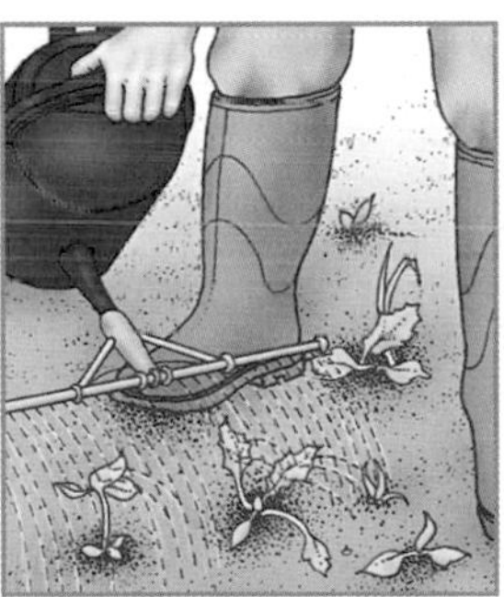

Crops are most vulnerable to weeds in their early stages, so early treatment saves effort later.

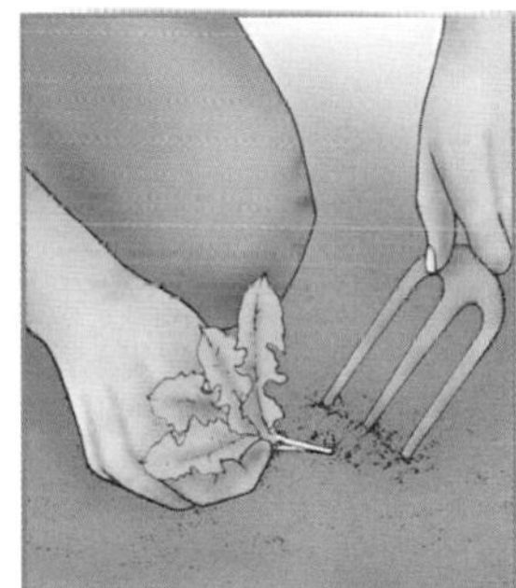

Weeding by hand is effective against small weeds and annuals. A hand fork may help.

APPLYING A LOOSE MULCH

If the soil is dry, water the soil well before mulching. This moisture will then be locked in by the mulch.

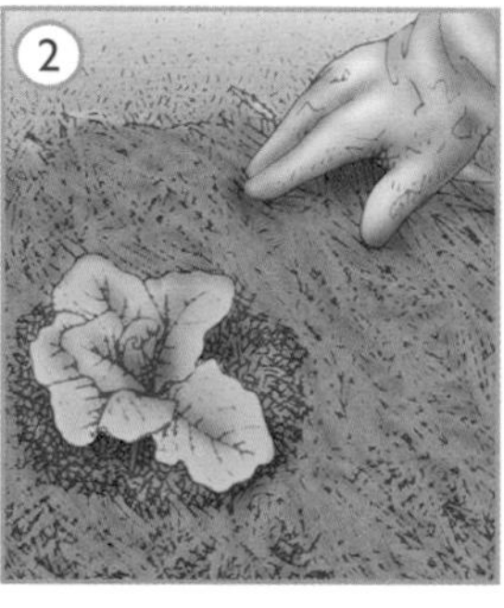

Spread the mulch evenly by hand around small plants, leaving a space around their stems.

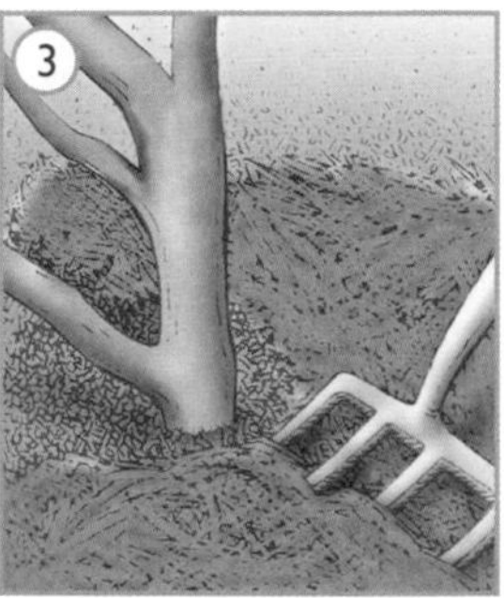

Keep the mulch clear of the stems of trees and shrubs, using a garden fork or rake around such plants.

and for spot treatment of perennial weeds, but are too powerful to be used safely around crops!

Mulches

By excluding light, mulches suppress weeds and conserve a limited amount of water. Up to the equivalent of about 2cm (¾in) of rain, or nearly two weeks' supply,

Dedicate a sprayer to applying weedkillers and use it for nothing else.

APPLYING A SHEET MULCH

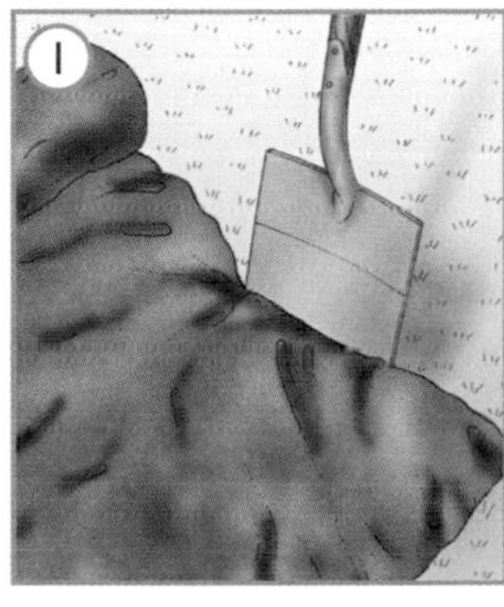

Anchor the sheet mulch in position by pushing the edges into soil that has been well dug and watered.

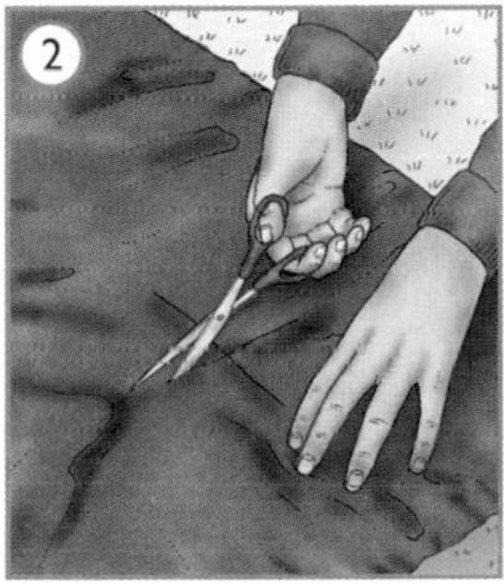

Cut a small cross in the sheet and, using a trowel, make a hole in the soil to plant in the normal way.

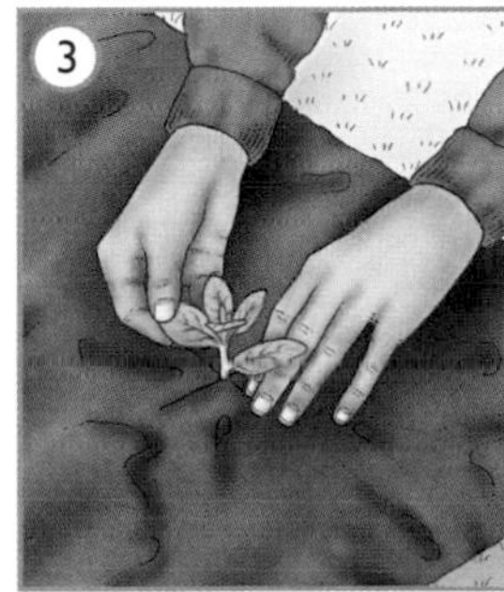

Put the plant through the cross into the hole and firm it in the soil. Cover the sheet with a bark mulch.

can be lost from the soil surface by evaporation. Sheets of opaque plastic or paper materials can be laid on the soil surface and crops planted through them. Widely spaced plants, such as tomatoes and pumpkins, are easiest to handle, while closely spaced carrots, for example, would be impractical.

Organic materials that are free of weed seeds, such as mushroom compost, need to be laid at least 5cm (2in) deep (but, ideally, 7cm/3in deep) to conserve moisture. Again, they are much easier to use around widely spaced crops.

Sheet mulches are effective against perennial weeds, but organic mulches offer insufficient resistance to perennial weed shoots.

Some losses from weeds, pests and diseases are inevitable, but by raising healthy, well-fed and watered plants and buying good-quality seeds, sets and other planting material, losses can be kept to a minimum. Garden hygiene is important, too, with the destruction of infected or infested material to limit the transfer of problems to new plants. Care also needs to be taken not to transfer weed seeds on garden tools. Gardeners should beware of friends bearing gifts, as these can, unknown to the donor, often carry weeds, pests and diseases. Even so, intervention by the gardener in cases of serious attack will help improve yields, quality and reliability of crops (see pp58–63).

• PROTECTED CROPPING •

Protecting crops from weather can start cheaply with horticultural fleece, which offers a slight (2°C/4°F) lift in temperatures or protection from frost. A crop covered in fleece will mature about two weeks earlier than an uncovered one and is protected from pests. Water and pesticides can be applied through fleece without removing it, and the protection it offers from wind damage is especially useful. On the downside, conditions beneath fleece support slugs and it is inconvenient to weed beneath it. In addition, fleece has a short life (usually no more than two seasons), is almost always made from non-renewable resources and cannot be recycled, so its environmental cost is significant.

Cloches are usually low tunnels of transparent material and more expensive than fleece per unit area of ground covered. Almost all cloches now sold are plastic and have a life of three to five years. They cannot be heated.

Well-designed cloches allow better ventilation and, therefore, higher-quality plants than the tunnel alongside, but are heavier, relatively expensive and more prone to damage.

COVERING CROPS

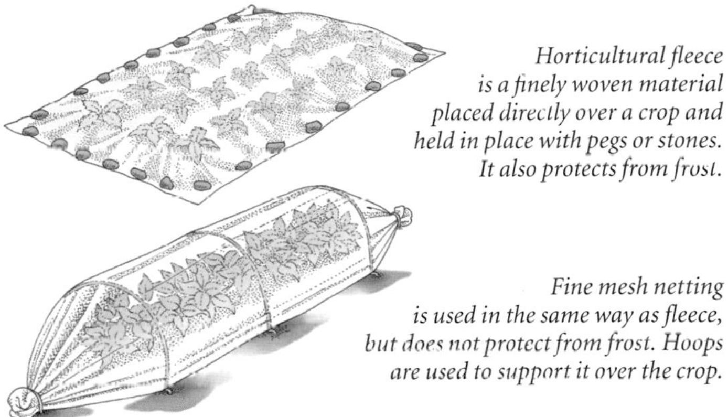

Horticultural fleece is a finely woven material placed directly over a crop and held in place with pegs or stones. It also protects from frost.

Fine mesh netting is used in the same way as fleece, but does not protect from frost. Hoops are used to support it over the crop.

TYPES OF CLOCHE

Glass and plastic cloches make a low tunnel of continuous design, while individual ones are like a hat for each plant. Both give more protection than fleece, advancing early crops by 3–4 weeks and ripening tender crops almost as well as a greenhouse in summer. They cost much more than fleece, and covered plants need frequent watering. Like fleece, they are easily blown away in exposed gardens.

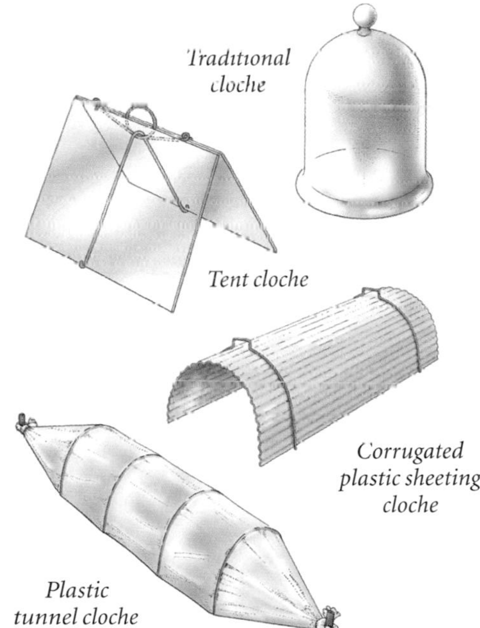

Cold frames are boxes with glazed lids and, usually, sides. They confer more protection than cloches but often cost more per unit area of ground covered. They are especially useful for 'hardening off' tender plants raised indoors (see p44). Well-made glazed frames should last for 10 years.

Polythene tunnels give similar protection as cold frames and, being 'walk in', are easier to use. However, it is not so easy to prevent overheating or exclude cold in winter. Their cost per unit area of ground covered is good compared to other forms of protection, except fleece. They are ideal for raising tender crops, such as peppers and tomatoes in summer and hardy salads in winter. They are costly to heat. Polythene covers should last up to five years.

Glasshouses, usually glazed with glass or rigid plastic such as polycarbonate, are more expensive than polythene tunnels but longer-lasting and offer better temperature control, are more economical to heat and give better winter protection. Glass is superior to plastic, as it traps heat more efficiently, but it is heavier, less robust and, unless safety glass is used, potentially hazardous. Those available to amateur gardeners should last for about 10 years.

WINDBREAKS & SUPPORTS

Damage from wind is often subtle and underestimated but an exposed garden can suffer two to three weeks' delay in maturity and reduced quality of produce compared to a sheltered garden.

Barriers slow the wind to some extent – about 30 times the barrier height downwind and five times the height upwind – but significant protection is only conferred to about seven times the

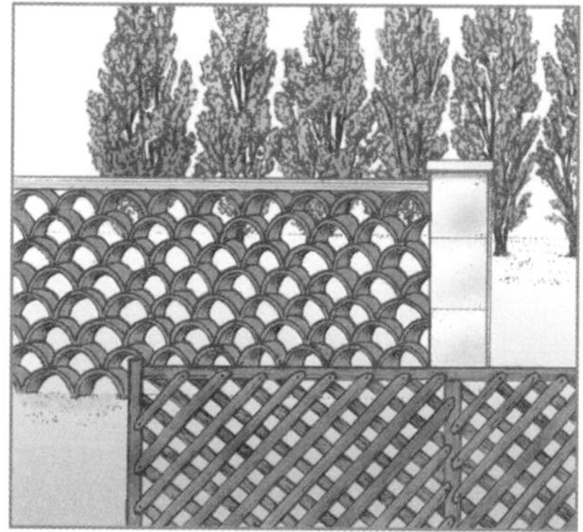

TYPES OF WINDBREAK

The best windbreaks allow some wind to filter through. They can be hedges or natural screens (top), porous walls (centre) or fences (bottom). Such barriers are also useful at the bottom of slopes, as they stop frost pockets forming.

SUPPORTING CLIMBING BEANS

Like runner beans, climbing French beans need a strong support. The simplest structure is a wigwam (far right) of 4 canes, in a 1m (3ft) square. Secure the canes at the top with string. Sow 3 seeds 5cm (2in) deep at the base of each cane, later thinning to leave 2 plants per cane. Alternatively, hammer 2 strong wooden stakes into the ground at each end of a row of beans and stretch netting across (above left). Space plants 15cm (6in) apart, thinning to 30cm (12in) apart.

height. Thus a 2m (6½ft) high hedge will shelter a 14m (130ft) width of garden.

Panel fences and walls are less effective than porous fences. To slow air flow without causing turbulence, an ideal ratio is 60:40 solid to porous. Other good windbreaks include closely clipped hedges or those that are half evergreen.

CONTROLLING THE WIND FLOW

Solid barriers cause turbulence on the lee side. In extreme cases, this can knock plants over and cause walls and fences to collapse.

Porous barriers, like screens of trees and shrubs, are ideal for shelter. They filter the wind, reducing its force and slowing it down.

• PESTS & DISEASES •

PESTS

Vegetables and herbs are prone to attack from seven main groups of pests.

Nematodes (eelworms)

These microscopic worms live in or on plants, sucking the contents of their cells. The potato cyst nematode, which forms barely visible golden or yellow cysts on potato and tomato roots, will cause the plant to wilt. It persists in the soil as a hardy cyst. There are resistant potato cultivars. Discard infested plants, rotate crops and buy pest-free planting material.

Slugs and snails

These are the commonest garden pests and attack most vegetables above and below ground. Slug pellets are the most effective remedy – those containing ferric phosphate are even safer than metaldehyde ones. Nematodes that on infecting slugs introduce bacteria that harm the slug can be watered on crops in warm weather and give good control, but are not effective against snails. Barriers of abrasive materials, such as grit or water-absorbent granules, may be washed away in storms or during watering, and as with copper, may be bridged by vegetation or soil.

Woodlice, centipedes and millepedes

These seldom cause damage. When present, they are usually taking advantage of damage done by slugs and snails.

Mites

Glasshouse red spider mite is the usual mite pest in vegetable gardens. It feeds beneath leaves, sucking plant sap often under fine webbings, which are barely visible except with a magnifying glass. Control under cover by introducing predatory mites before the mites become numerous.

Insects

These are the most significant pests, after slugs and snails. Sap-sucking insects include aphids such as whitefly and greenfly. These aphids suck sap, especially from young growth, and often cause severe distortion of infested foliage due to their injecting material that controls plant growth. The distorted foliage prevents access by many pesticides, although systemic ones are effective.

Glasshouse whitefly are best controlled by parasitic wasps called *Encarsia formosa*, but when the whitefly are too numerous for them to be effective, they can, like outdoor cabbage whitefly, be controlled with insecticides based on oils and fatty acids, which work by physical action.

Sap-sucking thrips, or thunderflies, are common on onions, leeks and peas, causing a silvery discoloration of foliage and pea pods. The remedies used to control aphids will work on thrips.

Caterpillars of leek moth, pea moth, cabbage moth, cabbage butterflies and, less commonly, other moths eat foliage or affect pods. Control with insecticides or protect crops with fine nets.

Soil-dwelling caterpillars (cutworms) can be very destructive in dry summers, affecting a wide range of crops. There is no remedy for these but watering can be highly effective if it catches the caterpillars at a vulnerable stage.

Pea and bean weevils are the most obvious beetle pests, although they are not very destructive to vegetables. Cover young plants with fleece to exclude the pest and hasten growth so the plants outgrow the damage. Control flea beetle, which can damage young cabbage-family plants, in the same way. Treat the rosemary beetle, which attacks herbs, and asparagus beetle by picking off or spraying with natural pyrethrins.

Certain fly larvae (bean seed fly, cabbage root fly, carrot fly and onion fly) mainly attack the roots of their host plants. Erect barriers of fleece or insect-proof mesh to protect carrots from attack, or grow resistant cultivars. Fleece and mesh work to exclude cabbage root fly, too, but you can also place barriers of card or fabric around the base of the plants.

Birds

Pigeons have been known to devastate green crops, and jays will steal ripening peas, beans and sweet corn. Netting of 50mm (2cm) mesh will deter these birds without harm.

Mammals

Animals are significant in some areas but are not usually widely destructive. Wire netting will protect against rabbits and deer, but sometimes trapping is required to control other pests. Deterrent substances, sprayed onto plants, can sometimes work but are usually short-lived, especially if it rains. Ultrasonic scarers have been reported to repel some individual pests, especially foxes and badgers. In many gardens, a 'fruit cage' for the vegetables will be a good investment.

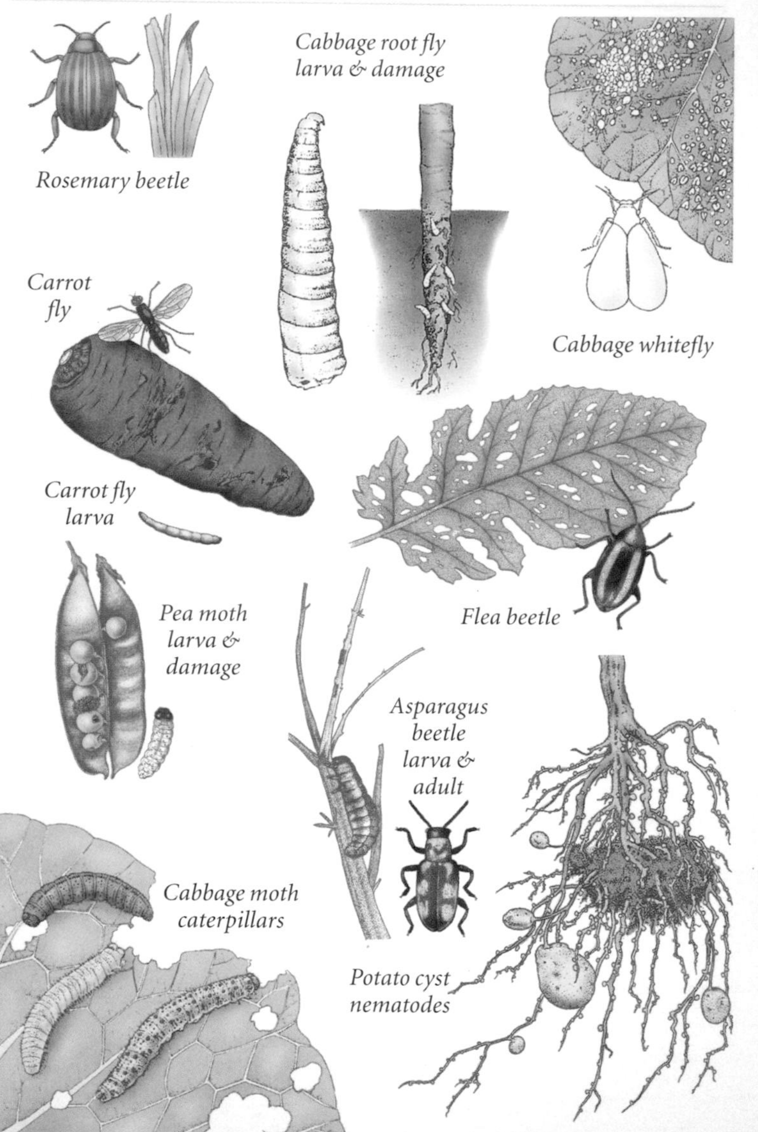
Rosemary beetle
Cabbage root fly larva & damage
Cabbage whitefly
Carrot fly
Carrot fly larva
Flea beetle
Pea moth larva & damage
Asparagus beetle larva & adult
Cabbage moth caterpillars
Potato cyst nematodes

DISEASES

Downy mildews strike in warm, wet weather; onion downy mildew can be very damaging to onions and shallots and hard to control with chemicals, but resistant onion cultivars are available. Like most fungal diseases, downy mildews are specific to their host and do not affect other crops. Downy mildews overwinter in infected plants and in the soil, so destruction or disposal of all infected plants and debris is an important control measure.

Potato blight behaves like downy mildews. In wet weather, the most that can be expected from the copper fungicides used to control blight is a two-week delay in the destruction of potato foliage and tomato foliage and fruits. Where foliage is kept dry in greenhouses, blight, and indeed all downy mildews, are much less damaging.

Powdery mildews are less dependent on warm, wet conditions than downy mildews, and they affect plants stressed by dry roots.

A limited range of fungicides is available to gardeners; organic gardeners can use sulphur fungicides. Enriching soil with organic matter, and watering to avoid drought stress are important measures to take.

Rust diseases include bean rust, leek rust and garlic rust. Remove and destroy all infected material at the end of cropping. Some leeks show more tolerance of the disease than others. Rusts, like downy and powdery mildews, are highly specific to their host plants and will not spread to other crops.

In wet weather, moulds can rot vulnerable plants. Grey mould, or botrytis, is common in glasshouses and outdoors in cool, wet weather. Prompt removal of dead rotted material is the only control.

Soilborne diseases include club root affecting cabbage crops, and onion white rot, which affects leeks, garlic and shallots. Both produce resting bodies in the soil, surviving at least 12 years so that rotation cannot entirely prevent these diseases. Club root-resistant brassicas are available, but no resistant onion-family plants are yet offered. In extreme cases, gardeners might have to raise onion-family crops in beds or containers of fresh, disease-free soil. Club root can be largely prevented by liming to raise the pH to 7.5 (see p19), ensuring good drainage and raising transplants in 15cm (6in) pots. Remove and destroy infected plant material or consign to the municipal green waste.

Viruses are less important in vegetable crops because they are usually raised

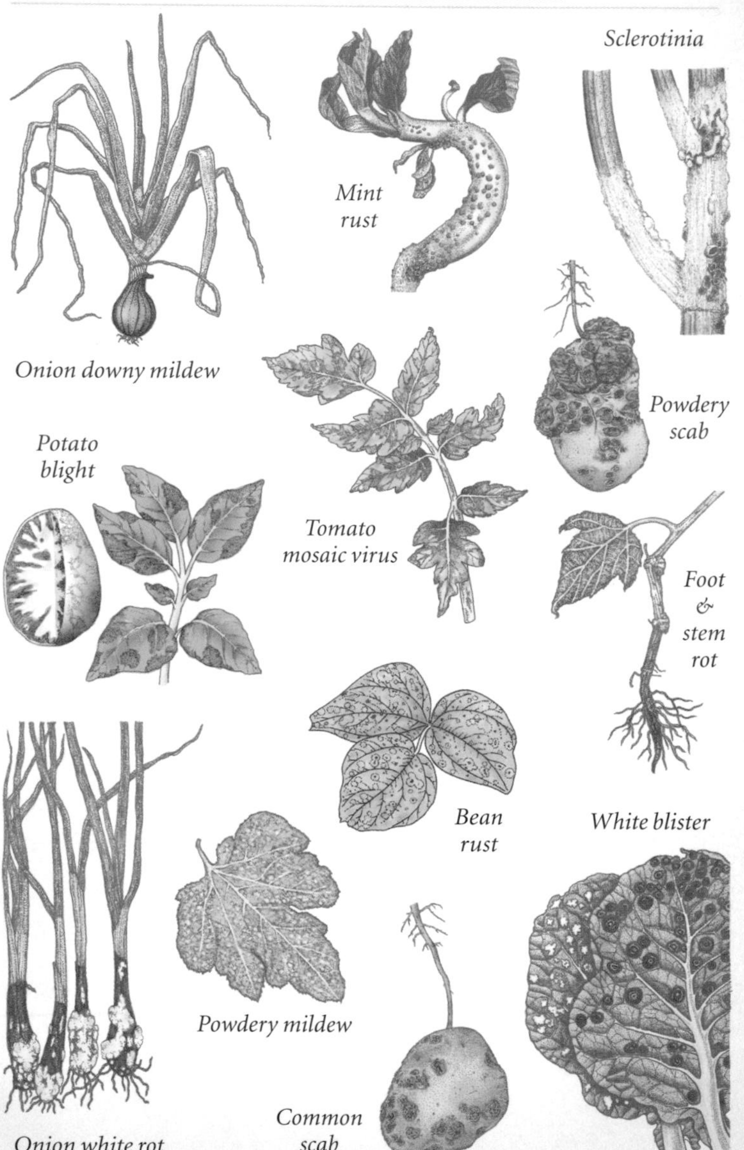
IDENTIFYING VEGETABLE DISEASES
Sclerotinia
Mint rust
Onion downy mildew
Powdery scab
Potato blight
Tomato mosaic virus
Foot & stem rot
Bean rust
White blister
Powdery mildew
Common scab
Onion white rot

from seed, and viruses do not readily cross from parent plants to the seeds, so each crop gets off to a virus-free start.

Potatoes are an exception because they are grown from seed tubers, which are an excellent vehicle for viruses. But good-quality, virus-free seed potatoes are widely available from parent stock raised in high-altitude cold regions such as Scotland – where aphids are relatively few – or in lowland regions such as Holland – where aphids are rigorously controlled by insecticides. Potatoes from this seed will usually be virus-free but subsequent crops from home-saved seed are often poor.

CULTURAL CONTROL

Good gardening techniques are the first priority in pest and disease control.

Plantings and sowing

Good soil preparation, good sowing and planting only when the soil is warm enough gives plants a head start so that they grow quickly and can shrug off insect attack and diseases. Protect young plants with fleece or insect-proof mesh.

Choice of plants

Plant breeders have responded to a reduced availability of pesticides by breeding crops resistant to potato blight, onion downy mildew and club root.

Hygiene

Careful destruction of infected material before it can shed spores or before insects disperse can limit damage in subsequent crops. Home composting seldom gets warm enough to kill disease spores, but can eliminate plants infested with insects.

Care of plants

Good growing conditions prevent physiological disorders and help plants fend off pests and diseases.

Biological control

Using living creatures to control pests is now widely practised in glasshouses, and insect parasitic nematodes are widely offered for a broad range of pests. It is not yet clear how effective they are.

Pesticides

Pesticides include insecticides, fungicides, slug pellets and even weedkillers. For cost reasons, few pesticides are offered to home gardeners, so they are seldom named here. Such information would also become out of date very quickly.

VEGETABLE DIRECTORY

• LETTUCES •

There are many forms of lettuce available and all are easy to grow.

● Butterhead, or cabbage, lettuces have a firm rounded heart within a rosette of soft pale leaves. They have a mild flavour, and are delicious when eaten fresh from the garden. However, they don't store well.

● Cos lettuces have taller, elongated heads of oval leaves and a more pronounced flavour than other types.

● Sucrine, or 'Little Gem'-type, lettuces are small, upright, crisp and well-flavoured. Crosses between cos and sucrine lettuces combine the best of both types.

● Crisphead, or 'Webbs Wonderful'-type, lettuces are headed like butterheads, but the leaves are crisp and crinkled with firm hearts; 'Iceberg' lettuces are crispheads with very firm hearts indeed. Crispheads have a mild flavour but keep well in the fridge.

● Looseleaf lettuces produce masses of loose leaves to cut as required, although if left to mature, they will make a big fluffy head. They are mild-flavoured and often highly ornamental.

FROM SOWING TO HARVESTING LEAF LETTUCE

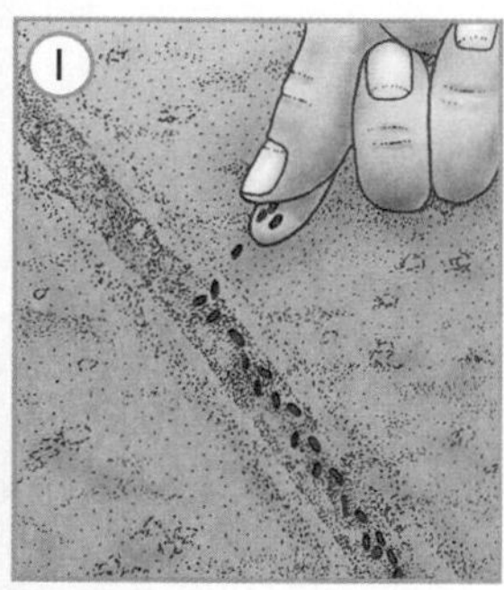

Sow in drills 1cm (½in) deep weekly in spring. Thin seedlings, as crowded plants will not form proper hearts.

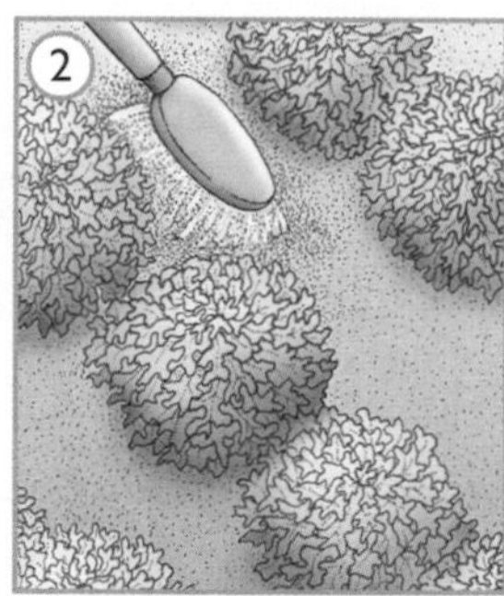

In hot, dry weather, apply two watering cans per square metre (yard) every 10 days to prevent bolting.

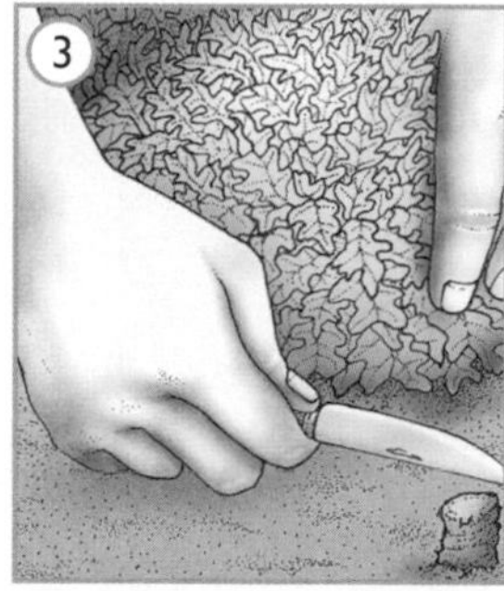

Harvest the leaves when still small, usually in 3–6 weeks. Leave a stump with side buds to regrow another crop.

A little of many different lettuces helps prevent gluts, adds variety and pleases the eye.

All these lettuces can be grown as 'baby leaf' similar to the pillow packs of leaves sold in supermarkets (see box on p69).

Lettuce seed is cheap, but it does not store well, and fresh seed should be bought every year. Packets of mixed lettuces are an excellent way of economically trying out different kinds.

Lettuces are ideal for intercropping (see p25) and catch cropping, but they will not heart properly in shade.

Grow spring lettuces outdoors from sowings in early autumn. They usually heart in mid- to late spring, but can be a week or two earlier if protected with a covering of fleece or cloches.

For late spring and early summer lettuces, raise plants indoors in late winter and early spring. For summer to early autumn lettuces, sow seed outdoors from early spring (under cloches or fleece) until late summer.

Protect winter lettuces in cold frames, polytunnels or glasshouses. Sow special 'short-day' cultivars indoors from early autumn until midwinter.

Lettuces benefit greatly from additions of organic matter (two bucketfuls of well-rotted compost or manure, and fertiliser per square metre/yard). Before sowing, rake in growmore or other general fertiliser, at 150g per sq. m. (4oz per sq. yd), and apply additional fertiliser as the crop grows.

Lettuces will not stay in peak condition for long before flowering (bolting), especially in hot dry weather. To overcome this, sow small batches of seed every 14 days.

Sow seeds 15mm (½in) deep in finely raked moist soil in rows 30cm (12in) apart. Thin the seedlings as soon as they can be handled to their final spacing:

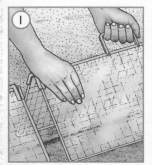

SOWING PROTECTED LETTUCE

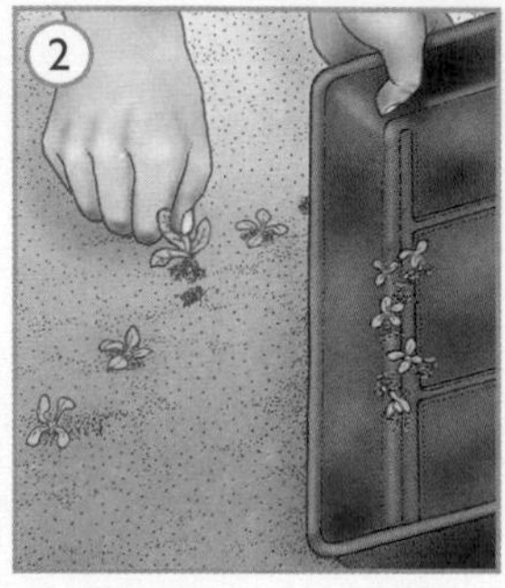

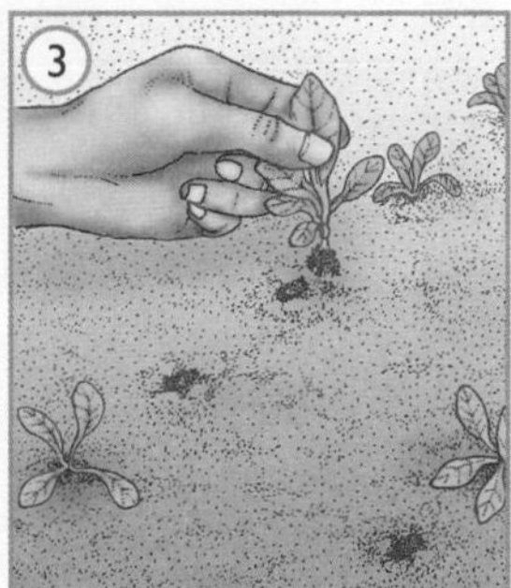

Sow in mid-autumn in drills 20cm (8in) apart. Station sow at 7cm (2½in) intervals. Protect with cloches.

Thin seedlings when 1cm (½in) high, leaving the strongest plant at each station. Protect plants over winter.

Make final thinnings in spring, leaving a lettuce plant every 15–23cm (6–9in) to grow on.

butterheads 25cm (10in), cos 30cm (12in), semicos 25cm (10in), 'Little Gem'-types 15cm (6in) and crispheads 30cm (12in). Overcrowding can prevent proper hearts forming. Thinnings can be used as baby leaves.

Sow seeds of larger lettuces in groups of three to seven, with seedlings singled later.

Lettuces can also be raised in celltrays, although if good hearts are required, they should be planted out as soon as their roots bind the potting medium.

A topdressing of nitrogen-rich fertiliser, chicken manure pellets at 100g per sq. m (3oz per sq. yd) for example, sprinkled along the rows before rain or watering, can greatly improve yields once the plants have started to grow vigorously.

Harvest lettuces as soon as they are big and firm enough to use or, in the case of looseleaf plants, when there is sufficient leaf to be worthwhile.

Lettuces have few serious problems. Birds can damage early sowings but are excluded by fleece. Slugs and snails thrive in wet periods and should be controlled

MINI-LETTUCES

Small lettuce cultivars are ideal for small gardens, intercropping, catch cropping and small households. Good ones include: 'Little Gem' (sucrine), 'Mini Green' (crisphead) and 'Tom Thumb' (butterhead).

BABY LEAVES

Leafy greens and salad vegetables, such as lettuces, can be harvested for their young, tender mild-flavoured leaves.

Harvesting at a young stage allows very close spacing of plants. Allow 10–15cm (4–6in) between rows, spacing seeds so that a seedling will grow every 1cm (½in). Broadcast sowing (scattering seed evenly over the soil surface, aiming for about 5cm/2in between plants) is also possible but weeding can be tricky. Avoid mixing seeds, as the different plants take different lengths of time to reach cutting size.

Cut-and-come-again leaves take little space and are suitable for the smallest garden, but the seeds can be expensive. Well-drained, moderately fertile soils are ideal. Containers filled with multipurpose potting media can also give good results.

RECOMMENDED CULTIVARS

Butterhead
'Diana': very reliable for summer

Cos
'Lobjoits Green Cos': overwinters

Semicos
'Winter Density': overwinters

Sucrine
'Little Gem': quick-growing, compact, sweet and succulent

Loose-leaf
'Concorde': red 'oak' leaves

Oakleaf
'Lollo Rossa': frilly, red leaves

because they often contaminate the edible portion of lettuce.

Lettuce downy mildew forms mouldy patches on the undersides of outer leaves in wet periods, especially in autumn, but as these leaves can be discarded at harvest, there is no need to attempt control.

Greenfly or aphids often need to be controlled. Aphid-resistant cultivars are sometimes available. Root aphids cause wilting, and can be very hard to control. In midsummer and in areas where these are common, grow resistant cultivars.

Soil-dwelling caterpillars can be troublesome in hot dry weather but are vulnerable to watering.

Viral diseases in lettuces are common but seldom damaging in gardens.

• ENDIVES & CHICORY •

Endives and chicory are quick-growing annuals and perennials respectively and are easy to grow. They resist drought, heat and cold weather better than lettuces and are especially useful in autumn and early winter.

● **Endives are grown for salads and are generally blanched. They may be frilly**

FROM SOWING TO HARVESTING BLANCHED ENDIVE

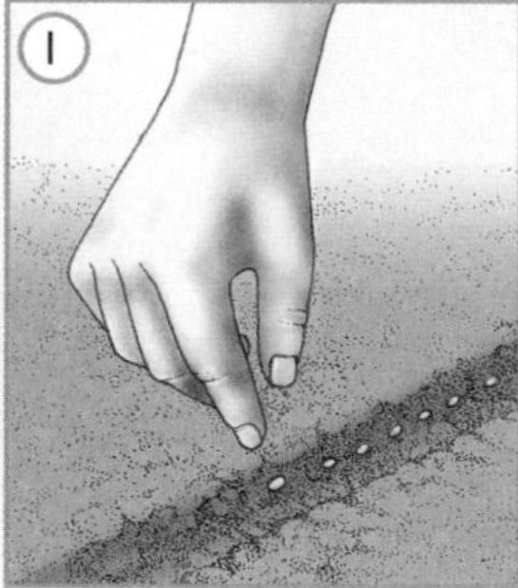

Sow in drills 12mm (½in) deep, 30cm (12in) apart, fortnightly from spring to late summer.

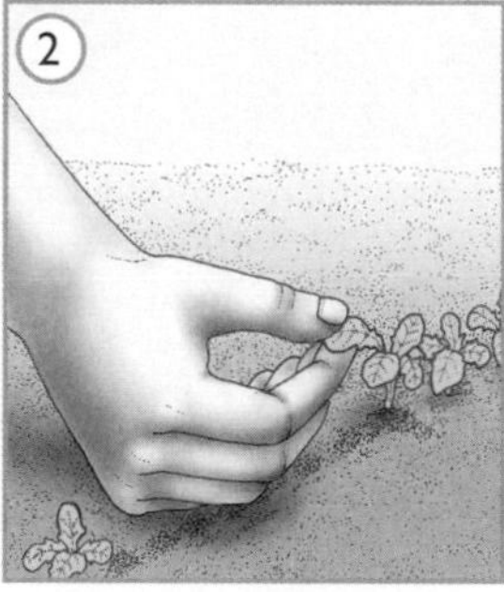

Thin seedlings to 25cm (10in) apart when the first four leaves appear. Water plants regularly.

When they are fully grown, loosely tie each plants around its stems with raffia to reduce the risk of rotting.

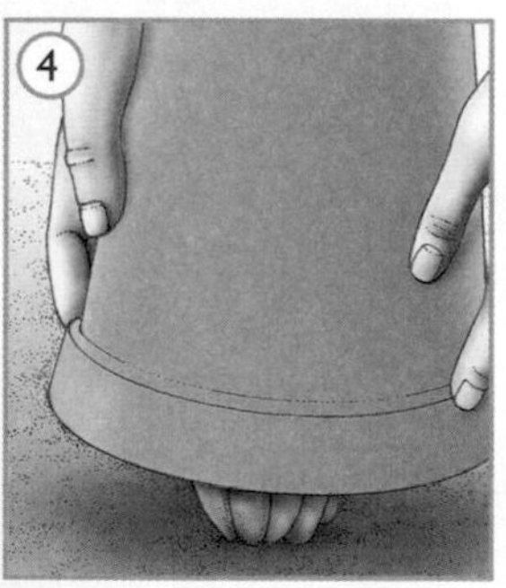

Begin to blanch about four months after sowing; set a large, light-proof container over the plant.

Leave a slight gap between the rim and the soil to prevent rotting. Blanching takes 2–3 weeks.

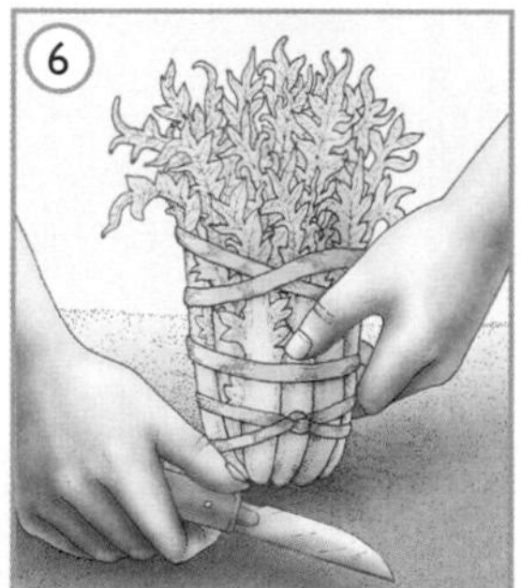

Harvest blanched plants by cutting just above soil level. Blanched endive does not store well.

or broadleaved. The young unblanched leaves may be added to salads.

- Heading chicories form hearts, which may be like a cos lettuce ('Sugar Loaf') or a butterhead lettuce (radicchio). Use the bitter hearts in salads or cooked.

- Forcing chicory (Belgian or Witloof) form chicons from its roots (see box right).

Two sowings after midsummer are usually enough for endive and chicory.

Endive and chicory benefit greatly from additions of organic matter – two bucketfuls of well-rotted compost or manure per square metre (yard) – and of fertiliser. Before sowing, rake in growmore or general fertiliser, at 70g per sq. m (2oz per sq. yd).

Sow seeds 15mm (½in) deep in finely raked moist soil in rows 30cm (1ft) apart; thin seedlings to 30cm (1ft) apart. Endive and chicory can also be raised in celltrays; plant out as soon as their roots bind the potting medium.

Water occasionally in dry spells. Endive and chicory attract virtually no pests or diseases.

Cut the heads when large or when hearts have formed.

FORCING BELGIAN CHICORY

Sow chicory for forcing in late spring and thin to 20cm (8in) apart. Lift roots in early winter when the foliage has died down, discarding any small or forked roots; shorten the rest to 23cm (9in). Store in a box of sand (any type is suitable) until needed for forcing. To force, place the roots in pots of moist, but not wet, garden soil, with added sand if the soil is heavy clay, so that 12mm (½in) of each root is above the soil. Set in a warm place at 7–13°C (45–55°F) and cover with black polythene to exclude light. Chicons (pale, mild-flavoured buds) should form within four weeks.

RECOMMENDED CULTIVARS

Endive

'Pancalieri': curled leaves

'Cornet de Bordeaux': plain leaves

Chicory

'Sugarloaf': mildly bitter

'Pallo Rossa': seriously bitter

'Zoom': Belgian or Witloof chicory for forcing

• CABBAGES •

This nutritious crop yields very heavily indeed in any fertile garden soil in full sun. It is easy to grow and especially useful from late winter to early summer when other greens can be scarce.

- Spring cabbages are sown in late summer and gathered as greens from late winter and as hearted heads from mid-spring until midsummer.

- Summer cabbages are sown from late winter until mid-spring; autumn cabbages, including ones to be cut and stored, are sown in mid-spring; and winter cabbages follow on from these from a late spring sowing.

- Red cabbages and savoy cabbages take a little longer to grow than green

Sowing different types of cabbages spreads harvests and varies flavour and textures.

FROM PLANTING TO HARVESTING SPRING CABBAGES

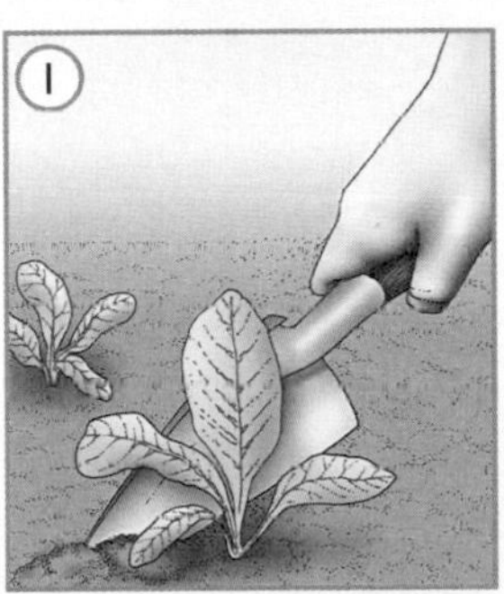

Pull soil around the base of young plants 2 weeks after planting. This protects against windrock in winter, which can loosen the roots and cause problems in later months. Firm any plants loosened later by adverse weather.

Hoe between growing plants from late winter to keep the rows free from competing weeds and maintain a good tilth to the soil. Some of the young cabbages can be cut from early spring if early greens are desired.

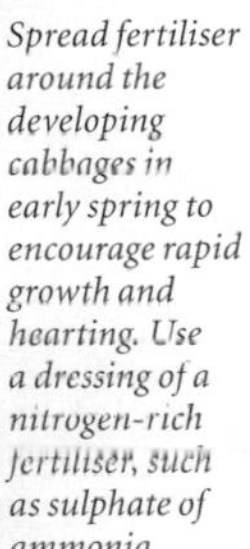

Spread fertiliser around the developing cabbages in early spring to encourage rapid growth and hearting. Use a dressing of a nitrogen-rich fertiliser, such as sulphate of ammonia.

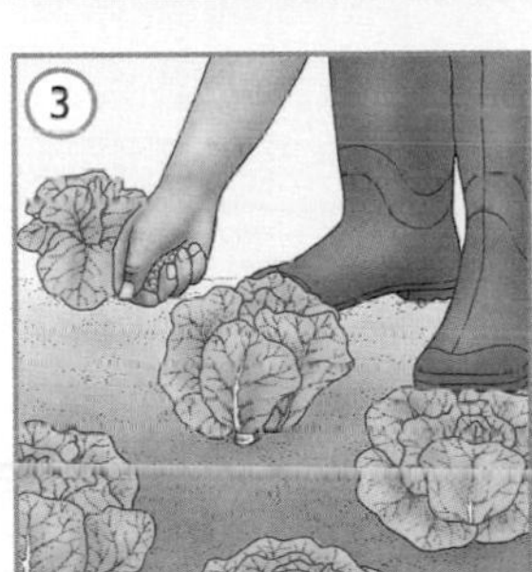

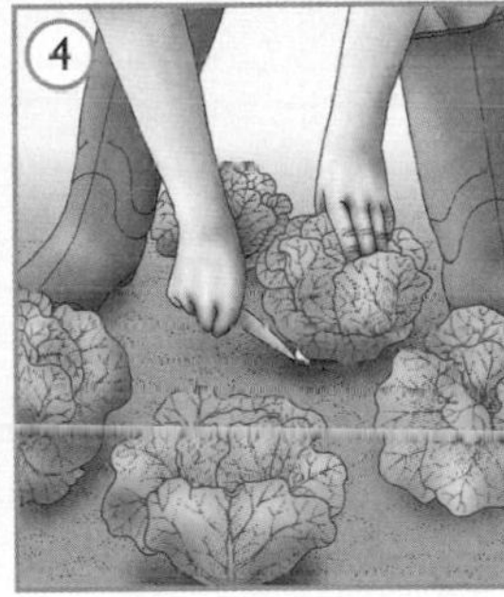

Cut mature spring cabbages from mid-spring. Clear away the stumps and roots, as this breaks the cycle of brassica whitefly, which may otherwise move on to other brassica plants in summer.

cabbages do, and should be started two weeks earlier than them.

Sow twice as many seeds as you will need plants in celltrays or pots filled with multipurpose potting media, and just cover the seeds with sieved potting media or fine vermiculite. They should germinate after 10 days at 12–22°C (54–72°F). As soon as they can be handled, prick out the seedlings into 7–9cm (2½–3in) pots or celltrays filled with multipurpose potting media. Place in good light and feed weekly starting after the first month. Plant out as soon as the roots fill the cell or pot.

Cabbages respond to fertile soil, so dig in two buckets of well-rotted organic matter such as manure every square metre (yard); before planting, apply growmore at 100g per sq. m (3oz per sq. yd) or chicken manure pellets at 150g per sq. m (5oz per sq. yd).

HARVESTING & STORING CABBAGE

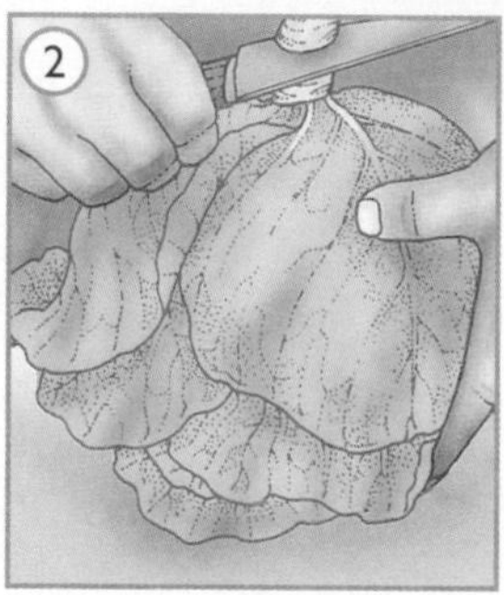

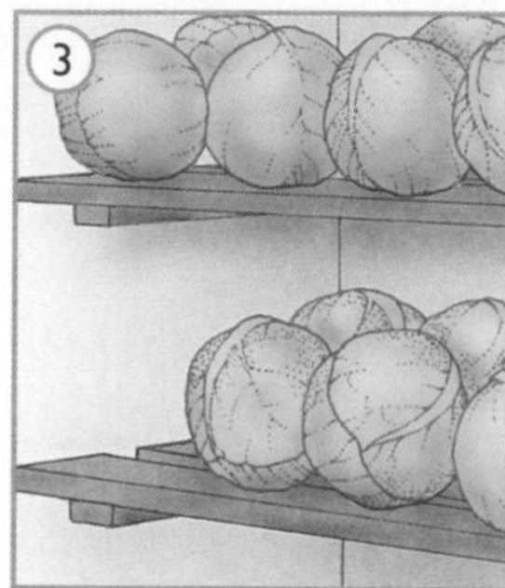

Lift winter cabbages for storing in late autumn and early winter. Some varieties can last through winter.

Trim the roots and bottom of the stem. Remove coarse outer leaves. Dense Dutch cabbages store best.

Store the heads in a cool but frost-free place. Slatted shelving allows air to circulate. Check for blemishes.

Plant spring cabbages 15cm (6in) apart in rows 30cm (12in) apart, with alternate plants cut first for greens and the remaining ones gathered later for hearts. Small summer cabbages need 40cm (16in) each way, but larger autumn and winter ones should be 45cm (18in) apart.

Plant out so the lowest leaves are flush with the soil level, and place a felt disc at the base of the plants to exclude cabbage root fly. Protect with slug controls and cover with fleece or insect-proof mesh for four to six weeks after planting. Water well at planting time and don't let plants dry out until they are growing strongly. When the hearts begin to form, give plants a good soak, wetting the soil to 25cm (10in) deep.

Adding extra nitrogen-rich fertiliser (topdressing), chicken manure pellets, for example at 100g per sq. m (3oz per

CHINESE CABBAGE

Chinese cabbages, which are botanically a form of turnip, are very easy to grow. Although they can be raised in celltrays like other cabbages, they are best sown in the soil, as you would turnips (see p127), in rows 30cm (12in) apart and thinned to 25cm (10in) apart. Sow between mid- and late summer in moist soil. Chinese cabbages are very susceptible to flea beetle, cabbage root fly and caterpillars, so grow under insect-proof mesh. The heads are very dense and store well in a fridge.

RECOMMENDED CULTIVARS

Spring

'First Early Market': tasty leafy greens from late winter

'Offenham I – Myatt's Offenham Compacta': sweet, pointed, reliable

Summer

'Duchy': F1 hybrid, 'Sweetheart'-type with pointed hearts

'Hispi': F1 hybrid, pointed hearts

Autumn

'Huzaro': F1 hybrid, red storing

'Kilaton': F1 hybrid, club root-resistant, white storing cabbage

'Rodeo': F1 hybrid, round red heads

'Sherwood': F1 hybrid, green round heads

Winter

'Deadon': F1 hybrid, 'January King'-type

'Endeavour': F1 hybrid, 'Savoy'-type for late winter

Chinese cabbage

'Kayoh': F1 hybrid, resists club root

sq. yd), when the plants are growing but not yet forming hearts, will often greatly increase yields. Topdressing spring cabbages in late winter is especially recommended.

Birds can be very destructive and netting is usually required throughout the life of the crop. Caterpillars, aphids and cabbage whitefly often need treating with approved insecticides, including those suitable for organic gardeners such as natural pyrethrins (which treat caterpillars and aphids) or soap or oils (used for aphids and whitefly).

Leaf diseases, especially white blister, can disfigure plants but there are no remedies available. The best solution is to choose resistant cultivars. Fortunately the yield is seldom seriously affected. Club root is more serious, but liming the soil to a pH of at least 7.5 (see p19) and raising plants in pots, ideally 15cm (6in) diameter, are usually effective. Club root-resistant white storing cabbage cultivars are available.

Gather heads as soon as they are firm; they store well in the fridge. A couple of 'cross-cuts' to the stump left after cutting the cabbage will promote several little leafy mini-cabbages, ideal for stir-fries or bubble and squeak. More than one crop can be produced in this way.

• BRUSSELS SPROUTS •

Modern Brussels sprouts cultivars have a light flavour and a long period of maturity on compact plants that are ideal for even small gardens.

Early, mid-season and late cultivars are offered for autumn and early winter; for midwinter including Christmas; and for midwinter until early spring, respectively. However, a midwinter maturing cultivar will supply sprouts over a long enough period for most people. Novelty red or leafy sprouts are available.

For the best results, add up to two buckets of well-rotted organic matter, such as manure, and 100g per sq. m (3oz per sq. yd) of growmore or chicken manure pellets before planting.

FROM PLANTING TO HARVESTING BRUSSELS SPROUTS

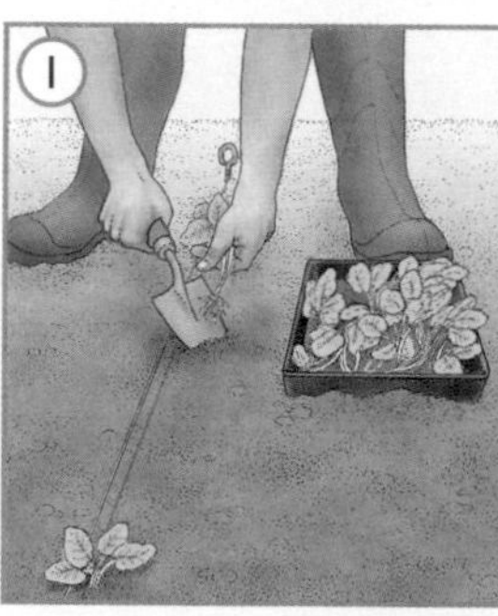

Transplant young plants into well-prepared soil. Space the plants about 60cm (24in) apart in rows 75cm (30in) apart. Plant them firmly with the lowest leaf at soil level.

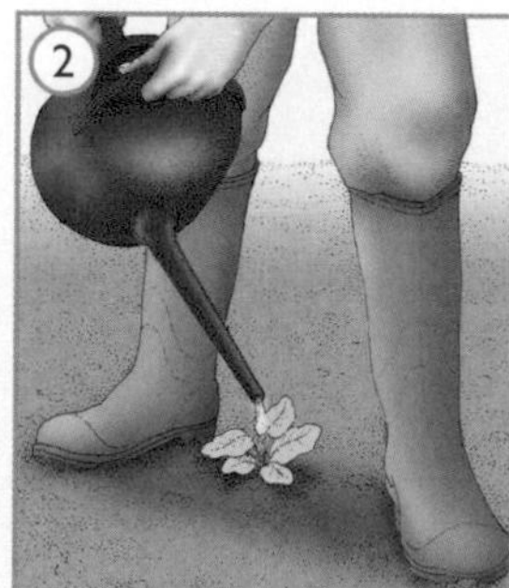

Puddle in the young plants and check that they are firmly planted. Firm planting is essential, as the plants can become top-heavy and planting them in firmly helps them become more stable.

Protect young plants from cabbage root fly by positioning a tightly fitting root collar around the base of each plant at transplanting time. The collar prevents the female laying eggs in the soil.

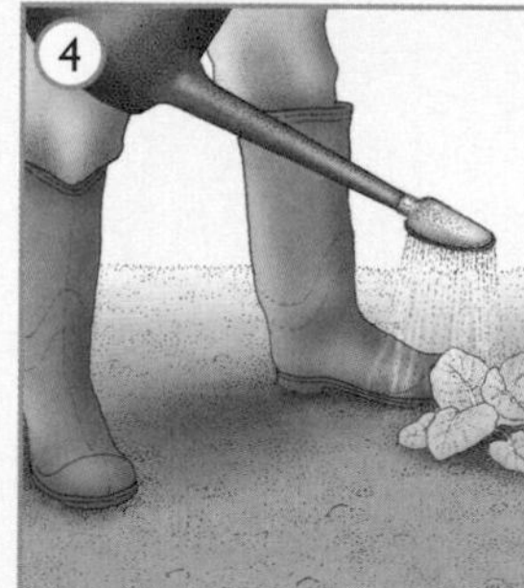

Continue to water young plants through spring and early summer until they are well established. Further watering will not be necessary, unless plants begin to suffer during prolonged dry weather.

Late-winter or early-spring sowing is very advantageous to get a good yield. As few sprout plants are needed in most gardens, raising plants in celltrays or pots in a glasshouse is ideal. Otherwise, cover the seedbed with cloches, a cold frame or even fleece.

Sow twice as many seeds as you will need plants in celltrays or pots filled with multipurpose potting media, and just cover the seeds with sieved potting media or fine vermiculite. After about 10 days at 12–22°C (54–72°F), the seeds should germinate. As soon as they can be handled prick out the seedlings into celltrays or 7–9cm (2½–3in) pots filled with multipurpose potting media. Place in good light and feed weekly after the first month. Plant out as soon as the roots fill the cell or pot.

Draw up some soil around the base of each stem during summer in light soils or on exposed sites, to make the plants more stable. Hoe around the plants regularly to keep them free from weeds.

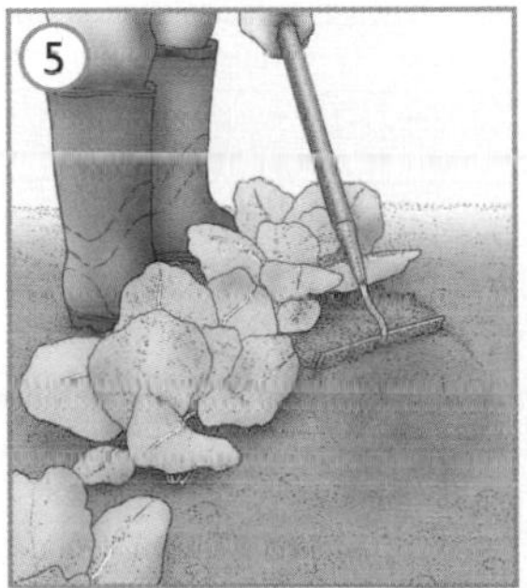

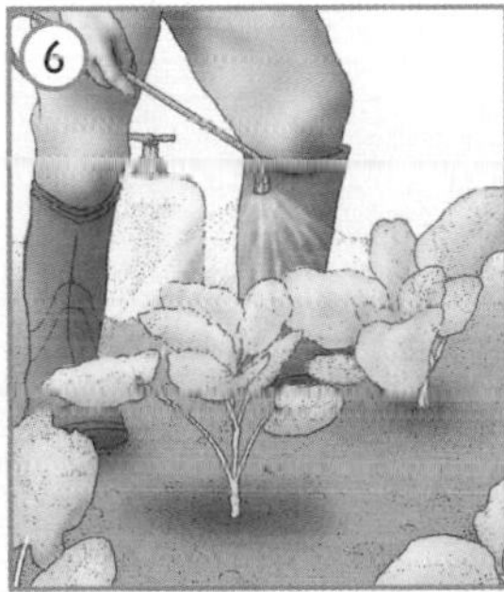

Apply nitrogen-rich fertiliser at the base of plants in midsummer at about 30g (1oz) per square metre (yard). To protect the crop from cabbage white butterflies and pigeons, cover with a fine-mesh netting.

From late summer onwards, remove loose or open sprouts from the lower stems, and any yellowing leaves, consigning them to the compost bin. This will reduce foliage disease and suppress slugs.

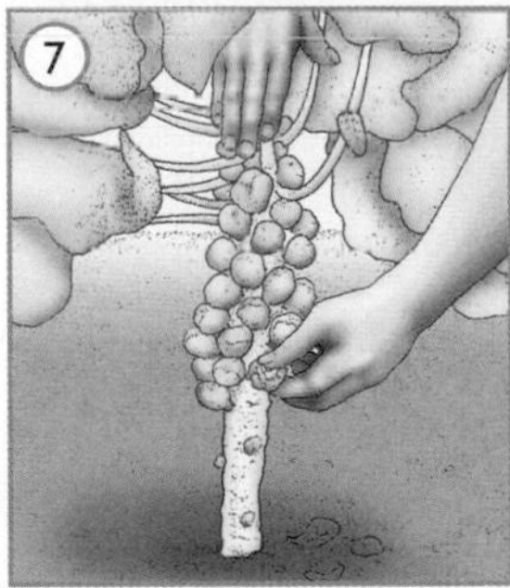

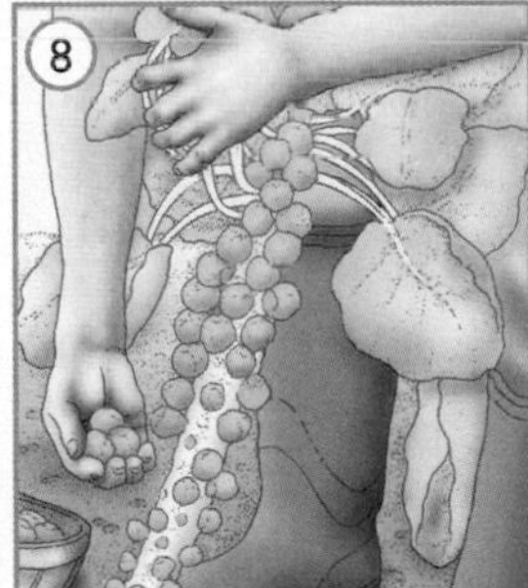

Gather sprouts when they are firm, as required, starting from the bottom of the stem. The leafy tops of the plants can also be removed for eating, but not before most of the sprouts have been collected.

Plant out so the lowest leaves are flush with the soil level and firm very well. A quick test is to tug a leaf of a newly planted sprout – the leaf should tear before the plant comes out of the ground. Place a felt disc at the base of the plants to exclude cabbage root fly. Protect with slug controls and cover with fleece or insect-proof mesh for three to four weeks after planting. Water well at planting time and don't let plants dry out until they are well established and growing strongly.

BRUSSELS SPROUT VARIETIES

Conventional varieties (right) *compare poorly to modern F1 hybrids* (left). *They produce fluffy, poor-quality sprouts that are less abundant and have less resistance to disease.*

Bare-root transplants are grown by sowing seeds under fleece, 12mm (½in) deep, in soil free of club root disease. Allow for one seed every 3cm (1in), in rows 20cm (8in) apart. Plant out the seedlings in fertile garden soil in full sun when they have about seven true leaves. Allow 60cm (24in) between plants and 90cm (36in) between rows.

Modern sprouts have been bred to resist diseases and to remove bitterness, which can make them unpalatable.

Aim to soak plants well every 14 days in rainless periods, but even this may not be necessary in rich, heavy soils. In late summer, applying extra nitrogen-rich fertiliser (topdressing) – chicken manure pellets at 100g per sq. m (3oz per sq. yd), for example – will encourage large, healthy and productive plants. In windy gardens, draw earth 25cm (10in) up plant stems in early autumn or stake individual plants.

Snap off sprouts as soon as large enough, starting with the earliest at the base of the stem and finishing several months later with those at the top of the stem. The head makes valuable greens.

Caterpillars, aphids and cabbage whitefly often need treating with approved insecticides. Cabbage root fly can sometimes attack the sprouts as well as the roots, so cover the crop with insect-proof mesh until winter.

Insect-parasitising nematodes are sold to control caterpillars and also cabbage root fly. They need moisture to work and are, therefore, more likely to be successful against cabbage root fly than against caterpillars which inhabit the drier, aerial parts of the plant.

Bird netting is often required ,especially in late winter when spoilage from bird droppings is as destructive as their feeding. Leaf diseases such as ringspot can make the sprouts unappetising, especially in wet regions, so choose resistant cultivars.

Club root is more serious, but liming the soil to a pH of at least 7.5 (see p19) and raising plants in pots, ideally 15cm (6in) diameter, are usually effective. Club root-resistant cultivars are available.

RECOMMENDED CULTIVARS

Hybrids greatly outperform open-pollinated cultivars, which are no longer worth raising. Best cultivars are seldom offered as plants and raising from seed is the only option.

Early

'Abacus': F1 hybrid
'Maximus': F1 hybrid

Mid-season

'Cronos': club root-resistant F1 hybrid
'Montgomery': F1 hybrid
'Petit Posy': leafy sprouts, F1 hybrid
'Red Bull': red sprouts, F1 hybrid

Late

'Revenge': F1 hybrid

• CAULIFLOWERS & CALABRESE •

Calabrese is exceptionally easy to grow in any fertile, well-drained garden soil in full sun. If spaced widely enough, it can crop over a long season in summer and autumn due to the sideshoots that follow the cutting of the first and main stem. Cauliflowers are a little harder to grow and need deep, fertile, moist but well-drained soil, but are valued for their early ripening in summer and for

FROM SOWING TO HARVESTING SUMMER CAULIFLOWER

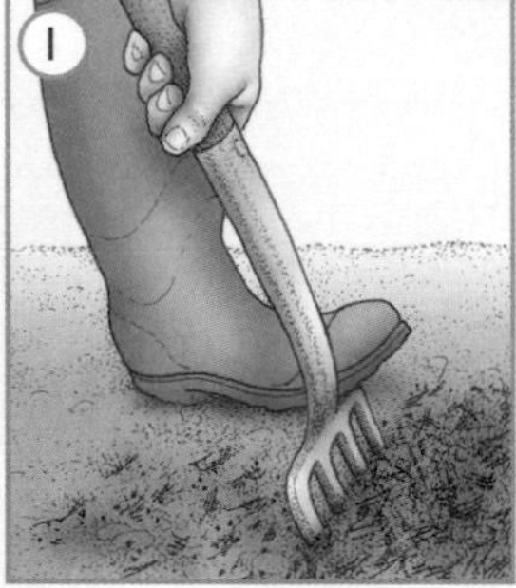

Cultivate the soil deeply in winter, and dig in plenty of well-rotted manure or garden compost.

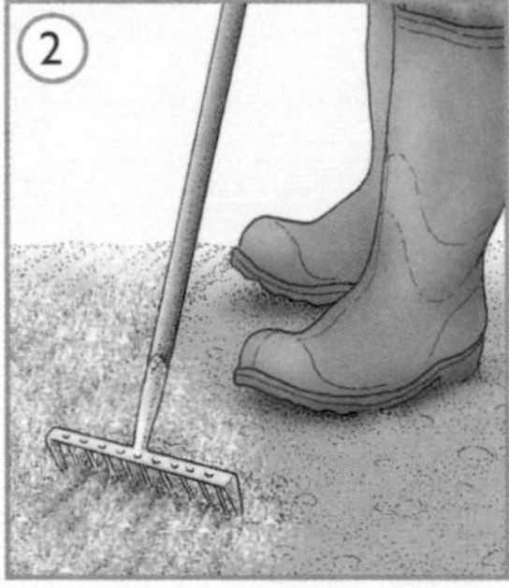

If the soil is still poor rake in extra fertiliser 1–2 weeks before sowing or planting out.

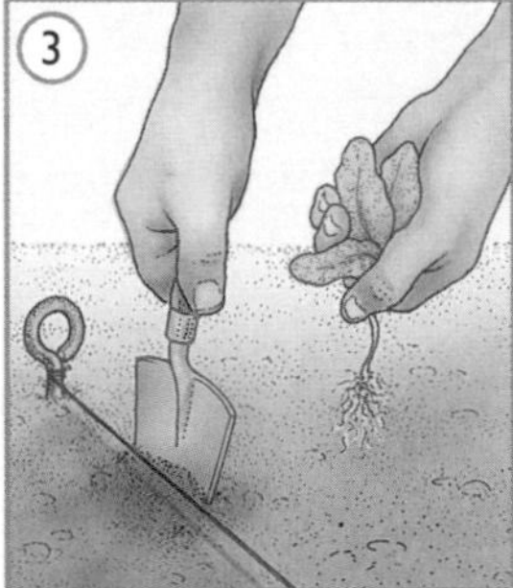

Water seedlings and soil the day before transplanting the seedlings at desired spacings. Then water well.

Water in nitrogen-rich fertiliser in late spring for transplanted crops or in midsummer for those sown direct.

Water weekly in dry weather, two watering cans per square metre (yard). Also water as the curds form.

Cut cauliflowers when the curds are firm and well developed, but not yet beginning to open.

their ability to produce heads in autumn and spring, or even, in very mild regions, in winter. Mini cauliflowers offer an easy-to-grow alternative for gardens with poorer soil.

- Summer cauliflowers are sown in late winter or early spring, in glasshouses or with other protection. Plant out in mid-spring to harvest in summer and early autumn.

- Autumn cauliflowers are sown in mid- to late spring. Plant out in early summer for cutting in autumn.

- Winter cauliflowers are sown in late spring to early summer. Plant out in summer for harvesting in winter. They are feasible only in mild regions, where hard frosts are unlikely.

- Overwintered cauliflowers (also called, confusingly, broccoli) are sown in late spring to early summer. Plant out in summer for cutting the following spring in regions where hard winters are unlikely.

- Calabrese (again, also called broccoli) is sown from late winter to late summer. Plant out from mid-spring to late summer for cutting from early summer until early winter. Some calabrese has very large central heads; others emphasise their shoots and stems, and may be called 'tender stem'.

- Romanesco is a cauliflower type plant with tasty, whorled, light green curds and is grown for autumn crops. It is more tolerant of adverse conditions than cauliflowers but not as reliable as calabrese.

Calabrese can quickly run to flower so prompt harvesting is needed.

MINI-CAULIFLOWERS

Spacing summer cauliflower plants 15cm (6in) apart in rows 25cm (10in) apart causes them to form small heads. Seed suppliers usually have some recommendations, but sowing batches every two to three weeks is required, as the mini-heads mature together, potentially causing a glut.

Sow twice as many seeds as you will need plants in celltrays or pots filled with multipurpose potting media, and cover the seeds with sieved potting media or fine vermiculite. They should germinate after 10 days at 12–22°C (54–72°F). As soon as they can be handled, prick out the seedlings into 7–9cm (2½–3in) pots or celltrays filled with multipurpose potting media. Place in good light and feed weekly, starting after the first month. Plant out as soon as the roots fill the cell or pot.

Give cauliflowers and calabrese two buckets of well-rotted organic matter such as manure, and 100g (3oz) of growmore or 150g (5oz) of chicken manure pellets every square metre (yard) before planting.

Plant out so the lowest leaves are flush with the soil level. Plant summer cauliflowers 45cm (18in) apart but larger autumn, winter and overwintered cauliflowers and Romanesco 50cm (20in) apart. Plant calabrese 45cm (18in) apart for single large heads; allowing a space of 40cm (16in) between plants in rows 50cm (20in) apart yields large heads followed by successive sideshoots over several weeks.

Cover spring-planted crops with fleece for four to six weeks, to avoid the check in growth that can cause premature head formation and to give protection from cabbage root fly. In summer, use insect-proof mesh. When the crop outgrows the mesh, place a felt disc at each plant base to exclude the cabbage root fly.

Water the plants thoroughly at planting. Keep cauliflowers moist at all times, but if this is not possible, a good soak at the beginning of head formation will give fair results.

To increase yields, add extra nitrogen-rich fertiliser (topdressing) – chicken manure pellets, for example, at 100g per sq. m (3oz per sq. yd) – when the plants are growing but not yet forming heads. Topdress overwintered cauliflowers in late winter.

Cut heads as soon as they are large enough, before they open and coarsen.

Bird netting is usually required throughout the life of the crop. Caterpillars, aphids and cabbage whitefly often need treating with approved insecticides. Leaf diseases such as ringspot can disfigure plants but the yield is seldom significantly affected. These crops are very susceptible to club root but liming the soil to a pH of at least 7.5 (see p19) and raising plants in pots, ideally 15cm (6in) in diameter, are usually effective. Club root-resistant summer and autumn cauliflower cultivars are available.

RECOMMENDED CULTIVARS

Summer

'Aviso': vigorous, robust

'Clapton': club root-resistant

Autumn

'Graffiti': purple

'Moby Dick': vigorous

'Talbot': high-quality heads

Winter

'Belot': high-quality cauliflower for early winter

Overwintered

'Aalsmeer': very robust; for mid-spring heads

'Evita': hardy; for early summer heads

Calabrese

'Fiesta': very productive all year

'Kalibroc': stem type

'Marathon': heavy yielding

Romanesco

'Celio': quick-growing

'Veronica': large heads on strong plants

• BROCCOLI •

In addition to the traditional spring crops, sprouting broccoli now matures from late winter until late spring, and from summer until autumn.

One especially useful form is purple cape broccoli (some call it a cauliflower), which produces one purple, very tasty head in late winter usually just before sprouting broccoli begins. Only moderate fertility is required, but full sun and a well-drained soil are essential.

Sow in mid-spring for summer and autumn sprouting cultivars, and in late spring and early summer for the overwintered ones. Summer-heading types sprout as soon as they are big enough, but the overwintered ones need the stimulus of a period of cold.

Dig in two buckets of well-rotted organic matter, such as manure, per square metre (yard). Add extra fertiliser only if the soil is very poor.

Sow twice as many seeds as you will need plants in celltrays or pots filled with multipurpose potting media, and just cover the seeds with sieved potting media or fine vermiculite. The seedlings will emerge after about 10 days. As soon as they can be handled, prick out the seedlings into 7–9cm (2½–3in) pots or celltrays filled with multipurpose potting media. Place in good light

FROM PLANTING TO HARVESTING SPROUTING BROCCOLI

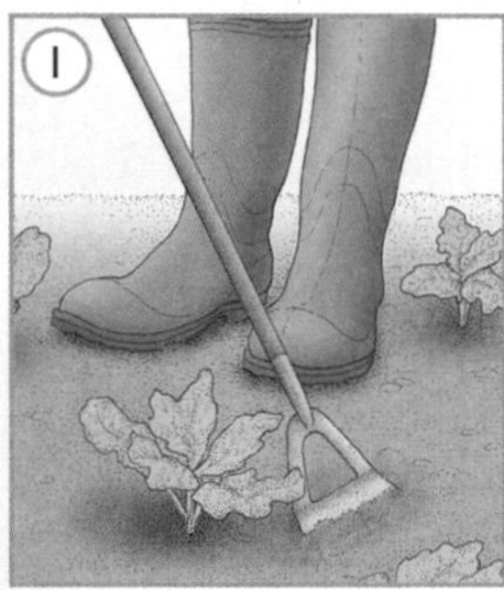

Set transplants in their final position in early to midsummer. Keep weed-free and water in dry spells.

Cut off any central head that forms, or the topmost shoots. Water in a fertiliser at this stage.

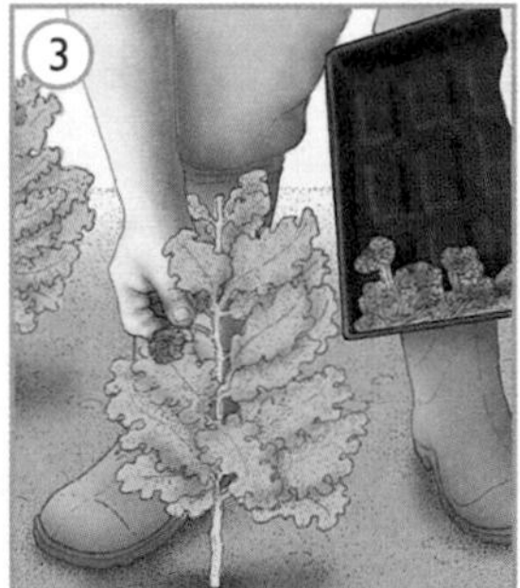

Harvest any sideshoots that develop further down the stem, every few days for as long as possible.

and feed weekly, starting after the first month. Plant out as soon as the roots fill the cell or pot.

Plant out allowing 75cm (30in) between plants in all directions. Set the lowest leaves flush with the soil level and place a felt disc at the base of the plants to exclude cabbage root fly. Water well at planting time, but after that watering should seldom be required. Suspend netting above the crop throughout its life. Feed summer crops as you would calabrese (see pp80–83).

Gather shoots as soon as they are usable and keep cropping so that none is allowed to flower. Cropping may continue for several weeks. After harvesting, destroy the plants to prevent any carry-over of pests and diseases.

Caterpillars, aphids and cabbage whitefly occasionally need treating. Leaf diseases such as ringspot can disfigure plants in wet regions but yield is seldom badly affected. Lime the soil to a pH of at least 7.5 (see p19) to protect against club root.

RECOMMENDED CULTIVARS

'Bordeaux': early to mid-spring
'Claret': early to mid-spring
'Late Purple Sprouting': early to mid-spring
'Rudolph': midwinter to early spring
'Summer Purple': summer cropping
'White Star': white, early to mid-spring

The central head of sprouting broccoli will need pigeon protection.

• KALE •

Kale are probably the easiest of all cabbage plants to grow and even beginner gardeners can be certain of good results. It is a very versatile, hardy and nutritious crop, with new cultivars offering a mild fresh flavour and crisp textures. Kale seedlings are often used in mini-leaf salads. Red and black kales are both appetising and easy on the eye.

Dig in one or two buckets of well-rotted organic matter such as manure per square metre (yard) before planting. Use extra fertiliser (100g per sq. m/3oz per sq. yd of growmore or chicken manure pellets) only if the soil is poor.

Sow twice as many seeds as you will need plants in a pot, pan or seedtray of multipurpose potting media, from mid-spring for autumn crops and again in early to midsummer for winter and spring crops. Just cover the seeds with sieved potting media or fine vermiculite. The seedlings emerge after about 10 days. As soon as they can be handled,

Kales are a winter proof, tasty and heavy yielding asset for greens, salads and stir-fries.

HARVESTING KALE

Pick only young leaves and shoots, pulling off and discarding yellowing or tough old leaves. Sideshoots will form in response; again, harvest when young, from the top downwards.

prick them out into 7–9cm (2½–3in) pots or celltrays filled with multipurpose potting media. Place in good light. Plant out when their roots fill the pot, allowing 40–50cm (16–20in) between plants, depending on the size when mature. Water in very well and place a felt disc around each plant stem. Little further watering is usually required, although fortnightly soaks might be needed in prolonged droughts.

If growth is poor, apply extra nitrogen-rich fertiliser, such as chicken manure pellets, at 100g per sq. m (3oz per sq. yd) and water in.

Draw soil 25cm (10in) up around the stems of tall cultivars in late summer in exposed gardens (note that dwarf cultivars are available).

Gather young shoots and leaves as soon as they are big enough and when required. By spring, new shoots form that should be picked while young and tasty. Once plants flower, the crop is over and must be consigned to the compost bin.

Bird netting is advisable. Caterpillars, aphids and cabbage whitefly very occasionally need treating with approved insecticides. Those suitable for organic gardeners such as natural pyrethrins (caterpillars and aphids) or soap or oils (aphids and whitefly) are usually sufficient for good control. These crops are not very susceptible to cabbage root fly nor to club root. Liming the soil to a pH of at least 7.5 (see p19) is adequate where club root occurs.

RECOMMENDED CULTIVARS

'Black Tuscan': strap-like black leaves, used for baby leaf salads
'Dwarf Green Curled': low-growing
'Redbor': red leaves
'Winterbor': tall, hardy

• CHARD •

Chard and leaf beets are the same species as beetroot and agricultural beets such as sugar beet. Being easily grown, they are ideal crops for beginner gardeners.

Leaf beets have abundant green tender leaves. Chard has thickened midribs and is offered with a range of leaf colours from green through yellow to red, although colour is lost on cooking.

These leaf beets, especially spinach beet, are hardy, and late summer sowings survive winter to yield abundant foliage from mid-spring until early summer – they are more reliable in this than autumn-sown spinach. Similarly, leaf beets are very much less likely than spinach to go to seed or spoil where soils are light and retain little moisture.

FROM SOWING TO HARVESTING SPINACH BEET

Sow 3–4 seeds at 20cm (8in) intervals in 2cm (¾in) deep drills from late winter for spring crops, in mid-spring for summer crops, and in late summer for crops the following spring.

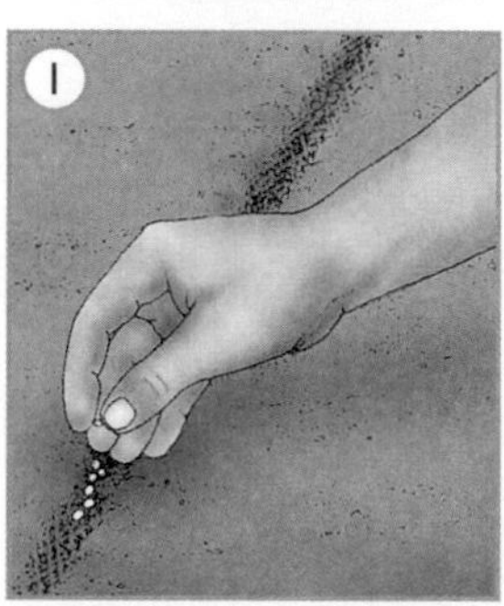

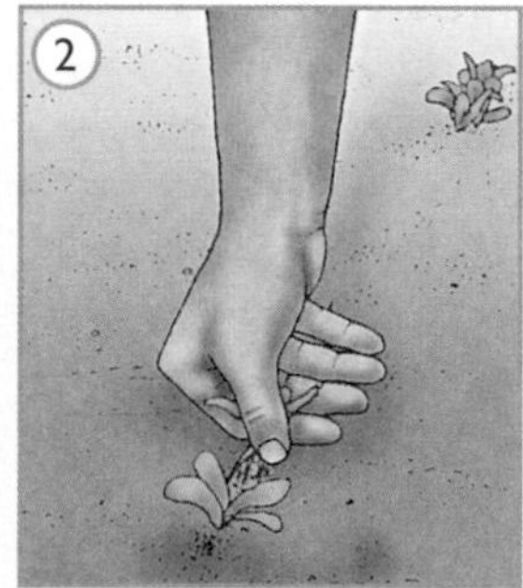

Thin the seedling clusters when each seedling is big enough to handle. Leave one seedling per station. Thinning can be done over several weeks, as the thinnings are useful eaten either raw or cooked.

Hoe regularly between the rows during the growing season. Water the growing plants liberally, approximately 2 watering cans per square metre (yard) every 5–10 days in hot, dry weather.

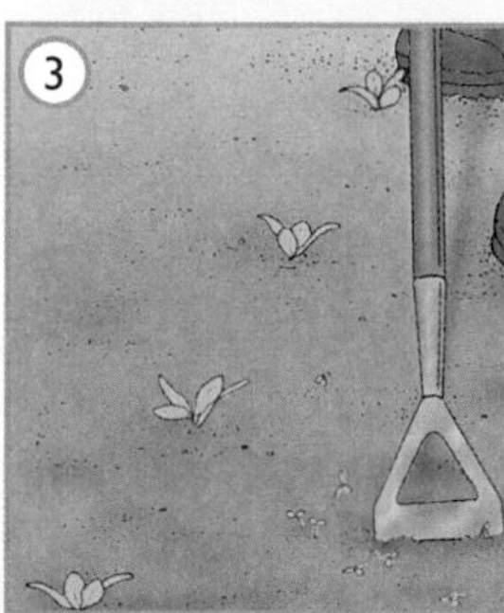

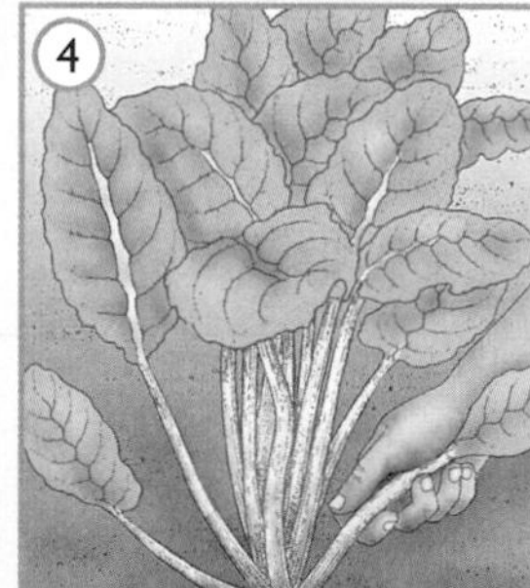

Harvest a few of the largest leaves after 60–80 days or as soon as the plants are large enough, picking them as close to the ground as possible. Gather the leaves regularly to encourage further production.

Leaf beets and chard are not fussy about their growing conditions, as long as the soil is well drained and in full sun. Enrich the soil with at least half a bucket of organic matter such as garden compost, with 100g per sq. m (3oz per sq. yd) of growmore or other general-purpose fertiliser raked in before sowing. Use twice as much organic fertiliser, such as chicken manure pellets. Produce grown in areas where a preceding crop was well fertilised usually need no extra fertiliser. Overwintered crops should, however, receive fertiliser in spring.

These robust plants grow well in containers at least 45cm (18in) deep and wide, filled with any good multipurpose potting media.

Where a constant succession of mini-leaves is needed, sow every three weeks from mid-spring until early autumn outdoors. Supplies for at least some of the winter can be had from an autumn sowing in a glasshouse or similar protected environment.

Give plants a thorough soak every 14 days during prolonged dry spells. Topdress with nitrogen-rich fertiliser, at 35g per sq. m (1oz per sq. yd), where growth is slow, especially for overwintered crops.

Harvesting could not be easier, with leaves being gathered as required. New leaves are produced over a long period, particularly if regular and thorough cutting is carried out.

Leaf beets have few pests and diseases, with leaf miners and leaf mildews and spots being occasional problems. Discarding affected foliage is often sufficient. Blackfly are an occasional pest and can be controlled with insecticides based on fatty acids or oils, which leave no residues.

RECOMMENDED CULTIVARS

'Bright Lights': a mixture of red, white, pink, violet, green, gold, orange, yellow and striped plants

'Lucullus': abundant large green leaves with wide tender midribs

New Zealand spinach: a sprawling plant that needs the same growing conditions as other leaf beets; when sown from mid-spring, it will grow where no other leaf beets really thrive, even in hanging baskets

Rhubarb chard: red stalks and purple foliage

Spinach beet: hardy selection to overwinter

• SPINACH •

Spinach is a short-lived annual grown for its tender, succulent and tasty leaves. It has gained a new popularity as a 'mini-leaf' in leafy salads.

- Plain-leaved: spinach is the robust ordinary one with barely any leaf puckering, which can be grown all year. It has the expected flavour and texture of spinach and grows in an upright habit, making it easy to wash before use.

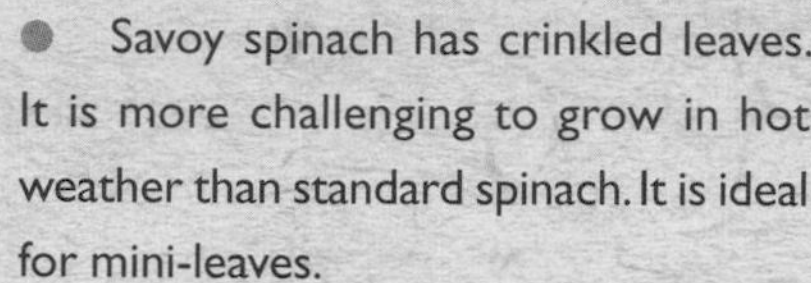

- Savoy spinach has crinkled leaves. It is more challenging to grow in hot weather than standard spinach. It is ideal for mini-leaves.

- Semi-savoy is more upright and less crinkled than savoy spinach and, therefore, easier to pick. It is good for mini-leaves.

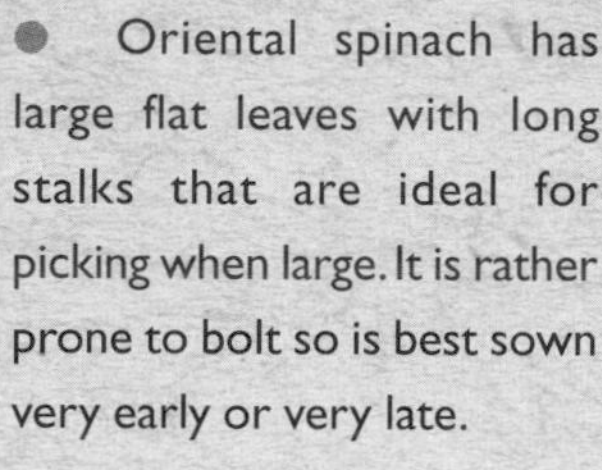

- Oriental spinach has large flat leaves with long stalks that are ideal for picking when large. It is rather prone to bolt so is best sown very early or very late.

Spinach will bolt very quickly in hot dry weather, unless grown in fertile soil that holds ample moisture. Therefore, before sowing add a bucketful of organic matter, such as garden compost or farmyard manure, to every square metre (yard) of soil and also 100g per sq. m (3oz

Older leaves can be picked, but as the plants mature the whole plant can be taken.

per sq. yd) of general-purpose fertiliser, or 200g per sq. m (6oz per sq. yd) of organic fertiliser such as chicken manure pellets. In spring, give overwintered spinach a nitrogen-rich fertiliser such as sulphate of ammonia, at 35g per sq. m (1oz per sq. yd) or chicken manure pellets, at 100g per sq. m (3oz per sq. yd).

Start sowing, under fleece, in late winter and continue every three weeks until early autumn. Although full sun is advisable for early and late sowings, in midsummer spinach is actually a little easier to grow in light shade.

Sow seeds 2cm (¾in) deep and two finger widths apart in rows 30cm (12in) apart. Water to keep the soil moist; this is critical in summer. Thin plants to 15cm (6in) in stages (use the thinnings in the kitchen), and then gather leaves from the remaining plants until they bolt.

For mini-leaves, sow seed 1cm (½in) apart in rows 15cm (6in) apart. Pick the leaves as soon as usable and go on plucking until the plants give up. Grown in this way, spinach is an easy crop for containers and also for containers in an unheated glasshouse for early and late crops. Fill the containers, which should be at least 15cm (6in) deep but preferably 30cm (12in) deep, with any fertile moisture-retentive potting media. Water them often to avoid dry periods and feed regularly, often weekly, with liquid fertiliser.

Slugs and snails can be troublesome. If aphids infest young plants on mini-leaves destined to be eaten young, then treat with non-persistent insecticides such as those based on oils or soap (fatty acids). Downy mildew is seldom a serious problem with widely spaced crops.

RECOMMENDED CULTIVARS

'Boeing': F1 hybrid with very good bolting resistance, so especially suitable for summer sowing

'Bordeaux': F1 hybrid with red stems and leaves; ideal for mini-leaves where its colour can be best appreciated

'Galaxy': F1 hybrid robust oriental type that can be grown over winter

'Monza': F1 hybrid plain leaf with strong bolting resistance; ideal for sowing in summer

'Rakalia': F1 hybrid 'savoy'-type leaf spinach ideal for mini-leaves, but not suited to midsummer sowing

• ASPARAGUS •

Despite being expensive to buy, asparagus is not difficult to grow and crops heavily in spring at a time of year when little else is in season. The two-year delay between planting and harvesting puts many gardeners off, but the wait is worthwhile.

A plantation can last for 10 or more years with little work needed other than rigorous weeding, as perennial weeds are hard to control in asparagus.

Asparagus will grow in any well-drained, sunny spot where frost does not linger because young shoots are vulnerable to damage, and where there is shelter from winds. Where drainage is poor, plant asparagus on a raised bed or ridge. It is worth getting the soil into top condition before planting because, once planted, any shortcomings are hard to remedy. If a pH test shows the soil to be acid, liming to pH 6.5–7 will promote good crops. Before planting, weed very thoroughly and add at least two bucketfuls of well-rotted compost or manure every square metre (yard).

Old-fashioned, non-hybrid cultivars consist of male and (less productive) female plants, and compare poorly to the more vigorous all-male F1 hybrids, where the spears are bigger, tastier and more numerous and there are far fewer asparagus seedlings to weed out (the odd female plant can crop up within male hybrid plantings).

Sow seed in late winter in celltrays or modules in a heated propagator. Pot on the seedlings before setting them out in mid- to late spring to grow on. Grown like this, asparagus can crop in

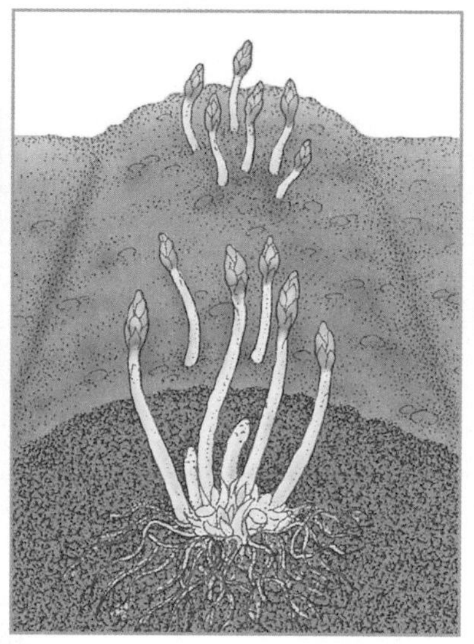

HOW ASPARAGUS GROWS

Emerging shoots, or 'spears', grow from a rootstock deep underground. The plant dies back to this rootstock over winter.

GROWING ASPARAGUS: THE FIRST YEAR

Dig to the depth of one spade blade in winter. Add plenty of well-rotted organic matter (scatter it with a fork) and lime as required, so the soil pH is between 6.5 and 7. Ensure that the ground is clear of weeds before you plant.

In spring, dig a trench 30cm (12in) wide and 20cm (8in) deep. Lightly rake into the trench 100g (3oz) of general-purpose fertiliser every square metre (yard). Make a ridge 10cm (4in) high at the base of the trench.

Plant the crowns in spring at 40cm (16in) intervals. Spread the spidery roots evenly over the ridge, with the buds pointing upwards. Pull back soil into the trench over the roots so that the crown tops are just covered.

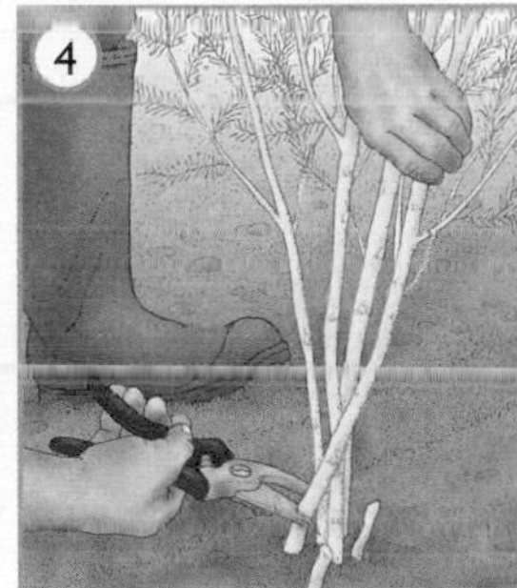

Cut back stems in autumn once they turn yellow. Remove any weeds by hand; do not dig deeply as asparagus roots are easily damaged. In late winter spread a 5–8cm (2–3in) layer of organic matter over the row.

year three, or even year two, if the plants grow especially well.

Seed can also be sown outdoors in mid-spring and the seedlings transplanted as dormant rootstocks or crowns in winter or the following spring. These asparagus plants will take two years to establish and will be ready to crop in year three.

Most home gardeners, however, buy one- or two-year-old crowns, which will be ready to crop in two years from a spring planting.

In spring, dig trenches 1.2m (4ft) apart and in the base add 100g (3oz) general-purpose fertiliser such as growmore or double the quantity of pelleted chicken manure. Plant the crowns and just cover them so that the final trench depth is 15cm (6in). The trench will gradually fill during watering and weeding. Make the ridges taller if you want to grow white asparagus, which is harvested as soon as it shows on the surface, cutting deep in the soil to get a long stem.

Water every 10 days in dry spells for the first two years, and each spring, topdress with 70g (2½oz) general-purpose fertiliser such as growmore or double the quantity of pelleted chicken manure. Mulch with well-rotted organic matter, 5cm (2in) thick, to suppress weeds and feed the plants. Mushroom compost is ideal because it has no weed seeds.

Handweed the bed, as the shallow roots are easily damaged by hoeing. Cover the bed with opaque landscape fabric in winter to suppress annual weeds. Very careful spot treatment with a ready-to-use weedkiller gun containing glyphosate can deal with deep-seated perennial weeds such as bindweed, but if

MANAGING AN ASPARAGUS BED

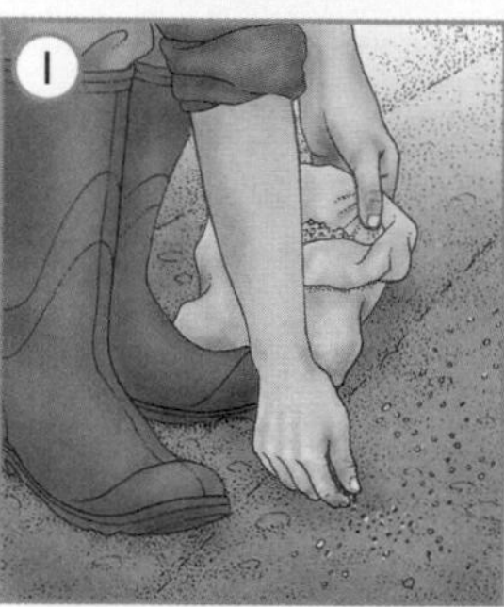

Topdress the bed with 100g (3oz) of general-purpose fertiliser every square metre (yard) in early spring to feed the coming growth. Double the quantity if you are using organic fertilisers.

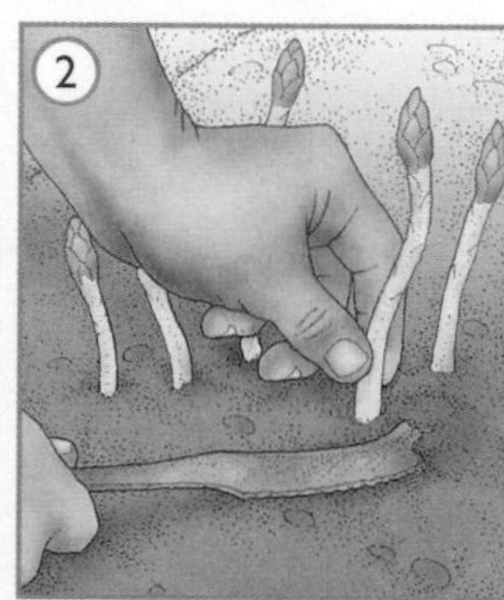

Cut spears with a sharp knife in mid-spring when 12–15cm (5–6in) tall. Cut each spear obliquely 2.5–5cm (1–2in) below the soil surface. Do not damage any underground shoots as you do so.

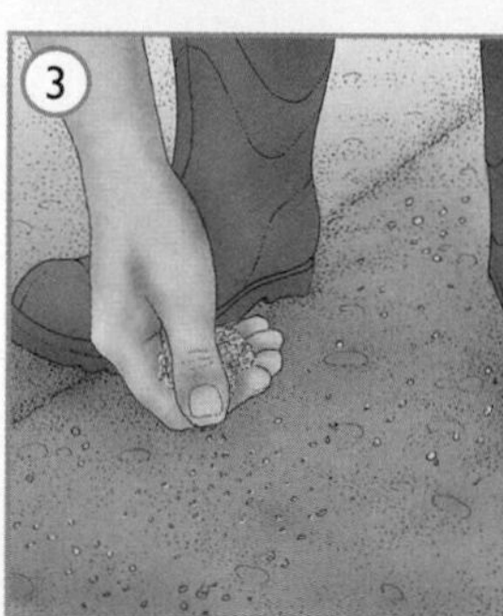

Apply a post-harvest dressing of general-purpose fertiliser at the same rate as in spring. This extra fertiliser is not essential but ensures a high level of fertility as the plant builds up energy for the next harvest.

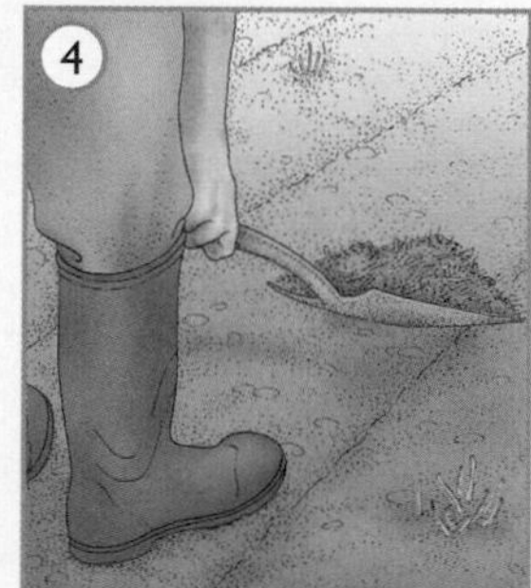

Cut down the yellowed stems and foliage in autumn and add to the compost heap or burn. Remove weeds by hand or with a trowel, then apply a mulch of well-rotted manure or compost.

asparagus plants are accidentally treated they will be severely damaged, although they should recover in time.

Allow the fern to turn yellow and straw-like each autumn before cutting it and consigning it to the compost bin or bonfire. Use stakes and string to support the fern in windy periods. It is traditional for culinary salt to be applied at 35g per sq. m (1oz per sq. yd) in winter, although not essential.

By the third spring, some spears can be cut, but cropping should be brief – six weeks only. An eight-week harvest period is allowed in subsequent years, but by early summer, the plants must be allowed to recover if crops the following year are not going to be compromised. All shoots must be severed for good cropping and to ensure that it continues for eight weeks.

Asparagus beetle is a major pest and has to be treated with natural pyrethrins if handpicking is insufficient. Where leaf diseases and root diseases occur, remove and destroy affected shoots and crowns. Slugs and frost can cause damage to emerging spears.

RECOMMENDED CULTIVARS

'Backlim': large crops of thick spears

'Gijnlim': large crops of spears with purple tips

'Mondeo': very heavy yields of high-quality spears

Strong fern supported by sticks and string gathers sunlight, leading to productive crowns.

• RHUBARB •

Rhubarb is a vegetable used as a fruit, and provides flavoursome stalks at a time of year when little else is available. To do this, the plants need to be strong and leafy in summer. This requires a position in fertile, well-drained soil in full sun, so they can store plenty of reserves in their fleshy crowns to support vigorous stalks that can be gathered the following year. Plants need replacing at intervals of three to five years.

Offsets from established plants are taken in winter, each with a length of root and at least one bud, from the vigorous areas at the edge of the clump. Plant immediately at the same depth in very fertile soil, enriched with at least two bucketfuls of well-rotted compost

FROM PLANTING TO HARVESTING RHUBARB

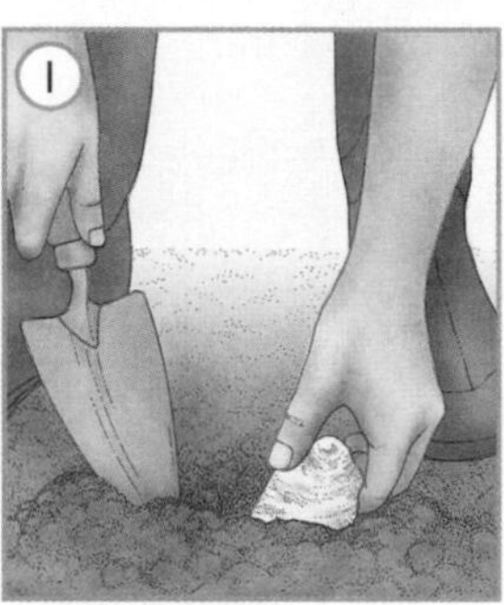

Take offsets with a strong bud from the edge of a parent plant in winter or early spring. Replant 1m (3ft) apart in enriched and well-fertilised soil. Plant the offset with the bud just above the surface.

Feed plants in spring with 100g (3oz) of general fertiliser per square metre (yard). Water well in dry spells, and keep weed-free. A spring mulch will prevent weeds and improve growth.

Remove old leaves in autumn, once they have turned brown and helped to build up reserves in the root. Apply a general-purpose fertiliser at 100g per sq. m (3oz per sq. yd).

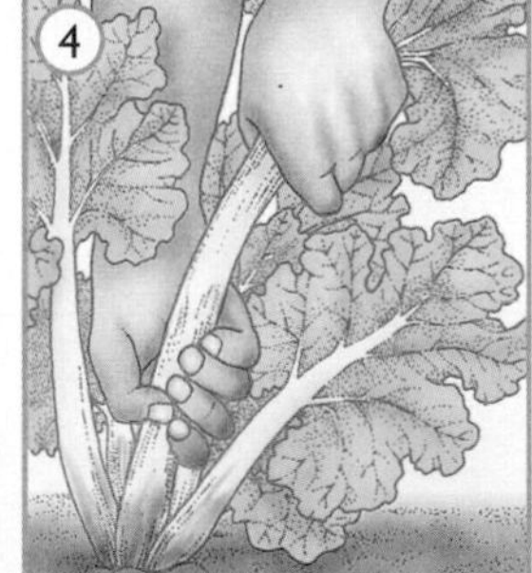

Harvest stems the following spring by gripping each at soil level and pulling so that each comes away without breaking. Discard the foliage – this is potentially harmful to eat but safe to compost.

or manure every square metre (yard). If a pH test shows the soil to be acid, liming to pH 6.5–7 (see p19) will promote good crops. Such hungry crops also need fertiliser. After planting, and every spring, apply a general-purpose fertiliser such as growmore, at 100g per sq. m (3oz per sq. yd), or twice that amount of pelleted chicken manure. If a 8cm (3in) mulch of organic matter can be given every late winter ,the fertiliser quantity can be halved.

FORCING RHUBARB

Pale, tender, mild stalks can be grown for harvesting before the main crop is ready. Dig up crowns in early winter and leave them on the surface until the New Year; then bring them into a warm dark place, water and allow to sprout. Discard crowns forced this way.

Alternatively, cover crowns with a box at least 50cm (20in) high in the New Year and cover this with manure. Usable stalks will be ready in five to six weeks. Crowns forced in place will recover after two years of being unpicked.

RECOMMENDED CULTIVARS

'Hawke's Champagne': high yields of bright red stems, mid-season

'Timperley Early': bred to give high yields of early thick, red stems when forced

By the second year, a light harvest of stalks can be taken in mid-spring, and from the third year stems can be harvested from spring until early summer. After early summer, leave the plants to grow good foliage and build up leaves. Remove any flower stalks.

Rhubarb is trouble-free, but honey fungus can kill crowns, and many stocks have viruses.

• FRENCH BEANS •

French beans show an amazing diversity, with dwarf and climbing forms, many of them highly ornamental and with delicate flavours and textures. They produce abundant crops, making them ideal for small gardens. Dwarf beans reach 45cm (18in) high, while climbing ones require wigwams 1.8m (6ft) high, or rows of canes, stakes and string.

Wigwams add height and colour, save space and ease management and gathering of the crop.

Grow these quick-growing tender annuals on any fertile, well-drained garden soil in full sun, in a sheltered warm site. In many gardens, these beans will have nitrogen-fixing bacteria in

FROM SOWING TO HARVESTING FRENCH BEANS

Sow seeds in drills 5cm (2in) deep at 15cm (6in) intervals. Grow in fertile soil in full sun, ideally where crops have previously been fertilised. Wait until after the last frost before sowing outdoors.

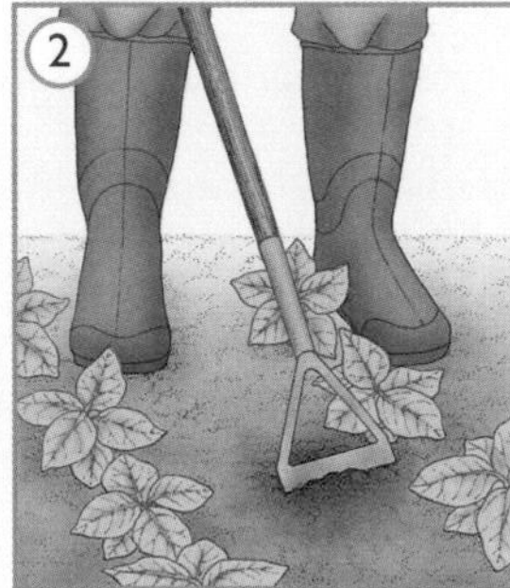

Hoe plants regularly to remove weeds before they compete with your crops for nutrients, moisture and sunlight. Take care not to damage the roots or top growth of the young plants.

Water the soil well every 10 days during dry spells. While dry soil at flowering time is less of a problem for French beans than for other types of beans, boosting the moisture will help increase the yield.

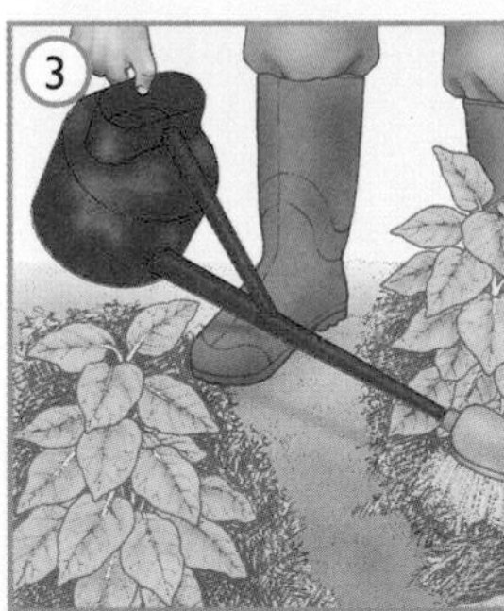

Harvest beans regularly so the plants keep producing. The young pods are delicious, but French beans also dry well: pull up a whole plant, hang it by the roots in a dry, frost-free place, then remove the beans.

their root nodules. Where these are lacking, a sprinkling along the bean row of soil from a garden where beans have these nodules (judicious checking with a trowel will clarify this point) should do the trick, but the other garden must be free of soilborne problems such as club root, onion white rot or potato cyst nematode. These nodules seldom fix enough nitrogen in cool countries such as Britain to meet all the crop's needs, and fertile soil is advisable, so enrich the soil with one bucket of organic matter, such as garden compost, per square metre (yard). Before sowing, rake in growmore or other general-purpose fertiliser at 100g per sq. m (3oz per sq. yd), or use twice as much organic fertiliser, such as chicken manure pellets.

The large French bean seeds produce big, quick-growing seedlings and it is easy for these to spoil if too many are sown or if they are sown too early. However, early and late crops are possible in glasshouses or under cloches, using sowings in early spring and again in late summer. In colder regions, cover dwarf cultivars with cloches or fleece. French beans are self-pollinating and insect access is not required.

Cultivars grown for their dried seeds are best sown early, as the seeds need a long time to ripen, and autumn rains may spoil the crop if seeds are sown too late in the growing season.

Although rows 45cm (18in) apart are easiest to manage and easiest to pick, beans in fact crop best at high density. In small gardens, it is worth sowing as close as 15cm (6in) between plants in all directions.

From mid-spring (for planting out in early summer), sow seeds indoors at 18–25°C (64–77°F) in celltrays or 7cm (2½in) pots filled with any good-quality multipurpose potting media. After germination, liquid feed every week and plant out seedlings as soon as the roots bind the potting media.

Seeds fail in cold soils, so pre-warm them by covering for four weeks with cloches or clear polythene; also cover sowings with fleece. Then, from late spring until midsummer, sow climbing cultivars direct in the ground; sow dwarf forms until late summer. A few extra seeds at the end of the row will provide spare plants for any gaps. Thin to one plant, if necessary, later.

Sow two or three seeds of climbing forms at the base of each cane, set 30cm (12in) apart, in a wigwam or row.

Unlike runner beans, which are perennials, annual French beans have a relatively short cropping period, and

RECOMMENDED CULTIVARS

Climbing

'Algarve': very high yields of flat pods

'Goldfield': flat yellow beans

'Trionfo Violetto': climbing purple podded bean

Dwarf

'Irago': early with high yields of beans held clear of foliage

'Maxi': high yield of long pods held above foliage

'Purple Teepee': moderate yields of purple pods held above foliage

'Safari': moderate yields of attractive thin, tender 'Kenya' beans

Drying

'Barlotto Lingua di Fuoco': climbing; pods streaked with red

'Brown Dutch': dwarf; golden brown beans

successional sowings every three weeks from mid-spring until late summer are needed for a constant supply. In some cases when crops languish, watering in a high-nitrogen fertiliser may be helpful. Although support is not essential for dwarf French beans, sticks and string to make a fence along the plants prevents flopping, thereby easing picking and enhancing airflow to reduce disease.

Pick beans as soon as they are usable and discard any that get overmature, as these will inhibit further cropping.

Being self-pollinating and, therefore, likely to come true to type, it is useful to save your own French bean seeds.

French beans can be attacked by blackfly and red spider mites, especially in hot summers. To reduce infestations, spray the entire surface of the leaves, including the underneath, with insecticides such as oils and fatty acids.

Caterpillars are an occasional pest, but can usually be picked off in most gardens. Slug controls are often necessary in rainy periods. Wet weather also promotes diseases for which there are no remedies except to remove and destroy affected material. In severe case, salvage what is possible from the crop and destroy the crop residues.

Where diseases are common, climbing cultivars are easier to manage than dwarf cultivars due to better airflow around the plants. Promptly remove all leaves infected with bean rust.

• RUNNER BEANS •

Being perennial (although usually treated as annual), runner beans can potentially flower and crop for many weeks so that successional sowing is less important than for many other crops, and the yield is usually enormous.

Runner beans relish cool, wet weather and climates, and thrive in any fertile, well-drained garden soil in full sun, with shelter from winds. Damaged and distorted beans are caused by windy weather, which also inhibits essential pollinating insects. Dwarf cultivars, which need no staking, are available and some climbing cultivars can have their shoot tips removed to make them low and bushy.

Some gardeners do not rotate their runner bean crops but have a permanent site, with supports left in place from year to year. This seldom causes problems, but if bean rust or root aphids strike, it is wise to use a fresh plot.

With such a long season of cropping fertile soil is essential. Bean trenches, where the soil is excavated to a depth of 60cm (2ft) and filled with kitchen waste, manure and shredded cardboard or paper, are a traditional way of increasing fertility and moisture retention, but equally good results can be achieved by digging in at least two bucketfuls of well-rotted compost or manure every

FROM SOWING TO HARVESTING RUNNER BEANS

Dig a trench and enrich the soil with plenty of organic matter. Runner beans like a moisture-retentive soil.

Rake the soil level and firm it in by treading lightly. Add a dressing of general-purpose fertiliser.

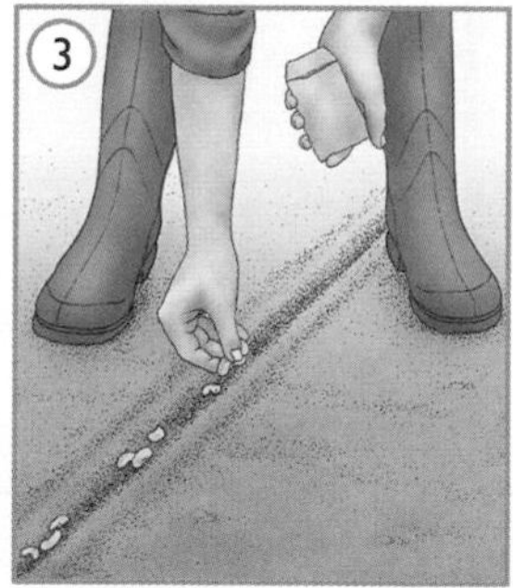

Sow 7cm (2½in) deep, 15cm (6in) apart, in drills 60cm (2ft) apart. Thin plants to 30cm (12in).

square metre (yard). Before planting, rake in general-purpose fertiliser such as growmore, at 100g per sq. m (3oz per sq. yd), or use twice that amount of pelleted chicken manure.

Before sowing in mid-spring, erect the bean support in a wigwam or single or double rows by pushing 2.4m (8ft) canes or sticks into the soil for at least 30cm (12in). Set rows a minimum of 1.2m (4ft) apart, with the canes 30cm (12in) apart. Position wigwam canes 1m (3ft) apart and each structure 1m (3ft) apart. Rows of bush or dwarf runner beans can be 70cm (28in) apart, with seeds sown every 15cm (6in) and thinned to 30cm (12in) apart.

Tie the canes at the top (in a bunch for wigwams) to a ridge wire or cane. String can replace some of the canes in sheltered gardens.

Tie the canes together to form supports. Secure them at the top and lay a cane across the ridge.

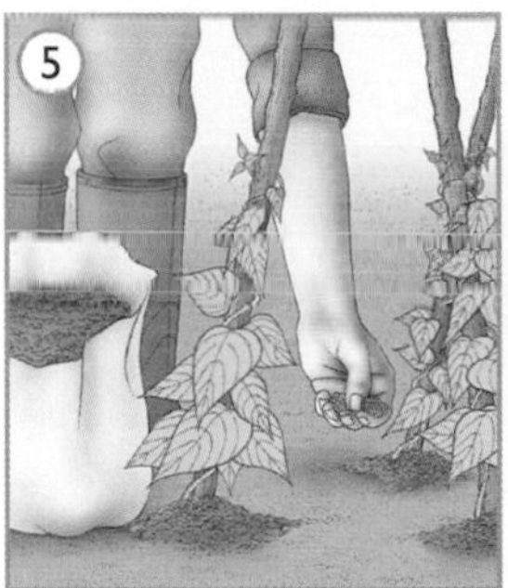

Feed young plants with a nitrogen-rich fertiliser, unless the growth is very green and lush.

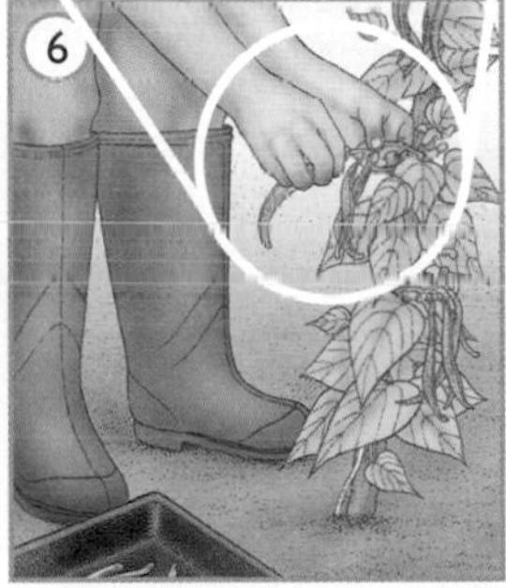

Harvest the beans after 13–17 weeks when the pods are 18cm (7in) long. Pick frequently to stimulate growth.

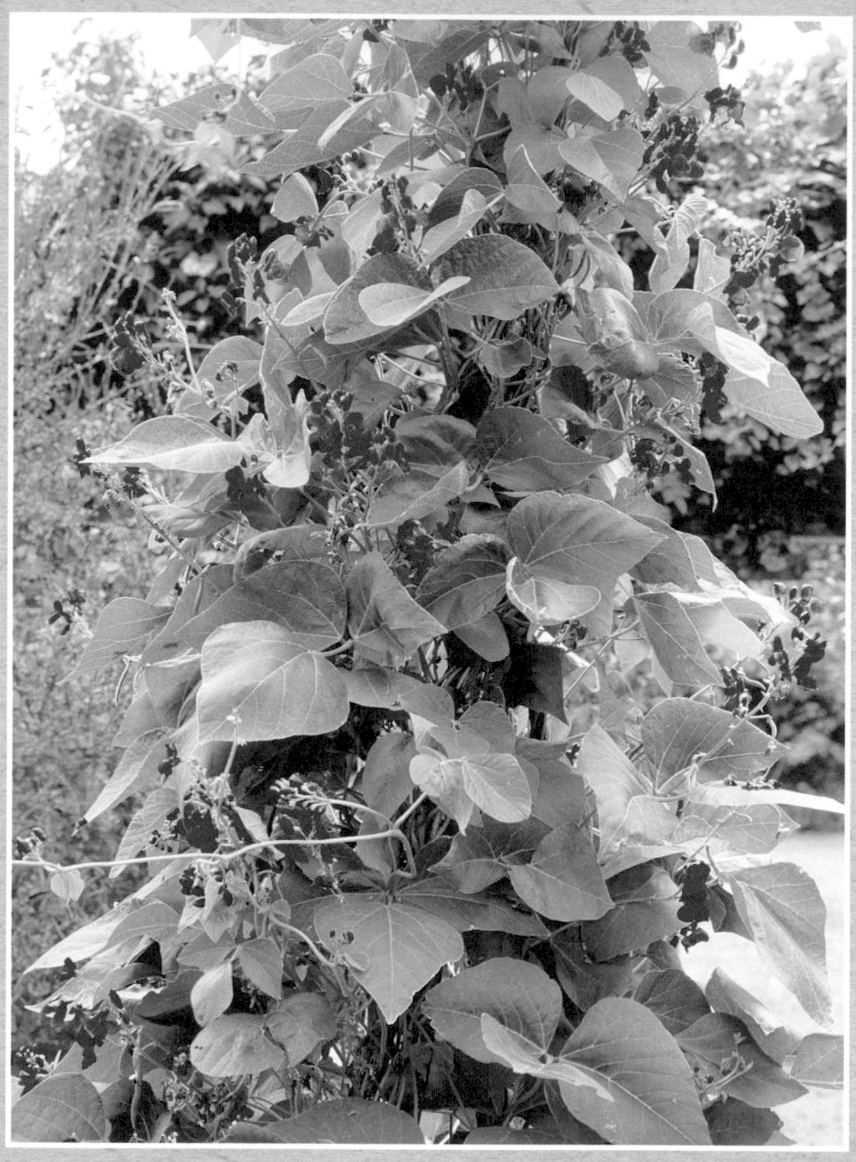

Runner beans crop more heavily than any other bean and look very attractive as well.

Raise early crops indoors in mid-spring, sowing two seeds per 7–9cm (2½–3in) pot, filled with any good multipurpose potting medium. Plant seedlings into the ground in early summer.

Sow runner beans outdoors in mid-spring, with three seeds at the base of each cane or string, thinning to no more than two plants later, if necessary. In warm regions, sow again in midsummer.

Guide the young shoots to the canes until they twine and climb naturally. If growth flags, topdress with a nitrogen-rich fertiliser, 35g per sq. m (3oz per sq. yd), or use double this quantity of organic fertiliser.

Water only after flowering starts, except for transplanted crops or in very dry spells. Once flowering begins, keep the soil moist by soaking it to a depth of 25cm (10in); this often requires two or more watering cans per square metre (yard). In very dry weather, you may need to water three times a week. Pod set is much reduced and often absent if the soil dries. In very hot weather, wetting the foliage at dusk may help cool the flowers and enhance pod set.

Gather pods as soon as they are usable and before the swelling seeds become visible bumps. Any pods allowed to mature suppress subsequent pod set.

RECOMMENDED CULTIVARS

'Hestia': dwarf, heavy cropping, for a dwarf bean, red and white flowers

'Red Rum': red flowers, heavy crop of beans even in hot weather

'White Apollo': white flowers, long beans of perfect texture and fine flavour

'White Emergo': white flowers, medium pods of good quality, performs well in hot regions

'Wisley Magic': red flowers, heavy crops of long beans

Runner beans can be attacked by blackfly and red spider mite, especially in hot summers and if watering is insufficient. Spray the entire surface of the leaves, including the undersides, with insecticides such as oils and fatty acids on a weekly basis. Root aphids and bean rust are occasional problems; grow on a fresh site in subsequent years. Pick off caterpillars and control slugs.

To save seed, collect it only from plants of one variety; keep any other bean varieties at least 100m (100yd) away, otherwise collected seed may not come true to type.

• BROAD BEANS •

Broad beans are hardy and can be sown early, or even in autumn in mild districts, for a succulent crop from early summer when little else is available.

Grow these hardy annuals in any sunny ,well-drained site, from mid-autumn sowings (in warm southern areas) or late winter to late spring ones.

FROM SOWING TO HARVESTING BROAD BEANS

Sow seeds 7cm (2½in) deep, every 20cm (8in) in double rows set 25cm (10in) apart.

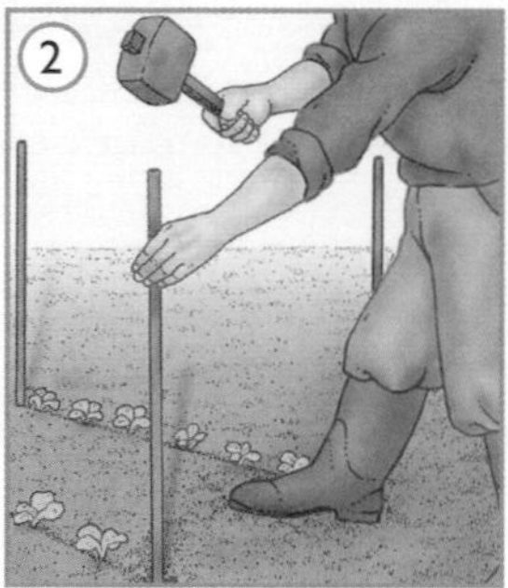

Hammer strong stakes at the end of each row. Run string along the row and attach it to the stakes.

Weed between the rows with a hoe, taking care not to damage the plants.

Water well when flowers first appear. Repeat 2 weeks later. This will encourage a good yield of pods.

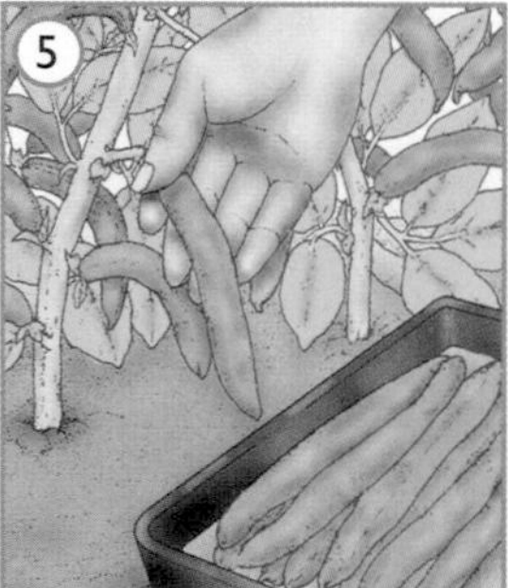

Harvest beans after 28–35 weeks for autumn-sown crops, or 12–16 weeks for spring-sown crops.

Dig spent plants into the soil to boost nutrient levels for the next crop.

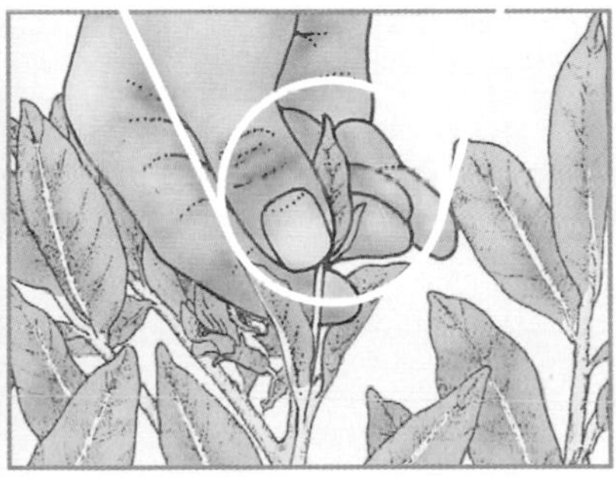

PICKING BROAD BEAN TOPS
Pinch out the tips of broad bean plants once they have flowered to deter blackfly. They can be eaten as 'greens' and are something of a delicacy. Lightly steamed, they taste a little like spinach.

Soils rich in clay often give better results than light soils, but any good garden soil that is not too acid (not less than pH6) is satisfactory. The early sowings are best yielding, with later crops, sown after mid-spring, more prone to attack by pests and disease. Where previous crops have been manured and fertilised, there is no need to add extra fertility, as these beans fix all the nitrogen they need via the bacteria in their root nodules. Otherwise, add a bucketful of well-rotted organic matter per square metre (yard).

Broad beans have a deep taproot and are best sown straight into the ground. Use surplus seedlings to fill any gaps. Leave a 70cm (28in) path around double rows for good airflow to reduce disease and also to ease staking, weeding, pest control and picking.

In small gardens and windy sites, sow dwarf cultivars – about 50cm (20in) tall – straight into the ground in single rows 25cm (10in) apart.

In cold, exposed gardens and where the soil is sticky clay, sow two seeds in each 7cm (2½in) pot, thinning to one plant later, if required. Plant out as soon as possible and keep watered if the weather turns dry.

As well as weeding, broad beans often need to be supported with three lines

At this growth, stage with flowering beginning, broad beans must not run short of water.

RECOMMENDED CULTIVARS

'Aquadulce Claudia': tall, long pods, very hardy and good for autumn sowing, but should not be sown after late winter

'Listra': white-flowered, small-seeded, mild flavour, good for eating pods whole

'The Sutton': dwarf compact plants ideal for smaller plots and exposed situations

'Witkiem': long pods, robust flavour, quick-growing

of string strung along 1.5m (5ft) high stakes set every 1.5m (5ft). Plants seldom need watering until the beginning of flowering, when they need a thorough soaking using at least two watering cans per square metre (yard); water again two weeks later.

As soon as the flowering finishes, pinch out the tips to slow down blackfly invasion and to divert the plant's resources into pod formation.

Tips can be used as greens, and young tender pods can be consumed whole in the same way as mangetout peas, but both are an acquired taste.

Once reasonable-size seeds have formed in the pods, they can be gathered for shelling. They soon become coarse, woody and strong-flavoured, so regular picking is essential. Pull up spent crops, and compost.

Every week, spray the entire surface of the leaves, including the underside, with insecticides such as oils and fatty acids to reduce infestations of blackfly (black bean aphid). These residue-free insecticides often allow ladybirds to mop up survivors. It is important to avoid spraying when bees are working the crop. If this is unavoidable, you should treat plants at dusk.

Pea and bean weevil will notch leaves, but unless 25 percent of leaf area is lost, this is no real cause for concern. Covering with fleece to boost growth is the best remedy. Foliage diseases such as chocolate spot and rust are usually only troublesome in wet years and in later crops; remove and destroy the worst affected plants. It is best to avoid growing broad beans in the same place each year as there are soilborne pests and diseases encouraged by overcropping.

• PEAS •

These hardy annuals are useful in the garden not only for their tasty, protein-rich seeds and, in many cases, edible pods, but also because they crop early in summer before other crops are ready.

As well as 'shelled' peas, where the seed is removed from the inedible fibrous pod, there are edible-podded forms: mangetout, with flat stringless pods; and sugarsnap, where the pods are stringless, but fleshy and succulent. Both are harvested slightly earlier than peas that have to be shelled. Petits pois are shelled peas with very small seeds.

Some peas are round-podded, with their seeds packed with starch. These are less likely to rot in cold, wet soil, compared to wrinkle-seeded cultivars, which are richer in sugar than starch.

Some peas have been bred to have tendrils in place of all, or some, leaves. This eases mechanical harvesting but, more important to gardeners, these peas are less attractive to pigeons and often require little or no support.

Early peas grow quickly to 40–60cm (16–24in) tall, while maincrop peas are 75–120cm (30–48in) tall and develop more slowly. Second-early peas fall somewhere in between. Older cultivars may be up to 1.8m (6ft) tall and troublesome to support. Modern pea

FROM SOWING TO HARVESTING PEAS

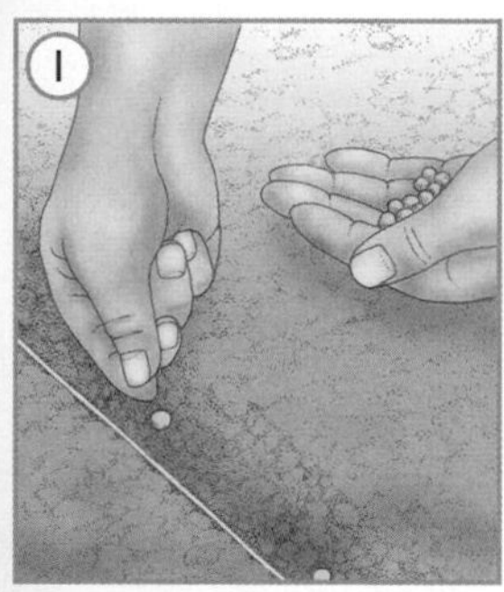

Sow seeds 1cm (½in) apart in drills 5cm (2in) deep and as far apart as the expected final height of the peas.

Rake soil into the drill gently. Firm down with the rake head so that seeds are held in close contact with the soil.

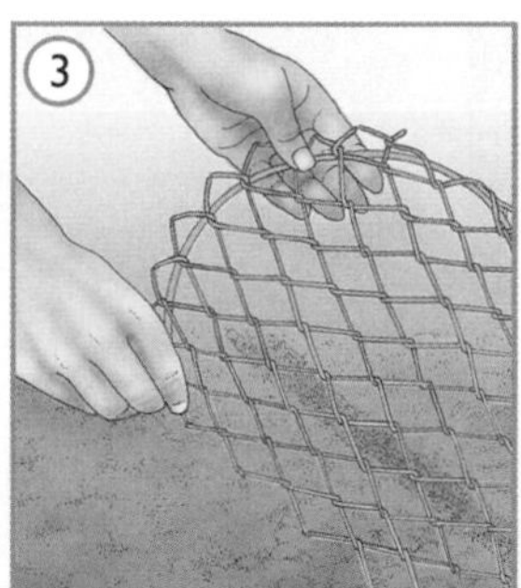

Place a wire netting tunnel over the rows. This prevents birds from digging up the seeds or seedlings.

cultivars tend to be on the short side and bear up to three pods per node (flower group) and they mature with only a few days between the earliest and latest.

Like broad beans, peas produce relatively few pods per plant, although the yields are very much higher with edible-podded forms.

Grow peas in sunny, well-drained sites. Light soils often give better results than soils richer in clay, and the pH should be 6 or above.

Where previous crops have been manured and fertilised, there is no need to feed the soil further, as peas fix all the nitrogen they need with the help of bacteria in their root nodules. Otherwise add a bucketful of well-rotted organic matter per square metre (yard).

Start sowing in mid-autumn in mild regions, and in late winter where the soil is light and well drained, using short, quick-maturing, early cultivars. Protection with cloches and fleece greatly increases the chances of success with early sowings, which have the best yields. Make subsequent sowings, using second-early and maincrop cultivars, as soon as the seedlings from the preceding sowing exceed 5cm (2in) high. To get a better spread of maturity, sow some of both second-early and maincrop at the same time. Some gardeners use first- or second-earlies for all their sowings.

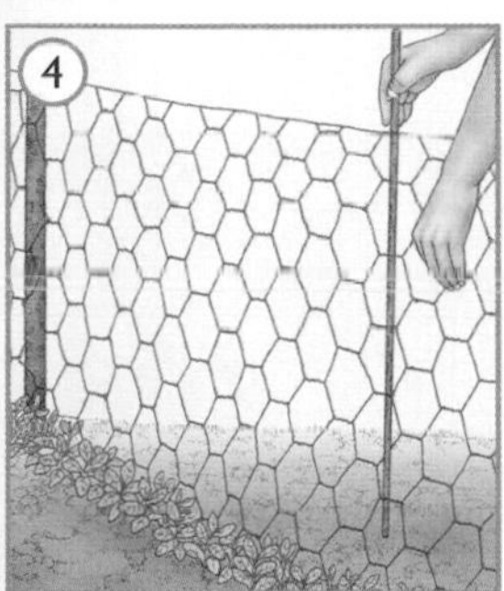

When plants are 8–10cm (3–4in) tall, erect netting supported on posts up to the mature plant height.

For the best crops, water peas well while in flower or when the pods are swelling.

Pick the pods about 4 weeks after flowering. Pods at the base of the plant develop first.

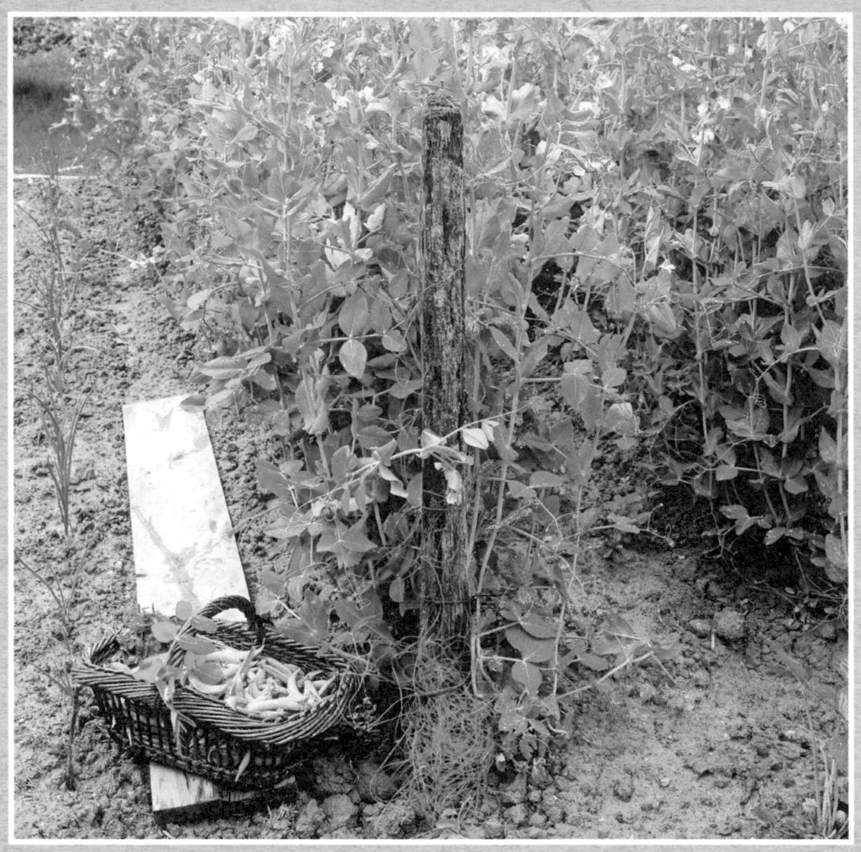

Well-supported, weed-free rows spaced at half their ultimate height are easy to access.

Sow peas in double or triple rows and thin them to about one pea plant every 8cm (3in). Control of mice may be needed, as these relish newly sown peas.

For an early sowing in gardens with wet, sticky, clay soil, sow peas in celltrays (one seed per cell), pots (three seeds per pot) or even strips of guttering. Plant the peas out later – in the case of guttering, slide the peas out into the prepared soil.

Peas are vulnerable to weeds and once the peas grow tall, hoeing is no longer possible and handweeding may be needed. Semi-leafless forms lack the thick leaves of other pea varieties and do not suppress the weeds.

Watering peas before they flower tends to increase foliage and may actually decrease yield of pods, except during prolonged droughts. Once flowering begins, soak the soil using at least two watering cans per square metre (yard). Water well again two weeks later.

Pick edible-podded peas as soon as the pods are large enough, and peas for shelling when the seeds have swollen but before they turn coarse.

Young pea plants can be checked in their development if notching by pea and bean weevil is extensive. Covering peas with fleece to boost growth is the best and, in fact, the best remedy.

Pea moth is the most destructive pest. The moth lays eggs on pea flowers and, later, the caterpillar penetrates the pod and feeds on the seeds, spoiling the crop. Spraying with a synthetic pyrethroid insecticide at the beginning of flowering and again two weeks later will give good control of the moth as well as pea thrips and aphids, which are both troublesome in hot summers. Using a pheromone trap to catch male moths allows gardeners to time sprays more precisely to coincide with moth activity. Organic gardeners have to exclude the pea moth with insect-proof mesh, which also excludes aphids.

Pea thrips and aphids can be organically controlled using insecticides based on fatty acids or oils. Resistant cultivars are widely offered and give some protection against powdery and downy mildew as well as other diseases including the various root rots afflicting peas, especially fusarium root rot.

RECOMMENDED CULTIVARS

'Cascade': heavy crops of medium-size, tender sugarsnap peas

'Dorian': easy-to-harvest, large but tender shelling peas.

'Jaguar': second-early with heavy crops of peas for shelling and good powdery-mildew resistance

'Misty': short, robust, quick-growing; heavy cropping for an early pea

'Oasis': maincrop for shelling, heavy yielding

'Oregon Sugar Pod': medium crops of mangetout peas; very hardy and suitable for early and overwintered crops

'Quartz': very heavy crops of succulent sugarsnap peas

• SWEET CORN •

Sweet corn are easy to grow in southern areas of the United Kingdom. In colder northern regions, crops are grown using transplants and protection.

There are four kinds of sweet corn:

- Supersweet is the commonest.They are sweeter than standard cultivars but the texture is chewy.

- Extra tendersweet is a less chewy form of supersweet.

- Standard sweet corn is less sweet and best consumed soon after harvesting. The seeds are less liable to rot at sowing than the more sugary supersweet seeds.

- Mini-cobs, or baby corn, are specialist cultivars producing tiny cobs, which are eaten while still tender; they lack woody cores.

Grow sweet corn on a sunny, well-drained, fertile site. Dig in at least two bucketfuls of garden compost or manure every square metre (yard). Before planting, rake in a general-purpose fertiliser such as growmore, at 100g per sq. m (3oz per sq. yd), or use twice that amount of pelleted chicken manure.

In mid-spring, sow pre-germinated seed indoors in pots or celltrays. Plant out in late spring or early summer, and cover

FROM SOWING TO HARVESTING SWEET CORN

Dig in well-rotted organic matter in winter. Before planting, rake in fertiliser.

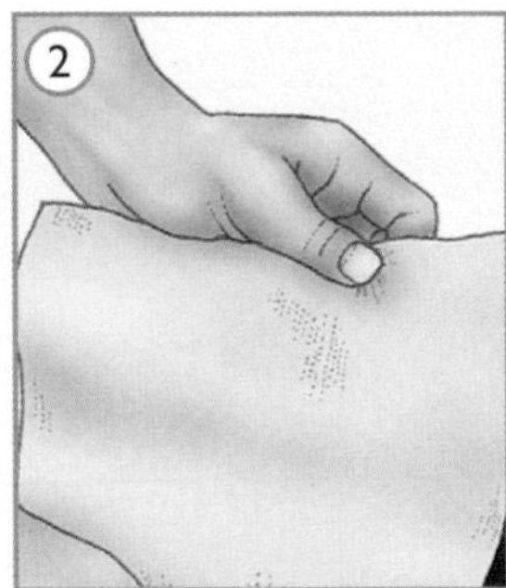

Scatter seeds on moist tissue paper in a closed container. Keep warm for 2–3 days, until sprouted.

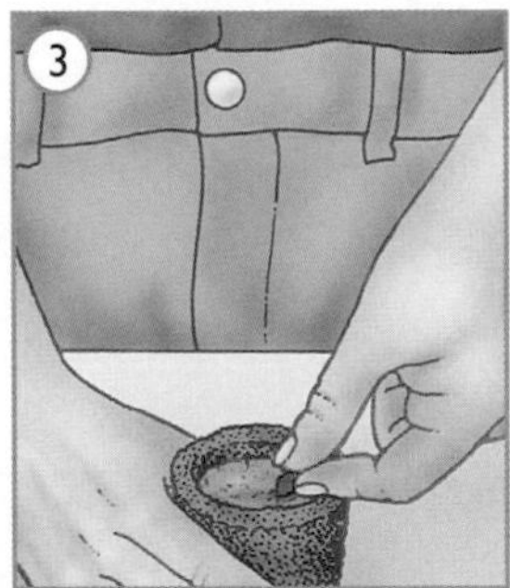

Sow pre-germinated seeds in individual pots. In the garden, sow 3 seeds at each station.

with fleece or cloches until plants get too big. As sweet corn is wind-pollinated, plant in blocks rather than in rows.

Sow seed outdoors 2.5cm (1in) deep in mid-spring in warm light soils. Thin to one per station. Where soil is cold, wet and rich in clay, transplants may be safer. Sowing beneath fleece or cloches is especially reliable. Make successive sowings until early summer whenever seedlings from the preceding sowing reach 10cm (4in) high.

Keep plants weed-free. If growth is poor or foliage lacks greenness, apply nitrogen-rich fertiliser. Watering is usually only worthwhile once the plants begin to flower – the male flowers appear first.

RECOMMENDED CULTIVARS

'Conqueror': supersweet
'Lark': extra tendersweet
'Seville': supersweet
'Swift': extra tendersweet

Cobs are ready when the silky strands go brown and the kernels ooze a milky sap when split with a knife or fingernail. If watery, they are immature, and if paste-like, overripe.

Sweet corn is virtually problem-free. Net the crop or cover individual cobs with plastic bags to deter birds and squirrels.

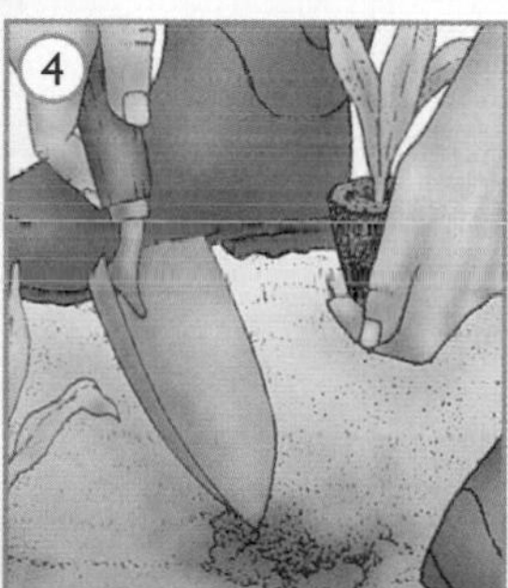

Plant sweet corn in blocks to assist pollination. Space plants 40cm (16in) apart, in each direction.

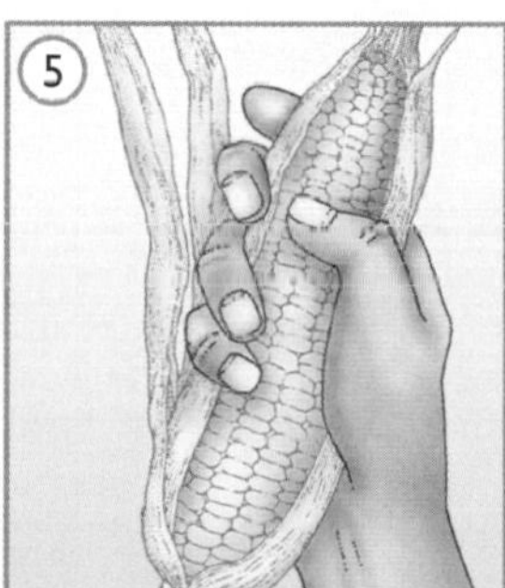

Harvest ripe cobs when pressing a nail into a kernel yields a creamy white juice.

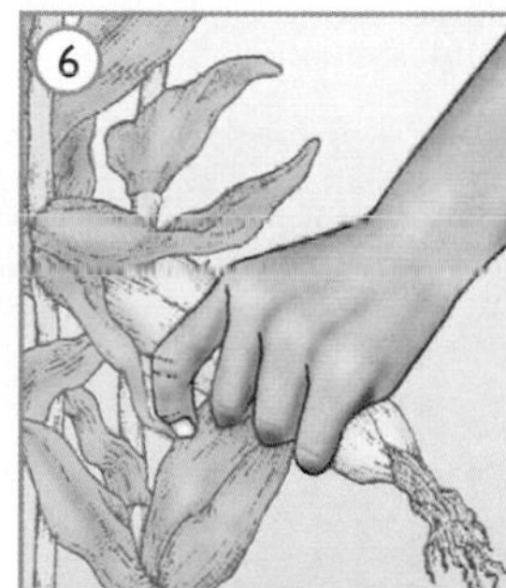

Twist the cobs downwards and pull away from the stem to detach them. Eat as soon as possible.

• ONIONS, GARLIC & SHALLOTS •

Onions have a two-year life cycle (biennial), making a bulb in year one that sends up a flower stalk in year two in response to the winter cold. Flowering is triggered by cold, and if onions are too large too early, they flower prematurely.

Early sowing is essential, and this is achieved in three ways: sowing in late winter in a greenhouse; sowing outdoors in early spring; or by making mini-bulbs, called sets, the previous year. These mini-bulbs are not readily triggered to flower by cold and will form a bulb instead of flowering. The only downside to sets is that the best onions for long-term storage are available only as seed.

Getting off to a good start is crucial for onions. A sunny, fertile, well-drained

FROM PLANTING TO HARVESTING ONION SETS

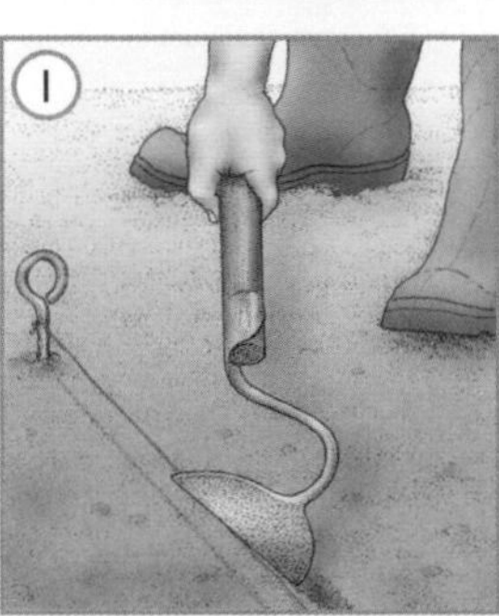

Make a drill 2cm (¾in) deep, with 25cm (10in) between rows. To help keep it straight, run the edge of a hoe along a length of string held taut between 2 pegs knocked into the ground.

Plant sets 5–8cm (2–3in) apart. Push each bulb firmly into the soil, burying it so only the tip is visible. Cover with fleece to deter birds and warm the crop.

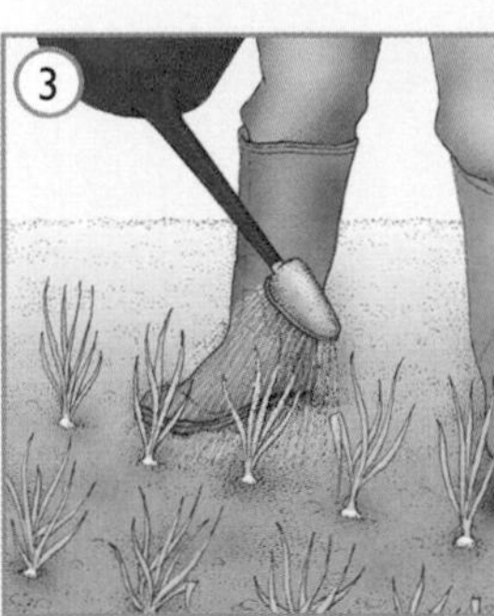

Water plants during dry spells. They need little water at other times, but they are easily swamped by weeds, so hoe around the plants regularly.

Harvest onions after 12–18 weeks. Pull them as needed. For onions to store, wait until their leaves bend over before digging up. Leave to dry for about 10 days.

light soil is ideal. Onions get off to a slow start on clay soils, so sets are best here. Acid soils (less than pH6) will need lime. Work in two bucketfuls of well-rotted manure or other organic matter every square metre (yard). For speedy strong growth, add growmore, at 100g per sq m (3oz per sq. yd), or twice the quantity of organic fertiliser such as chicken manure pellets. If well-rotted manure is not available, use more fertiliser, up to twice as much if the soil is poor.

Onions cast little shade and can easily become weed-infested. Planting through an opaque weed control film or fabric can reduce weeding.

In early to mid-spring, plant sets in drills or merely push them into loose earth. Cover with fleece to exclude birds, which inexplicably uproot sets, and also to hasten growth.

Use the same spacings for seeds as sets in the seedbed, which should be level, raked to be loose on top, and firm but not solid below.

Indoor sowing is more reliable, especially in cold regions. In celltrays, sow two seeds per cell, later thinning to one plant if necessary. Alternatively, sow six to seven seeds per cell and plant out the resulting clump, usually four to five plants, with 25cm (10in) between clumps. The space between rows is 25cm (10in).

In early autumn, plant sets to be grown overwinter for early crops, using the same spacings as for spring-planted onions. Seeds, too, may be sown in late summer, as above. The timings used are

SOWING ONIONS OUTDOORS

Sow seeds in previously enriched soil. Mark out a drill 1cm (½in) deep and sow seeds about 1cm (½in) apart, in rows 25cm (10in) apart. Sow bolt-resistant varieties in late summer, other varieties in early spring.

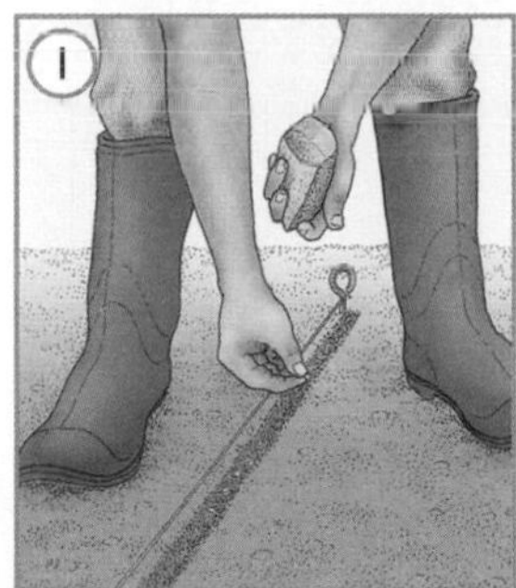

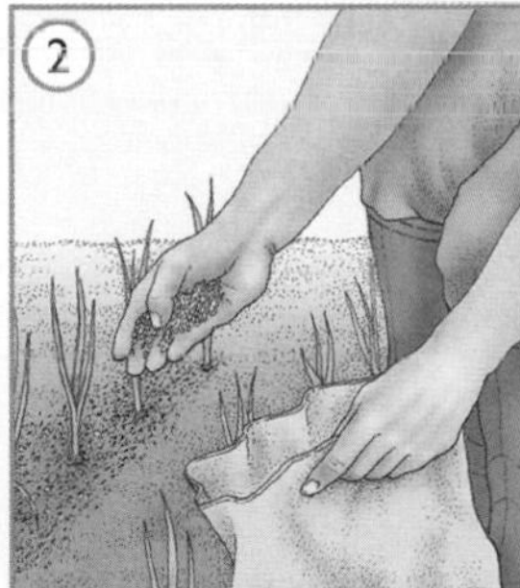

Feed plants in spring with 35g (1oz) of nitrogen-rich fertiliser. This will ensure bigger bulbs. Thin out plants to a spacing of 5–8cm (2–3in) apart. By late summer, your onions will be ready to harvest.

designed to produce plants 10–15cm (4–6in) tall before winter sets in. Any larger and they may bolt; if smaller, they may not survive. It is worth waiting until early spring before thinning, in case casualties occur over winter.

Salad or spring onions, also known as green onions and bunching onions, are almost always raised from seeds sown where they are to grow unless, the soil is wet sticky clay, in which case sow them in celltrays. In late summer, using hardy 'White Lisbon'-type cultivars, sow no deeper than 1cm (½in). Water carefully in dry summers if the seedlings are to emerge successfully. Smaller, follow-up sowings from early until mid-spring for pulling from early to late summer, are invaluable. Pull salad onions as soon as they are usable, and aim to clear the crop before bulbs form.

In late winter feed overwintered onions and spring-sown ones if growth is poor with nitrogen-rich fertiliser – sulphate of ammonia, for example – at 35g per sq. m (1oz per sq. yd).

From late spring, soak the soil every 14 days in dry spells. As ripening approaches stop watering to avoid soft bulbs, which will not store well.

Once the foliage has fallen, the bulbs will not swell further. For best storage, lift the plants before the foliage dies and becomes straw-like.

Onion white rot is the main onion disease and is especially damaging to overwintered crops. The spores of this rot remain viable in the soil for over 10

PLANTING & HARVESTING SPRING ONIONS

Sow seeds every 3 weeks, a finger's width apart in rows 10cm (4in) apart ,from early spring to summer for a continuous crop. Seed can be sown from late winter in mild areas, under a cloche.

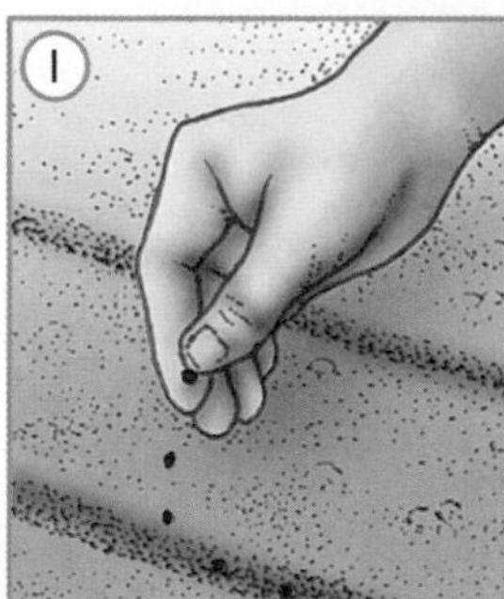

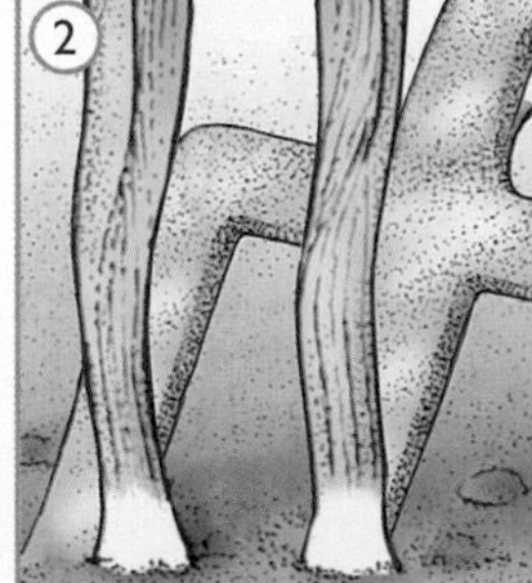

Thin out the developing onions to 2.5cm (1in) apart. The thinnings can be used in a salad. Salad onions are ready to harvest just 8 weeks after sowing. Lift them gently with a hand fork.

DRYING & STORING ONIONS

Loosen ripe onions with a fork on a sunny day and let them dry for a week. Onions are ripe once the foliage flops over. Let this process happen naturally; if you topple the foliage yourself, it will let in disease.

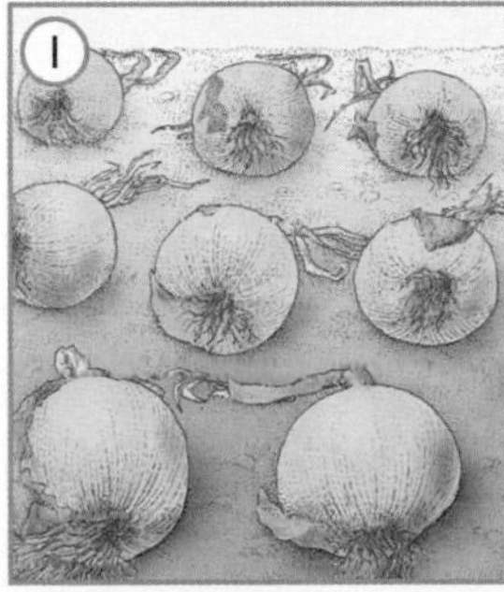

Lift onions and spread them out to dry in a well-ventilated cold frame or greenhouse if the weather is damp or wet. If you have room indoors, bring them in to dry on trays. It can take up to two weeks.

Inspect each onion, checking whether the skins feel papery. If not, leave them to dry further. Any onions with thick necks or those showing signs of rot should be used for cooking; only store blemish-free onions.

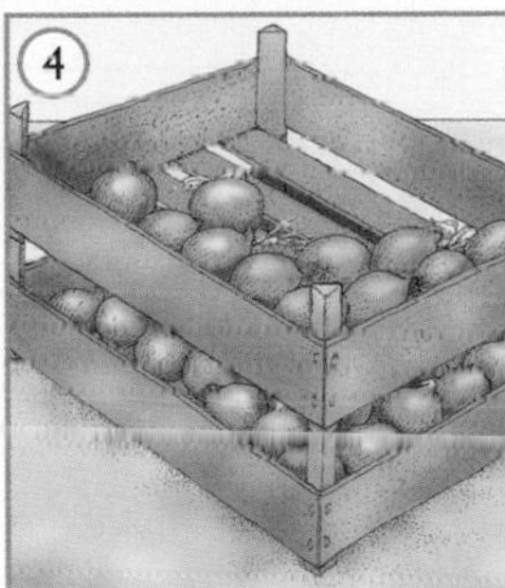

Store onions by placing them in layers in an open sided wooden box, set in a well-ventilated spot. Cold will not harm them, but dampness and poor air circulation will lead to rapid deterioration.

years, so rotation is ineffective. Prompt removal of infected plants, along with adjacent soil, will help limit build-up of the disease, but in severe cases, onions will have to be grown in raised beds or containers of imported soil.

Downy mildew is extremely destructive in mild wet weather. Overwintered crops often mature before severe damage occurs. There are no remedies except the prompt removal of infected leaves. Clearing all onions after harvest, and crop rotation, help because the disease can persist as spores in the soil, and in plants from previous years. Resistant cultivars are offered.

Neck rot fungus starts with rotting at the neck that spreads through the bulb. Avoiding bending down maturing onion stems and destroying affected onions help but the fungus spreads through infected seed and sets, so only good-quality propagating material should be used.

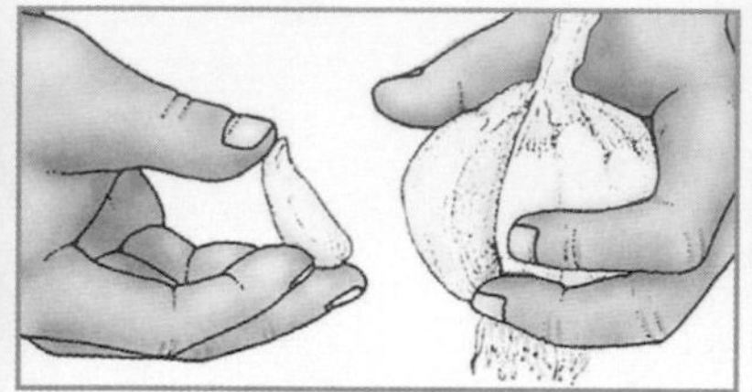

PLANTING GARLIC
Separate the individual cloves and discard damaged bulbs, which are prone to rotting. Plant cloves pointed end up.

Although onion fly and bean seed fly are seldom serious problems, it is a good idea to protect crops with insect-proof mesh. Use fleece to protect from thrips.

GARLIC

Garlic needs the same conditions as onions but is planted from bulb segments (cloves) in winter or early spring, depending on the cultivar. Allow

FROM PLANTING TO HARVESTING SHALLOTS

Plant shallot seed bulbs with their tips just showing. By early summer, each set will develop into a clump.

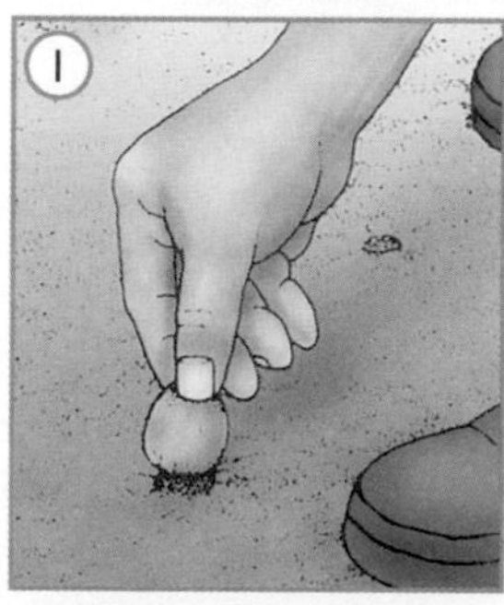

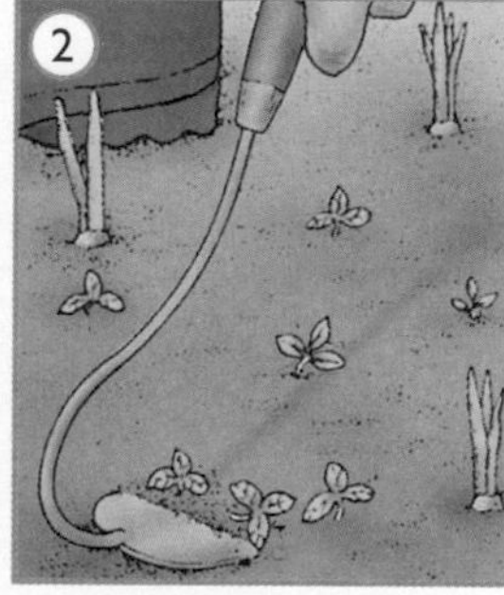

Hoe regularly between rows to keep the weeds at bay. You only need to water during prolonged dry spells.

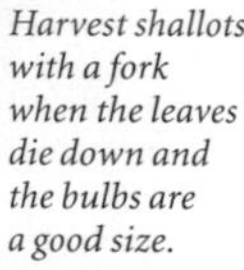

Harvest shallots with a fork when the leaves die down and the bulbs are a good size.

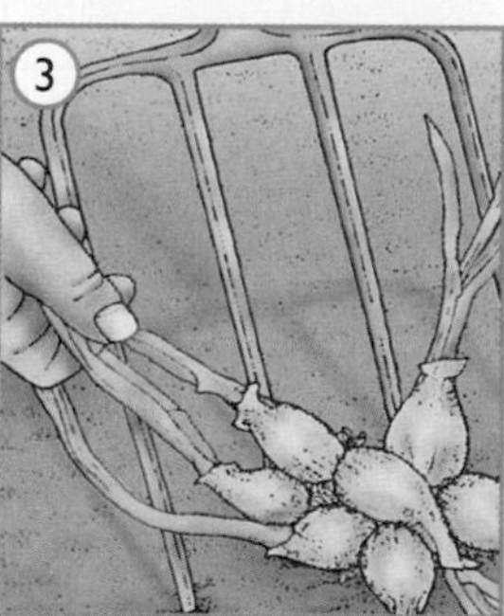

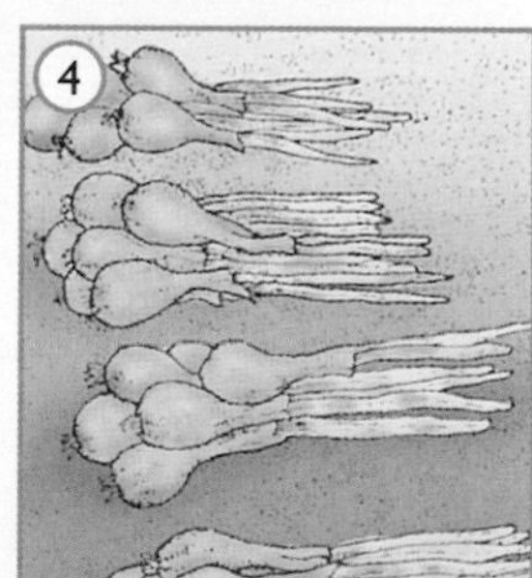

Dry bulbs for storing by spreading them out on the ground in the sun for a few days. If it rains, dry them under cover.

RECOMMENDED CULTIVARS

Onions

'Electric': red for overwinter (set)
'Marco': brown for spring planting (seed), good for long storage
'Red Emperor': red for spring planting (set)
'Santero': brown, downy mildew-resistant (set or seed)
'Senshyu': yellow globe, brown for autumn planting (set or seed)
'Shimonita': Japanese salad onion that forms thick tubular leaves
'Sturon': brown for spring planting (set or seed)
'Summer Isle': salad onion for spring sowing, forms no bulb
'White Lisbon': salad onion for overwintering and spring use, forms bulbs when overmature

Garlic

'Early Wight': early, will not store
'Germidour': purple cloves, late
'Solent Wight': late, good for storage

Shallots

'Ambition': often forms single bulbs (seed)
'Longor': brown, elongated, large
'Pikant': red skins, good yield, long-storing

10–15cm (4–6in) between cloves and 30–40cm (12–16in) between rows. Like onions, they need to be established by late spring so that large bulbs are formed by summer. Once the foliage goes yellow and straw-like, lift the bulbs and store as for onions. Garlic gets the same diseases as onions but is largely pest-free. Rust is the worst problem and, in the absence of controls, crop rotation and buying disease-free stock are the best remedy.

SHALLOTS

Although grown as onions, shallots are usually planted from offset bulbs in winter or early spring. Allow 30–40cm (12–16in) between bulbs and 45cm (18in) between rows. Like onions, they need to be established by late spring so that large bulbs can form. Once the foliage goes yellow, lift the bulbs and store as for onions. Shallots get the same diseases as onions but usually not so badly.

• LEEKS •

Leeks yield enormously, are completely hardy and very easy to grow.

Any sunny, fertile, well-drained soil is suitable. Acid soils (less than pH6) will need lime (see p19). Dig in two bucketfuls of well-rotted manure every square metre (yard). Also add growmore, at 100g per sq. m (3oz per sq. yd), or twice as much organic fertiliser, such as chicken manure pellets. If well-rotted manure is not available, use up to twice as much fertiliser if the soil is poor.

From late winter until mid-spring, sow leeks for harvesting from autumn until spring. Cloches or fleece greatly help early growth. From early to midsummer, transplant leeks to their final positions, making holes 10cm (4in) deep with a

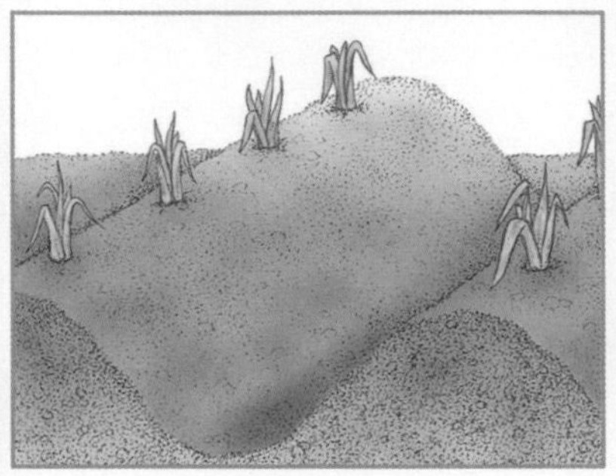

EARTHING UP

Leeks grow perfectly well planted on the level, but excluding light increases the length of the tender white stem and controls weeds. Blanching with a collar of opaque material, such as cardboard, can supplement or even replace earthing up.

FROM SOWING TO HARVESTING LEEKS

Sow the seeds in a well-prepared seedbed of finely raked soil with a level surface, loose on top and firm but not compacted below, in early spring. Sow 1cm (½in) deep, allowing a finger width between each seed.

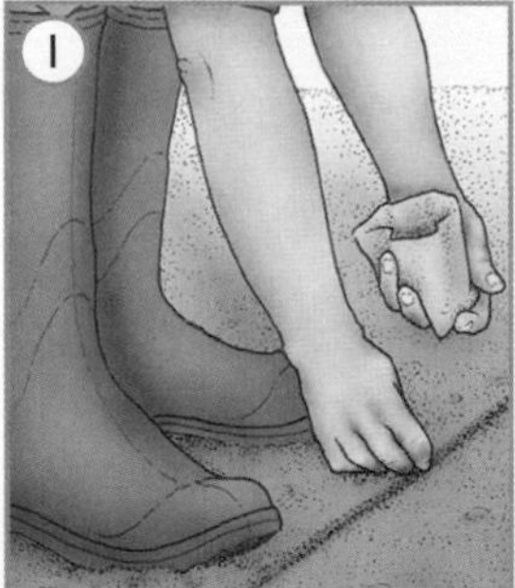

Thin to 2–3cm (¾–1in) between plants in early summer, and firm back the soil around the remaining plants.

dibber, and spacing each plant 10–15cm (4–6in) apart, in rows 30cm (12in) apart. Dribble water into each hole to fill it and settle the plants and roots in place.

If the soil is wet, cold, sticky clay and you requrie early autumn leeks from late winter sowings, sow indoors in celltrays. Sow two seeds per cell, later thinning to one plant if necessary; or sow four to six seeds per cell and plant out the resulting clump, usually three to four plants, 8cm (3in) deep, allowing 30cm (12in) between clumps. Row spacing remains at 30cm (12in). Fill the holes with soil by watering.

Water freely in dry spells, soaking to a depth of 25cm (10in), and topdress with nitrogen-rich fertiliser, at 35g per sq. m (1oz per sq. yd), if growth is not vigorous. Leeks cast little shade so need weeding.

When they are big enough to eat, ease the leeks out of the soil using a fork.

Leek problems are few, although rust and thrips can disfigure foliage in late summer. Fleece or insect-proof mesh gives good protection against pests.

RECOMMENDED CULTIVARS

'Atlanta': late winter
'Bandit': late winter
'Carlton': F1 hybrid, autumn
'Edison': F1 hybrid, late winter
'Oarsman': F1 hybrid, midwinter
'Toledo': midwinter

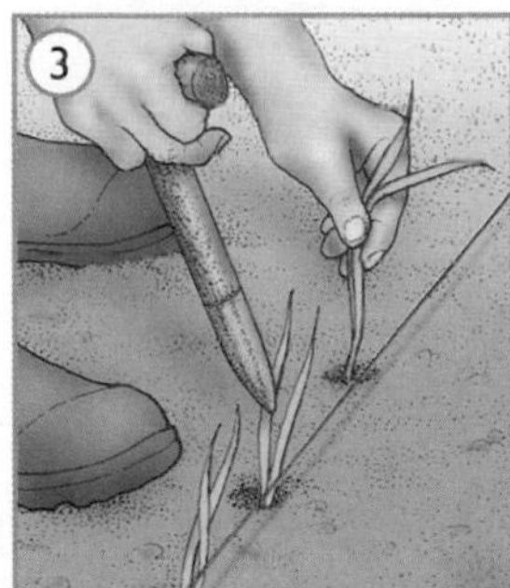

Plant out from early to midsummer; make a hole 10cm (4in) deep with a dibber and space each plant 10–15cm (4–6in) apart. Mulch around the plants or, if you want longer white stems, earth up.

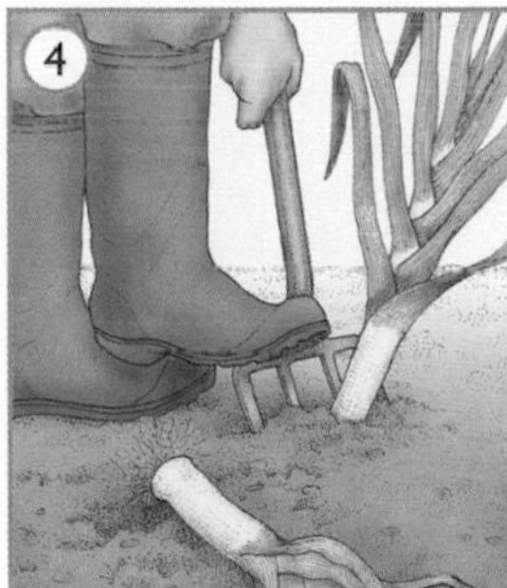

Harvest from late autumn. Cover a few with several layers of fleece so that you can lift them even during heavy frost.

• CARROTS •

Carrots are biennials, flowering in their second year from the tasty roots made during their first year. They crop heavily, and as well as orange roots, you can grow white, yellow, purple and red ones. There are also many forms suited to different seasons, soils and uses.

Any sunny, fertile, well-drained light soil is suitable. Acid soils (less than pH6) will need lime. Although it is not true that carrots will split if manured, there is no need to add organic matter. Neither is much fertiliser required: add growmore, at 50g per sq. m (1½oz per sq. yd), or twice that quantity of organic fertiliser, such as chicken manure pellets.

If the soil has not been improved for previous crops, use up to twice as much fertiliser if the soil is poor. Dig the soil over in winter and rake to a fine level surface, loose on top and firm beneath.

For early summer crops, sow from late winter to early spring – or even mid-autumn in mild regions. Sow into drills 10–15mm (¼–½in) deep, allowing a finger width between seeds, and set rows 25cm (10in) apart. Protect carrots with cloches, frames and fleece (essential for overwintered sowings).

Sow midsummer crops in mid-spring, and winter crops from late spring to early summer. On clay soils, the first

FROM SOWING TO HARVESTING CARROTS

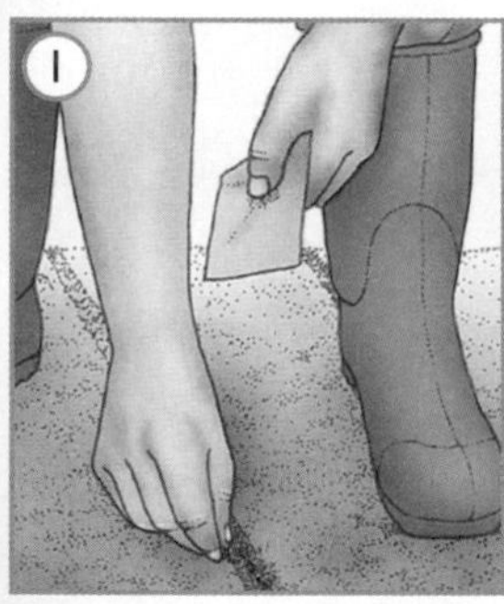

Sow seeds thinly in drills in well-raked soil. Cover with fleece to exclude carrot fly.

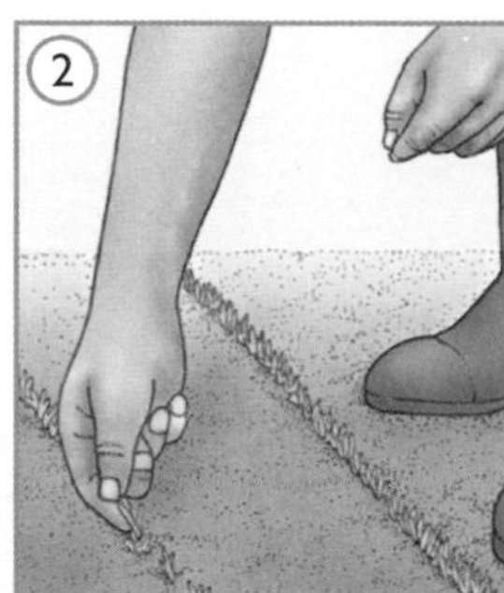

Thin the carrot seedlings when 4–5 small leaves appear. Remove thinnings.

Water in dry spells and hoe between the rows because carrot foliage is not effective at suppressing weeds.

sowings may not be possible until mid- to late spring, so raise 'Paris Market' and 'Amsterdam' cultivars in pots or celltrays and set out as soon as the potting medium is bound together by roots.

Thin to 2cm (¾in) apart for early and finger carrots, 10cm (4in) apart for summer and autumn carrots, and 15cm (6in) between plants for winter carrots.

Water only in prolonged dry spells, when a thorough soak every 14 days will give the best results. Feathery carrot foliage is no obstacle to weed growth, so weed the plot frequently.

Lift roots as soon as they are of a usable size. For winter, they are best left in the soil but protected from the frost and rain. If you are likely to want to lift carrots in severe frosts, protect the crop with a 15cm (6in) layer of cardboard or straw held in place with black plastic sheeting anchored by burying the edge in the soil. Alternatively, store indoors in boxes of sand (any type will do) or soil.

Carrot fly will generally ruin carrot crops, and resistant cultivars are not entirely damage-free. Fleece or insect-proof mesh over the crop for the growing season is the only sure way to ensure there is no damage. Barriers around crops, at least 60cm (2ft) high, that rely on the difficulty carrot fly has in surmounting barriers are often unsatisfactory. This is particularly true

Harvest carrots from summer onwards. Early sowings are usually best harvested young and tender.

In mid-autumn, mulch with straw if you plan to leave crops in the ground. The foliage will die back naturally.

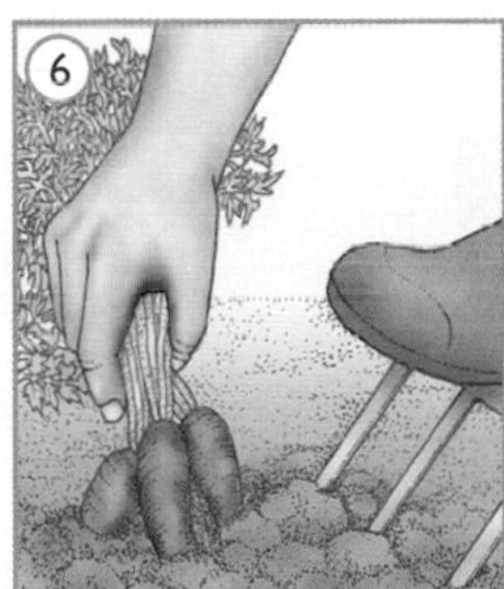

After lifting for storage, twist off the foliage: Space roots out in dry sand in a cool but frost-free place.

Purple is lost on cooking but in salads these carrots please the eye and the taste buds.

insect-proof mesh excludes them. Foliage diseases are seldom serious, and resistant cultivars are available. Prompt removal of infected foliage helps reduce losses. Unfortunately, mesh and fleece to exclude carrot fly reduces air flow and promotes disease. The wider mesh of insect-proof netting enables greater airflow and less disease.

in gardens where there is tall vegetation close by, upon which the fly is said to roost and from which it can descend and overcome the barriers. In exposed sites and where there are few tall plants nearby, the barriers may be more effective.

Companion planting is not fully proven to reduce damage from carrot fly. Although mixing carrots with onions is said to reduce the ability of carrot fly to find the plants because the onion scent interferes with that of the carrot, failure is often reported.

Root rots are common and crop rotation is the best control. Leaf miners and aphids are pests of carrots but

RECOMMENDED CULTIVARS

'Adelaide': F1 hybrid, early-maturing finger carrot for the earliest crops
'Bolero': F1 hybrid, maincrop 'Nantes'-type with good disease-resistance
'Carson': F1 hybrid 'Chantenay'-type for heavy soils
'Kingston': F1 hybrid, 'Autumn King'-type for winter use
'Nairobi': F1 hybrid, 'Nantes'-type for all seasons

• SWEDES, TURNIPS & KOHLRABI •

These humble biennial crops produce a very high yield of edible roots – actually swollen stems – that then go on to flower in their second year. The leaves, too, can often be eaten. Swedes, turnips and kohlrabi are, in fact, brassicas and are best grown in the brassica, or cabbage, part of the crop rotation scheme (see pp22–23).

Slow-growing swedes are gathered from early autumn until early spring, and their roots are very hardy. They grow best in cool, mild, rainy regions.

Turnips are quick-growing (taking 12 weeks from seed) and are gathered from early summer until early winter, but their roots are not completely hardy.

Kohlrabi is not closely related to the turnip, yet is grown in the same way. It is slightly hardier than a turnip and a little slower-growing.

For all these roots, dig in two buckets of well-rotted manure per square metre (yard), as well as growmore, at 100g per sq. m (3oz per sq. yd) or chicken manure pellets, at 150g per sq. m (5oz per sq. yd). Then rake to a fine level surface, loose on top and firm beneath.

In late winter and early spring, sow turnips, using bolting-resistant cultivars, and kohlrabi under fleece and cloches. Kohlrabi is easy to raise in celltrays at this time to plant out in mid-spring. Sow every two to three weeks until late summer for a continuous supply. Although invaluable as early crops to gather in early summer, turnips and kohlrabi soon 'go over' in hot weather. However, late summer sowings provide useful late season crops, and turnips can be sown in early autumn to provide 'spring greens'.

Sow swedes from late spring to early summer where they are to grow or in celltrays for planting out in midsummer.

Sow into drills, 5–10mm (¼–½in) deep, and set rows 30cm (12in) apart for turnips and kohlrabi, and 45cm (18in) apart for swedes.

Plants can be raised in celltrays, three seeds per cell, filled with multipurpose potting media, and covered with just enough sieved potting media or fine vermiculite to cover the seeds, singling seedlings as soon as they can be handled. Place in good light and feed weekly after the first month. Plant out as soon as their roots fill the cell.

Never allow plants to run short of water, although kohlrabi is slightly more tolerant of dry soil. Their strong foliage greatly suppresses weeds, but hoeing and weeding will be needed.

Feeding plants with nitrogen-rich fertiliser, at 35g per sq. m (1oz per sq. yd), in summer may increase yields.

Cut turnips and kohlrabi before they become coarse-textured and strongly flavoured (at cricket-ball-size). Swede roots can be used as soon as tennis-ball-size and are edible even when very big.

In mild regions during winter, cover turnips with a double layer of fleece,

FROM SOWING TO HARVESTING TURNIPS

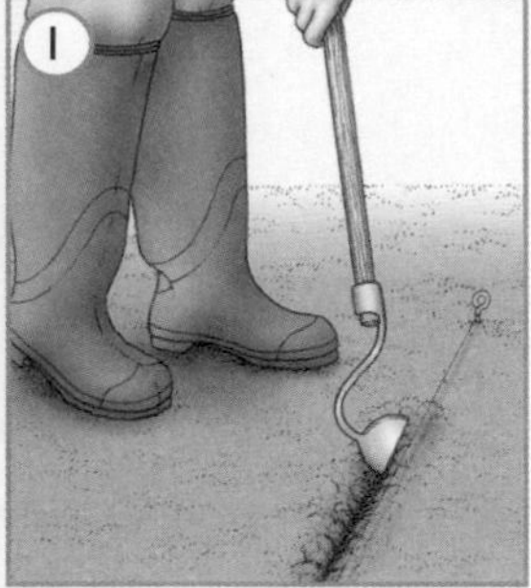

Water the day before sowing. Draw out drills and water the base of the drill if the soil is at all dry.

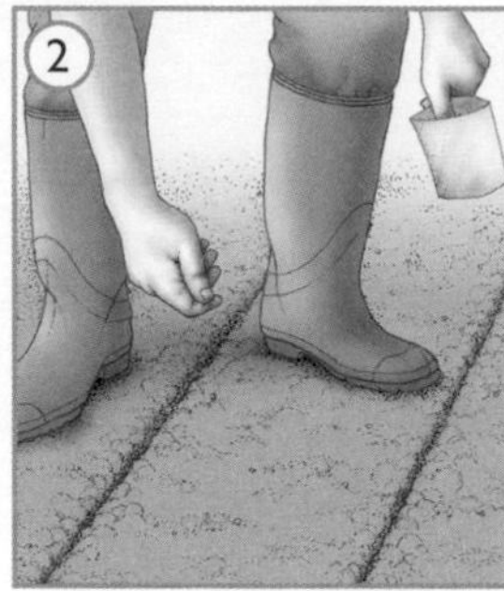

Sow, allowing about a thumb's width between seeds. Cover the drill, firm the soil and gently rake over.

Thin seedlings to 8cm (3in) apart as soon as they can be handled. Water after thinning.

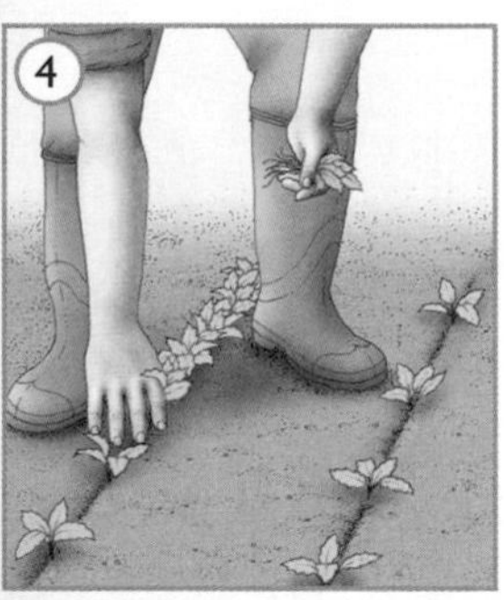

Thin plants again to 15cm (6in) when their leaves begin to touch. Firm the soil afterwards.

Hoe between rows, taking care not to damage the developing roots. Ensure that the plants never dry out.

Harvest young turnips as needed or by late autumn in all but the mildest areas. Store in a frost-free shed.

or store in boxes of potting media or soil. Swedes may, in cold regions, also require indoor storage. Kohlrabi is not well suited to storing.

Bird netting is often needed throughout the life of these crops. They are all very prone to club root but liming the soil to at least pH7.5 (see p19) and raising plants in pots are usually effective. Club root-resistant swedes are available.

Cabbage root fly kills seedlings and later tunnels roots, spoiling the crop. Growing under insect proof mesh thwarts the pest and also excludes caterpillars. Removing covers to weed can be irksome, however.

Fleece will protect crops against flea beetle, sawfly larvae and leaf miners. Control caterpillars and aphids with natural pyrethrin insecticides.

RECOMMENDED CULTIVARS

Swedes

'Invitation': club root-resistant, hardy

'Magres': good resistance to mildew, good for southern gardens

'Tyne': F1 hybrid, strong and hardy

'Wilhelmsburger': green top, good for southern gardens

Turnips

'Atlantic': white roots with purple top, small leaves, good for early crops

'Manchester Market': white roots with green top

'Snowball': white ball turnip, very quick-growing

Kohlrabi

'Kolibri': F1 hybrid, purple

'Logo': F1 hybrid, green

Harvest kohlrabi when golf-ball-size.

• CELERY & CELERIAC •

Celery and celeriac are biennials, forming a clump of tender stems (or a mild-tasting knobbly root in the case of celeriac). However, any stress from cold or drought leads to small, fibrous plants and often premature flowering.

In a trench, dig in two bucketfuls of organic matter per square metre (yard).

FROM SOWING TO HARVESTING CELERY

Dig a trench, 40cm (16in) wide and 15cm (6in) deep, in full sun. Fork manure into the bottom and refill.

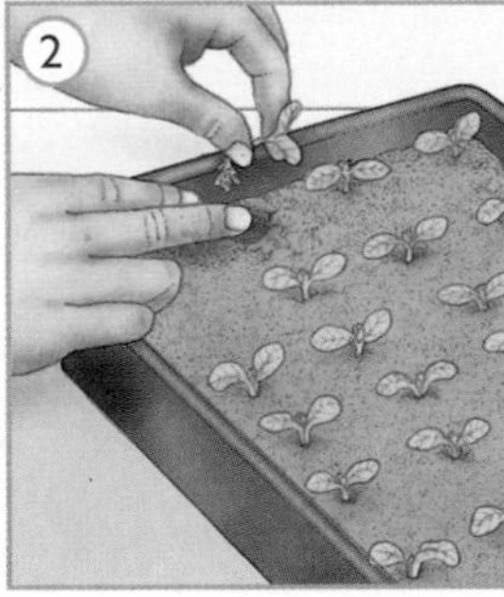

Transplant seedlings once they have a few leaves and are large enough to handle.

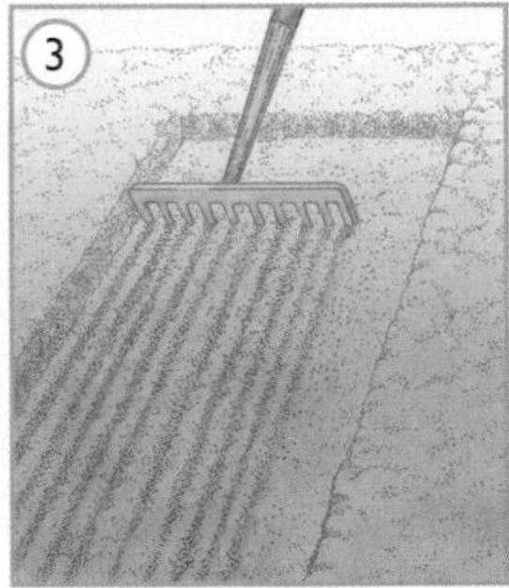

Just before planting rake in fertiliser, at 100g (3oz) per square metre (yard). Double this for organic fertiliser.

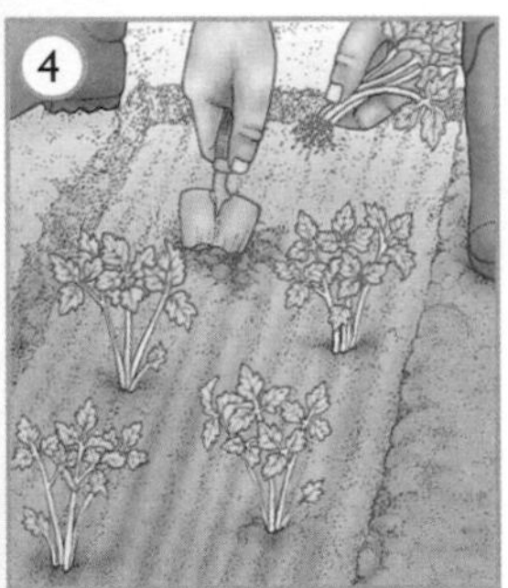

Plant self-blanching and green celery 25cm (10in) apart in a block to provide mutual shade.

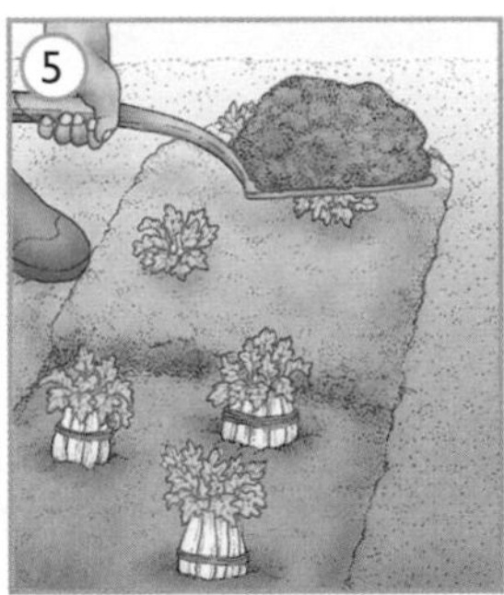

Blanch the stems by tying them and earthing them up or covering them with opaque porous fabric.

Cut whole heads at the base. Celery rapidly becomes pithy or rots as winter approaches.

Before planting rake in growmore, at 100g per sq. m (3 oz per sq. yd), or twice that quantity of chicken manure pellets. If organic matter is unavailable, increase the fertiliser by half .

In early spring, sow indoors at 15°C (59°F) in pots or celltrays, barely covering the seeds with fine vermiculite or sieved potting media. Pot on into 7–9cm (2½–3½in) pots once seedlings have a few leaves. Keep in good light and at a minimum of 10°C (50°F) to prevent bolting. By early summer, the plants will be big enough to plant out. Set out self-blanching and green celery in blocks. Plant celeriac in rows 45cm (18in) apart, allowing 25cm (10in) between plants. Cover with fleece to boost early growth.

Keep plants weed-free and well watered. Topdress with nitrogen fertiliser, at 35g per sq. m (1oz per sq. yd), once plants are established. Tie up celery stems and draw back the soil to exclude light, or blanch. Self-blanching celery goes white because of the mere presence of other plants nearby; similarly green celery is partially blanched that way. Remove fallen leaves and sideshoots from celeriac to ensure shapely roots.

Dig up celery from late summer and before frosts; harvest celeriac once roots are big enough, until hard frosts strike.

Use heat- or chemically-treated seeds to avoid celery leaf spot. Remove leaves affected by leaf spot or leaf mining flies. Control slugs with nematodes or pellets.

RECOMMENDED CULTIVARS

'Hopkins Fenlander': for trench cultivation (not self-blanching)
'Loretta': self-blanching celery
'Prinz': bolt-resistant celeriac
'Victoria': green celery, good flavour

Remove celeriac leaves as they die off.

• PARSNIPS •

Parsnips are hardy, undemanding crops. Cultivars vary, with roots that are conical, wedge-shaped or, best for clay soils because they are easy to dig out, bulbous.

Parsnips thrive in any sunny, fertile, well-drained, light soil. Acid soils (less than pH6) will need lime (see p19). There is no need to add organic matter. Feed with growmore, at 100g per sq. m (3oz per sq. yd), or twice that amount of organic fertiliser, such as chicken manure pellets. If the soil has not been improved for previous crops, use twice as much fertiliser, especially if the soil is poor.

In winter, dig the soil and rake it level when the soil is dry. Cover with clear

Parsnip foliage suppresses weeds, and surplus roots are a mild-flavoured treat.

FROM SOWING TO HARVESTING PARSNIPS

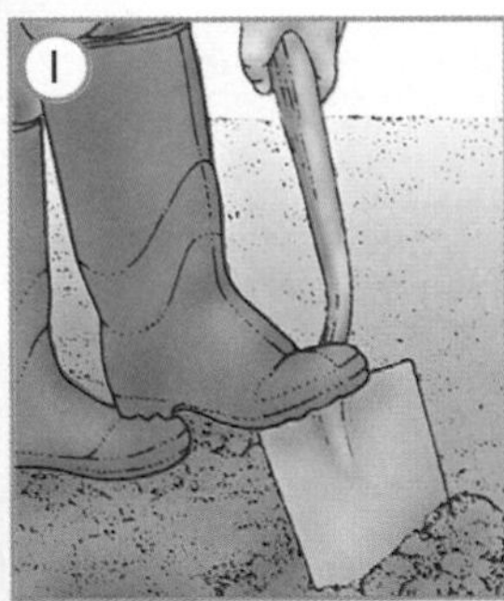

Dig heavy soils in winter or loosen lighter soils with a fork in spring to provide the right structure.

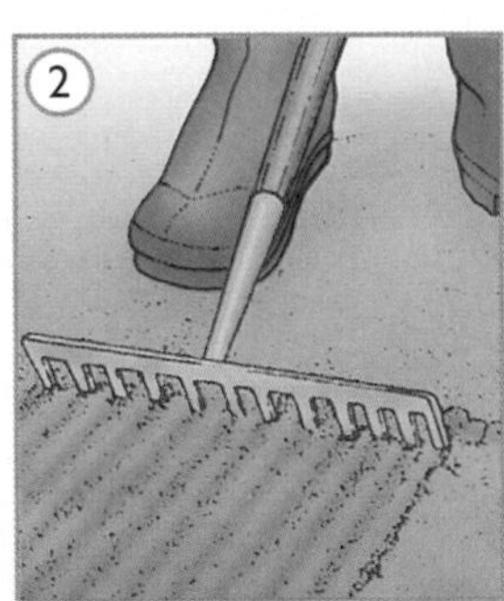

Rake in fertiliser at 70g (2oz) per square metre (yard) or double that rate for organic materials.

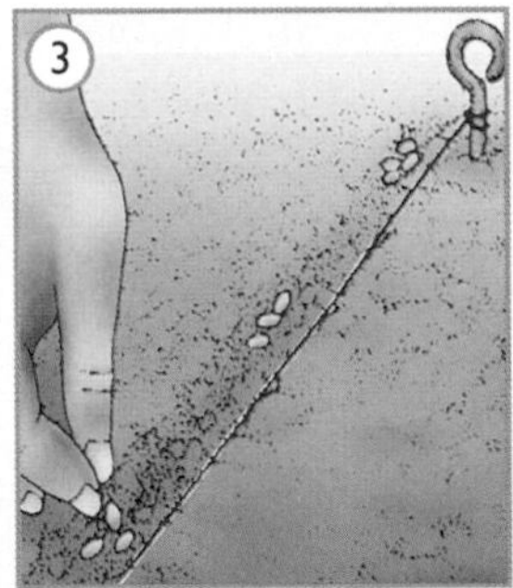

Sow seeds 10mm (½in) deep a finger's width apart, or station sow at 10cm (4in) spacings.

plastic in cold wet areas to keep the soil warm and dry until sowing time.

From late winter, sow into drills 25cm (10in) apart. On clay soils, wait until mid-spring to sow. Cover with fleece to speed germination.

Water only in prolonged dry spells, giving a thorough soak every 14 days. Parsnip foliage suppresses weeds well, but some hoeing is usually needed.

Parsnip flavour improves greatly after hard frosts. Roots are best left in the soil during the winter.

Carrot fly can damage parsnip crops, so cover seedbeds with fleece; later, replace this with insect-proof mesh for the rest of the growing season.

RECOMMENDED CULTIVARS

'Albion': F1 hybrid, long, pointed
'Countess': F1 hybrid, wedge-shaped, canker-resistant roots
'Gladiator': F1 hybrid, slightly bulbous roots with good canker resistance, good for clay soils

Root rot or canker is common, but resistant parsnip cultivars are available. Preventing carrot fly damage and crop rotation will also help reduce losses. Leaf miners and mildew are occasional but seldom serious problems.

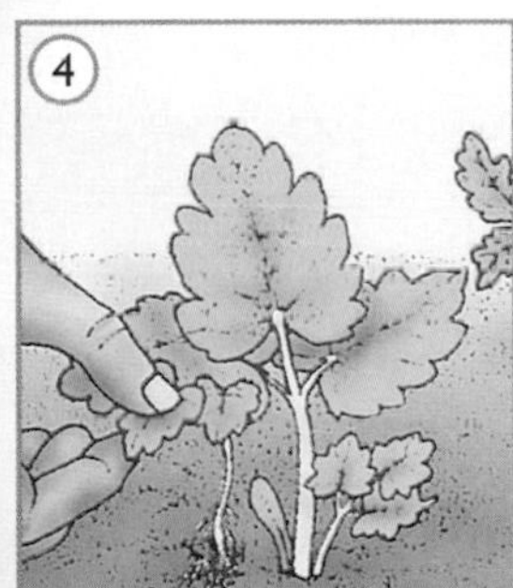

When 4–5 leaves appear, thin seedlings to 10–15cm (4–6in), removing weaker seedlings.

When hoeing, take care not to damage the 'shoulders' of the swelling roots, as injuries encourage canker.

Lift roots as soon as usable. In autumn, cover with sacking, and lift as needed.

• BEETROOT •

Beetroot yields heavily and grows fast. Its roots are usually ball-shaped, but may be cylindrical or long (often favoured for winter crops). As well as the usual red roots, there are also cultivars with yellow, white and even striped roots available.

The abundant red, sometimes green, leaves can be used as you would spinach.

FROM SOWING TO HARVESTING BEETROOT

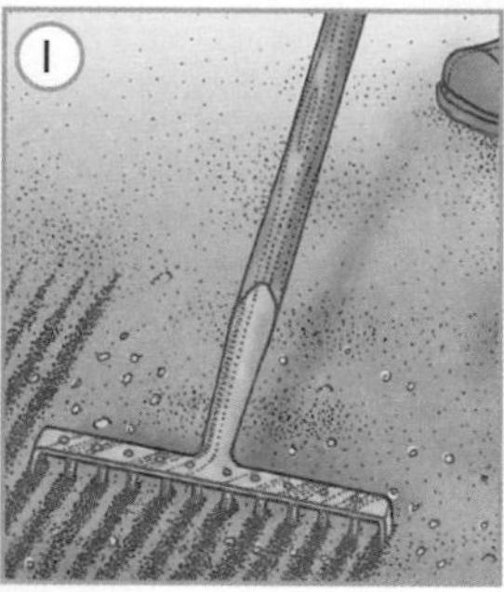

Rake the soil to a fine tilth ready for sowing or planting. Use bolt-resistant cultivars in early spring.

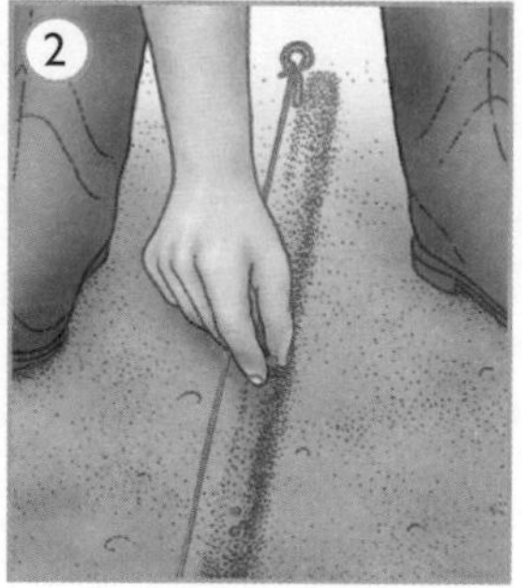

Sow thinly or station-sow as soon as the soil is warm and dry enough. Protect early sowings with fleece.

Thin seedlings in stages with small beetroot 10cm (4in) apart and large ones 15cm (6in) apart.

Hoe very carefully or pull weeds by hand. The thick foliage helps to suppress weeds.

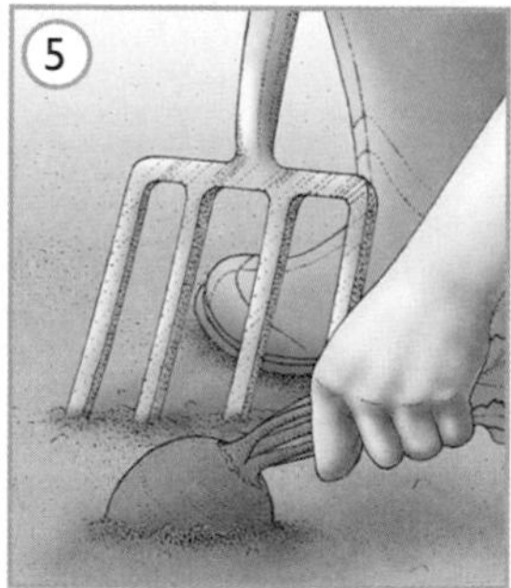

Harvest roots from late summer for immediate use or storage. Avoid breaking the skin.

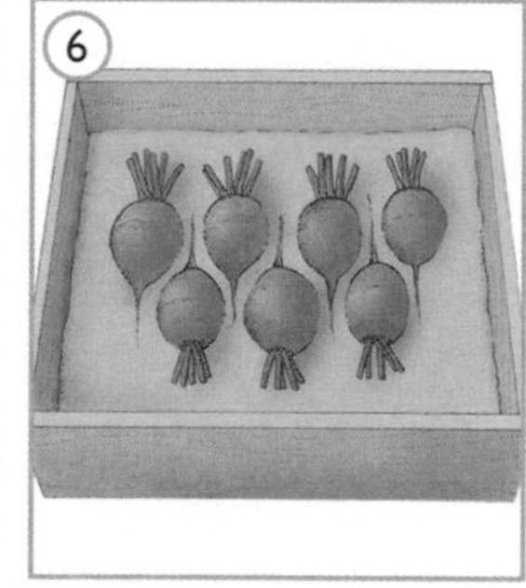

Store only undamaged roots in boxes of potting compost or sand for a ready-to-use winter supply.

Grow beetroot in any fertile, well-drained soil of pH6.5 or more and in full sun. Dig in two buckets of organic matter, such as garden compost, per square metre (yard). Before sowing, rake in growmore or other general-purpose fertiliser, at 100g per sq. m (3oz per sq. yd), or use twice as much organic fertiliser, such as chicken manure pellets. If organic matter is not available, increase the fertiliser by half.

Beetroot seeds, like those of leaf beets, are capsules containing several seeds, so thinning can be intricate. However, monogerm cultivars have seeds that contain just one viable seed.

For very early crops, sow bolt-resistant cultivars indoors in celltrays in any good multipurpose potting media using three to four seeds per cell. In mid-spring, plant out each cell with its cluster of seedlings at 15cm (6in) intervals, in rows 35cm (14in) apart. They will form baby beets.

From early spring until late summer, sow in drills 2cm (¾in) deep, in rows 35cm (14in) apart, placing seeds thumb's width apart. Make sowings every three to four weeks for a succession of tender young beet for summer use. For large roots for winter use, sow in late spring. Beetroot is sensitive to crowding, so thin plants as soon as possible.

RECOMMENDED CULTIVARS

'Boltardy': round, has good resistance to flowering when sown early

'Cheltenham Green Top': long roots, green leaves, good for winter

'Pablo': F1 hybrid, round, with good quality and good resistance to bolting

'Solo': F1 hybrid, monogerm – so thinning is reduced, round

Although drought-resistant, in dry spells soak plants with two watering cans per square metre (yard) every 14 days.

If growth flags at any stage, topdress with nitrogen-rich fertiliser, at 35g per sq. m (1oz per sq. yd).

Pull roots as soon as they are large enough (golf-ball-size). For winter crops, use larger roots as these keep better, either in the ground until early winter or indoors in boxes of sand or soil. Twist off the leaves rather than cut them to prevent loss of colour on cooking.

Voles, blackfly, leaf miner, leaf mildew and leaf spots present occasional problems. Discarding affected foliage is usually enough but leaf miner can be controlled with insecticides.

• RADISHES •

Radishes are brassicas but summer ones grow so quickly that they can be planted in any part of the crop rotation (see pp22–23). Winter radishes, including oriental mooli or daikon, are best kept with other brassicas, however. Since radishes grow so fast, they make good intercrops and catch crops (see pp24–25).

Grow in very fertile soil enriched with two buckets of organic matter, such as garden compost. Before sowing, rake in growmore, at 100g per sq. m (3oz per sq. yd), or use twice as much organic fertiliser, such as chicken manure pellets.

Sow summer radishes from late winter in containers indoors, and from early spring until late summer outdoors under fleece or cloches. In late summer, sow winter radishes – they tend to bolt (flower) if sown earlier.

Sow 1cm (½in) deep in rows 15cm (6in) apart, allowing a thumb's width between seeds. Thin seedlings to 2–3cm (¾–1in) apart – they hate to be crowded. Winter radishes are allowed to grow larger, so leave 30cm (12in) between the rows. Water crops in dry spells, as only quick uninterrupted growth will give a mild flavour and crunchy texture.

In cold regions store indoors in boxes of sand or soil until needed for winter soups, stews and, when grated, salads.

FROM SOWING TO HARVESTING SUMMER RADISHES

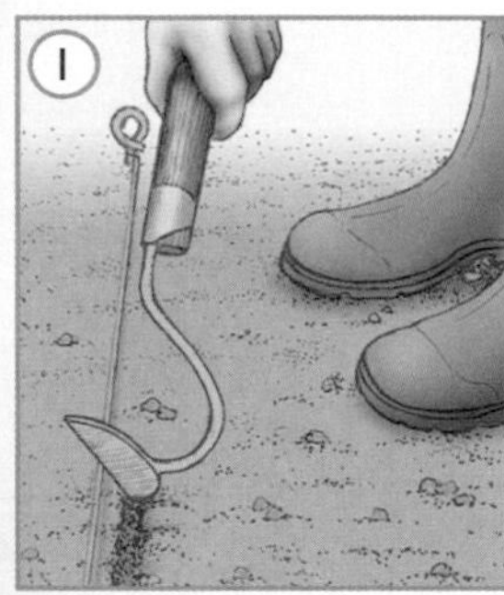

Sow seeds in drills where they are to grow, or for early crops, sow indoors. Sow every 2–3 weeks.

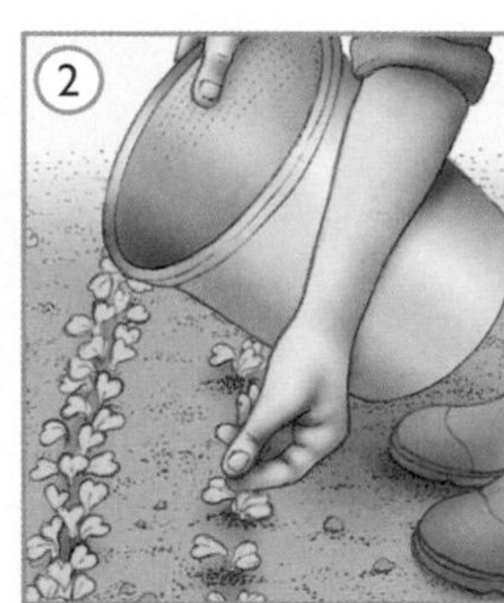

Thin seedlings as soon as they can be handled – they emerge rapidly in warm weather.

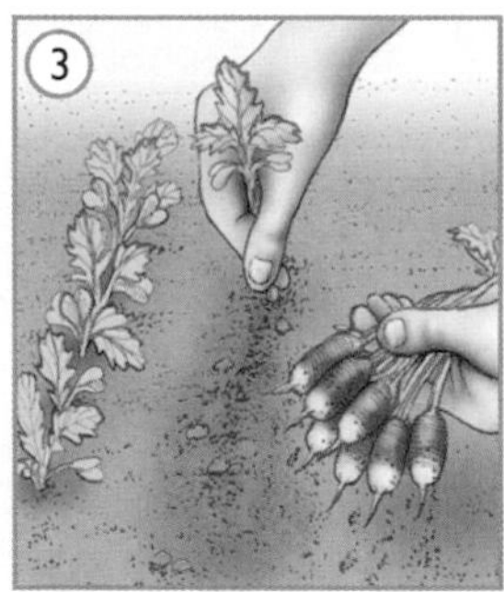

Lift roots when they are 2cm (¾in) in diameter, after 3–4 weeks (6–8 weeks for early sowings).

RECOMMENDED CULTIVARS

Summer radishes

'Amythyst': F1 hybrid, purple

'Short Top Forcing': round

'Zlata': golden yellow roots

Winter and oriental radishes

'Leaf Radish': oriental greens crop

'Mantanghong': multicoloured roots, oriental, winter use

'Neptune': F1 hybrid, mooli, winter, long white, oriental, bolt-resistant

'Round Black Spanish': black-skinned, winter, very hardy

In addition to their roots, radishes are also grown for their leaves, especially in China, using cultivars with a mild but deliciously spicy flavour. Sow seeds thickly, allowing about a thumb's width between seeds, and gather the young leaves when 5cm (2in) high.

Cabbage root fly can be devastating unless crops are grown beneath fleece or insect-proof mesh.

Winter radishes, especially mooli and daikon, are seriously harmed by cabbage root fly in late summer. Protect with fleece, which will also exclude flea beetles. Aphids and caterpillars are occasional pests that might need treatment with insecticide.

FROM SOWING TO HARVESTING WINTER RADISHES

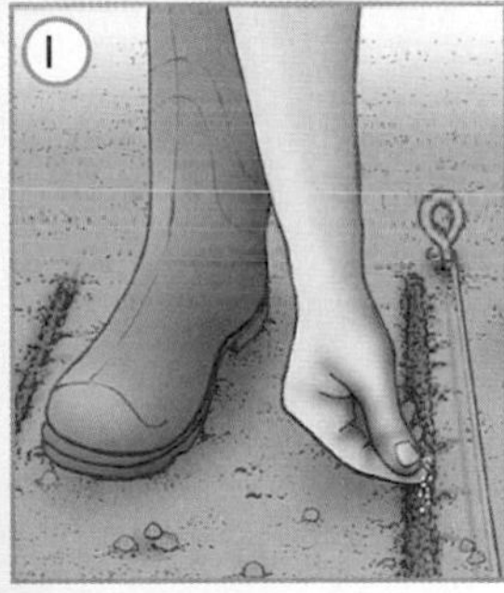

Sow groups of 3–4 seeds at 25cm (10in) intervals in drills in late summer.

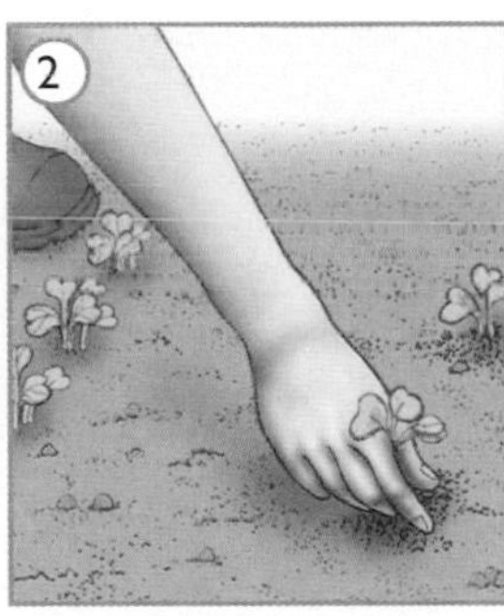

Thin seedlings as soon as they can be handled, leaving one plant at each station. Water the seeds afterwards.

Lift for storage in mid-autumn in cold regions. Elsewhere, winter radishes are hardy.

• ARTICHOKES •

JERUSALEM ARTICHOKE

This obliging vegetable is a close but perennial relative of the sunflower. Plant tubers in late winter. In most gardens, it is consigned to out-of-the-way spots where it is grown year after year. This avoids the tendency of Jerusalem artichokes to become an irksome weed.

FROM SOWING TO HARVESTING ARTICHOKES

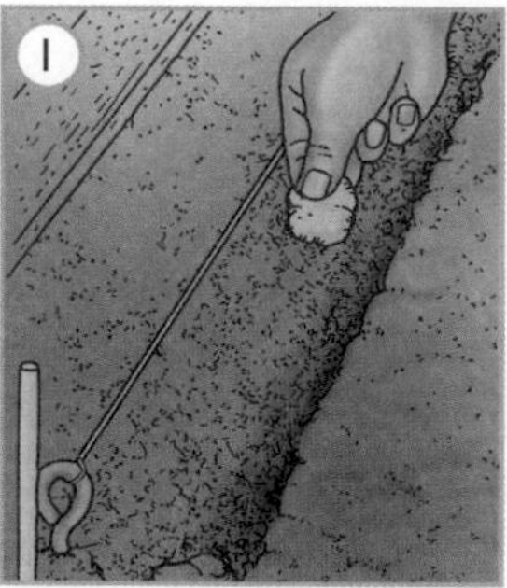

JERUSALEM ARTICHOKES: In late winter, plant tubers 10cm (4in) deep and 60cm (24in) apart.

In early summer, tie the plants to wires 20–30cm (9–12in) apart, between stakes 60cm (24in) apart.

Earth up plants to protect them against windrock and encourage tuber formation near the surface.

Water plants regularly in dry weather. In poor soils, apply liquid fertiliser every 2–3 weeks.

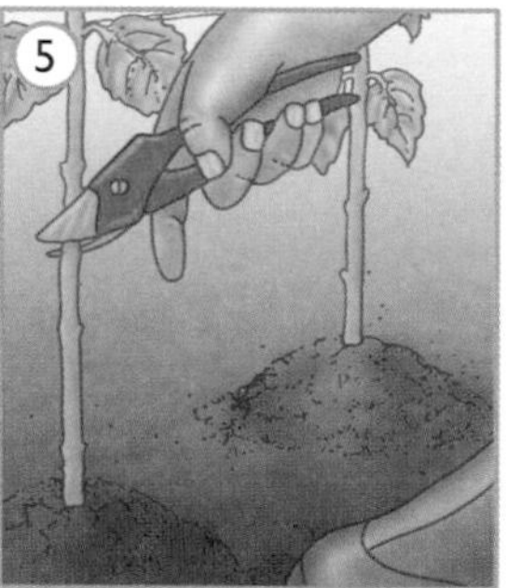

In autumn, shorten stems to 15cm (6in). Leave the tubers in the ground, for lifting as needed.

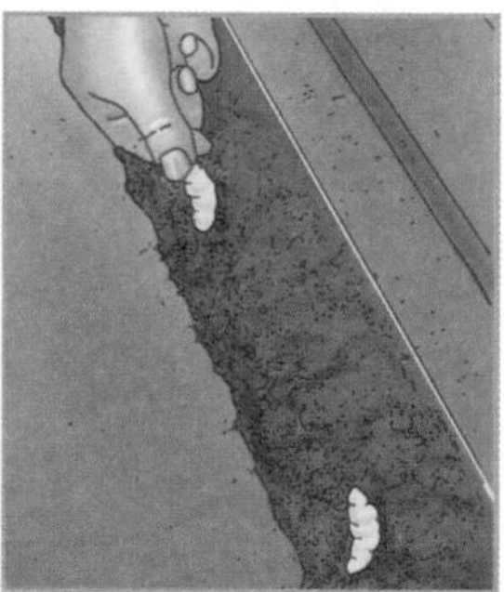

CHINESE ARTICHOKES: Plant tubers 5cm (2in) deep at 75cm (30in) intervals.

Any soil will do, as long as it does not get waterlogged in winter and gets at least six hours of sun each day in midsummer. Moderate fertility is enough – if in doubt, add a bucket of manure or other organic matter every square metre (yard). Before planting, rake in a general-purpose fertiliser, at 70g per sq. m (2oz per sq. yd). Set tubers in rows 1.5m (5ft) apart. Watering and weeding are not required.

Support the stems in early summer, or shorten them to 1.8m (6ft) to stabilise them. Also, draw earth around the base. Artichokes can be boxed in sand in case freezing weather prevents lifting.

Blackfly and powdery mildew do not affect yield.

GLOBE ARTICHOKE

In mid-spring, sow in celltrays indoors, or, better, raise from offsets of named clones such as 'Green Globe'. Plant out in early summer, in rows 1.2m (4ft) apart, in fertile soil. Harvest flowering shoots before flowers form. In cold regions in winter, cover plants with straw and fleece. Lift congested plants in mid-spring, divide and replant. Globe artichokes seldom need watering, and a spring topdressing of general fertiliser, at 70g per sq. m (2oz per sq. yd), is sufficient.

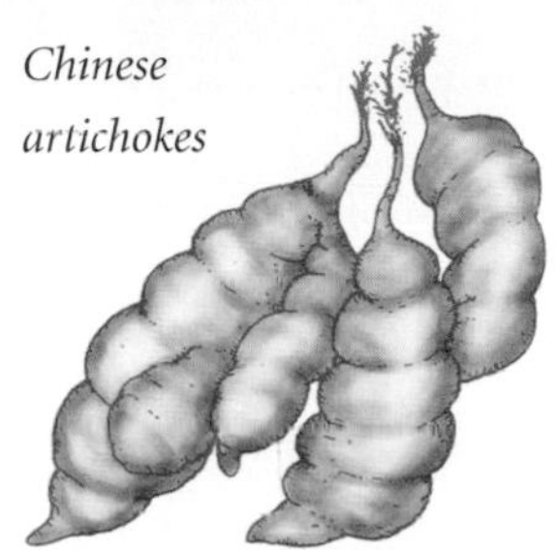
Chinese artichokes

CHINESE ARTICHOKE

These little-finger-sized, squiggly roots are formed at the base of an herbaceous perennial of the Stachys *family, and are exceptionally easy to grow. Plant the tubers 5cm (2in) deep, in early spring in any fertile, well-drained, weed-free soil in full sun. Allow 45cm (18in) between plants in all directions. The plants grow vigorously and suppress weeds, but good tuber formation requires moisture, so watering in dry spells is helpful. Removing tubers from the soil is laborious, so growing them in tubs of any multipurpose potting media is often done, and the compost easily washes off them. Lift tubers when the foliage dies and store in boxes of soil or compost.*

• POTATOES & SWEET POTATOES •

Potatoes are easy to grow, popular, widely cultivated and nutritious. They also have a multitude of uses. They are grouped by maturity period:

- Early: planted in early spring, or even in late winter indoors or in very mild coastal or urban areas, to crop from early summer, with high yields

- Second-early: planted from early to mid-spring to crop from midsummer. Their foliage matures and dies back in summer, after which the tubers are gathered and stored. Heavier yielding than early potatoes, but not as heavy as maincrop ones.

- Early maincrop: planted in mid-spring and lifted in early autumn, so may escape slug, blight and weather damage, unlike maincrop potatoes.

- Maincrop: planted in mid-spring to be lifted by mid-autumn but difficult to protect from slugs and blight.

Potatoes are also grouped by uses and other properties, so that some are good for salads or have a waxy or floury texture when cooked.

Dig in two buckets of organic matter, such as garden compost, per square metre (yard). Before planting, rake in

FROM SOWING TO HARVESTING POTATOES

Prepare the ground well with manure and fertiliser, and cultivate the fine tilth needed for earthing up.

Dig drills 10–15cm (4–6in) deep and row-spaced for the type of potatoes you are planting.

Place the tubers in the drills with the shoots of the rose end uppermost. Space them according to crop type.

growmore, at 100g per sq. m (3oz per sq. yd), or use twice as much organic fertiliser, such as chicken manure pellets. If organic matter is not available, increase the fertiliser by half.

Any well-drained garden soil in full sun will produce good crops, but wet clays may require late planting and early lifting, so second-earlies (see left) are especially useful. Potatoes prefer

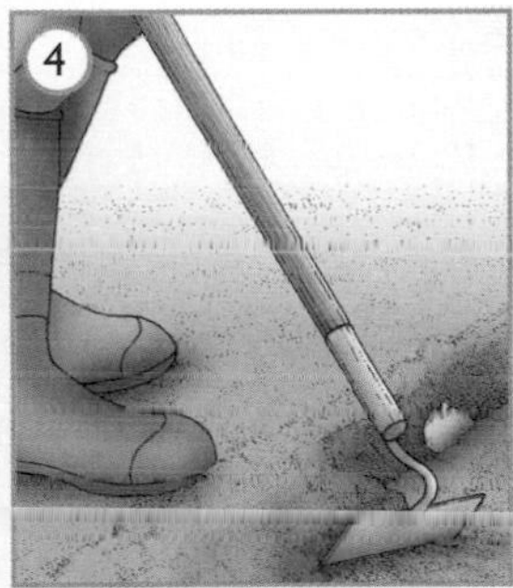

Cover the drills using a draw hoe. Mound the soil over the drills into a ridge 10–15cm (4–6in) high.

Water during dry weather in the growing season, particularly just before flowers open. Hoe weeds.

Earth up rows regularly, drawing soil up from the furrow to prevent light reaching the tubers.

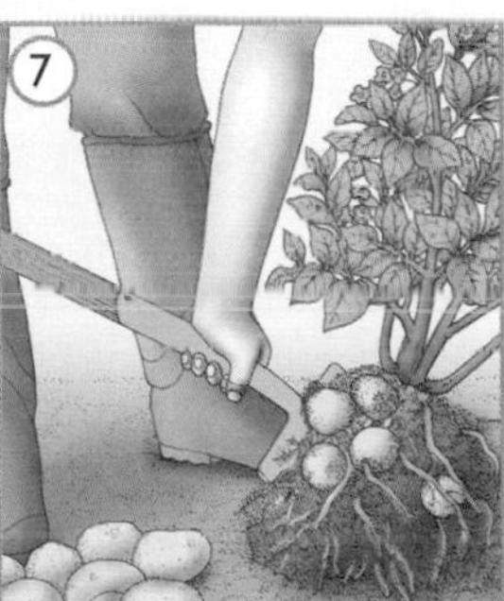

Lift early potatoes when the flowers are fully open. Using a flat-tined fork will help to avoid damage.

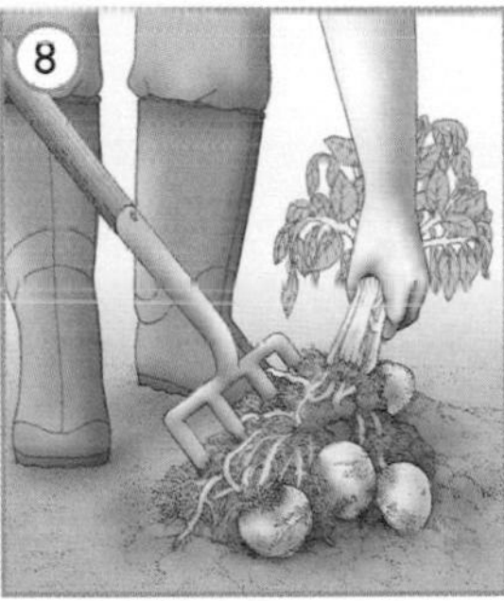

Lift second-early and maincrop potatoes when the foliage tops begin to die down.

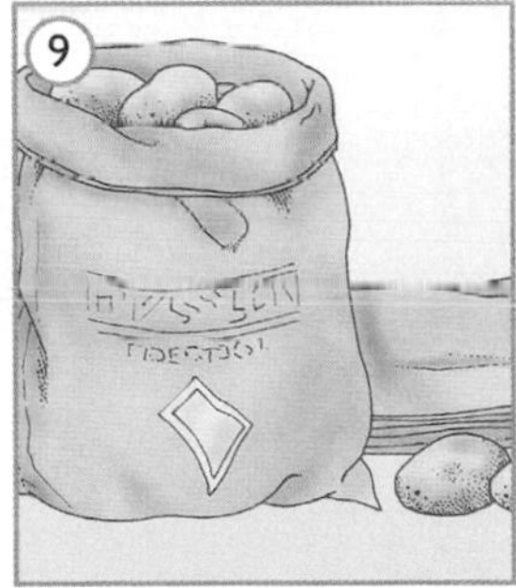

Store the potatoes in sacks or trays in a frost-free place. Remove any rotten tubers.

acid soils, but will crop well at higher pH levels, although these encourage common scab disease, so gardeners growing on alkaline soils should consider scab-resistant cultivars.

Although potatoes can be raised from true seed, it is usual to buy 'seed' tubers that are certified free of pests and diseases. They can be planted in the soil without any treatment, but if bought early, in winter,

GROWING POTATOES UNDER BLACK POLYTHENE

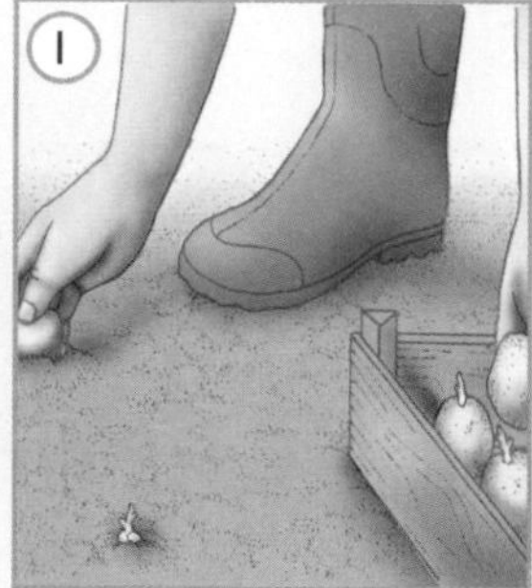

Plant the 'seed' tubers in spring after watering the ground. Space the tubers according to the type of crop.

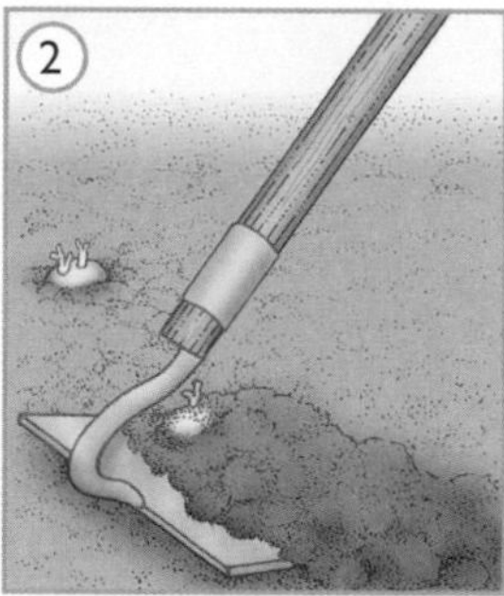

Cover the tubers with soil, mounding it slightly. Apply slug controls over and around the ridges.

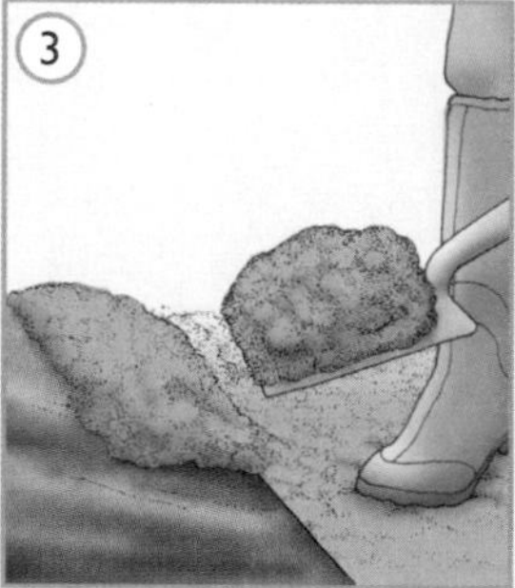

Cover the bed with a black plastic sheet. Mound earth over the edges of the sheet to hold it down securely.

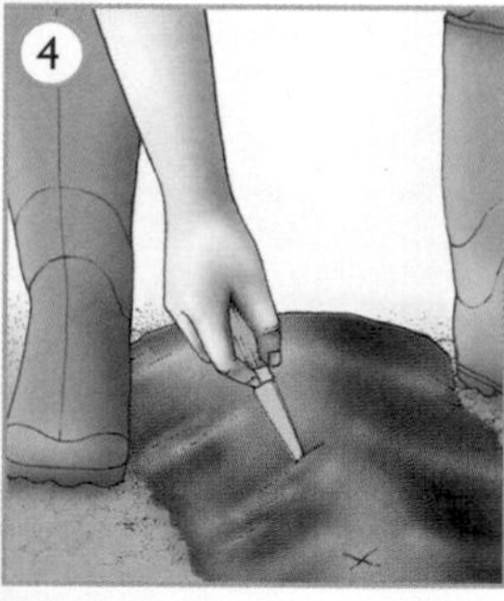

Cut small crosses in the plastic sheet as shoots develop. Keep cuts small so tubers are not exposed to light.

The plastic sheet suppresses weeds, retains moisture and protects tubers as the shoots push through the slits.

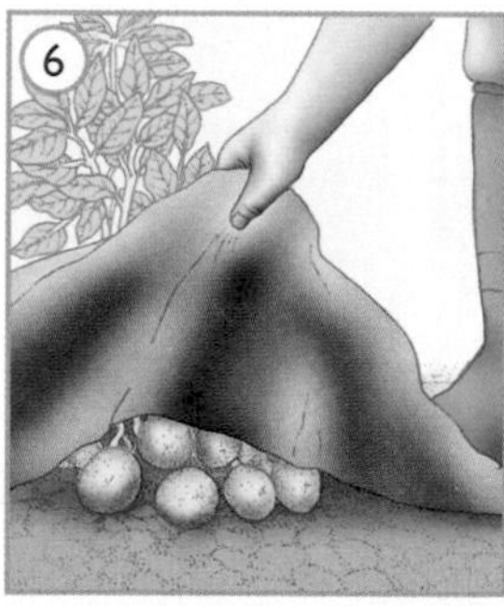

Harvest at the same time as earthed-up potatoes by pulling back the plastic sheet to expose the crop.

CHITTING POTATOES

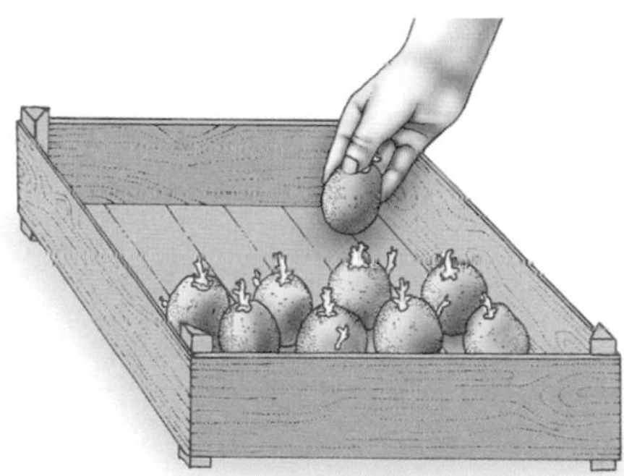

Buy 'seed' tubers as early as possible – those the size of hens' eggs are best. Large ones have numerous eyes and can produce masses of crowded shoots; they grow better if you can rub off all but four or five of the eyes.

After purchasing, place each tuber pointed end uppermost in a tray or shallow box, rejecting any that are damaged. Place in a cool, frost-free place in good light. Tubers soon get into a tangled mess if neglected and left in their packaging.

'chit' them (see box above). This 'ages' the tubers, enhancing early yield (ideal for early crops) and shortening the period to maturity, foliage die-back and harvest. When the shoots are 5–10cm (2–4in), long the tubers are ready to plant. Thin elongated shoots, produced when there is too little light and too much warmth, are poor and will seldom survive planting.

For earlies, place 'seed' tubers every 30cm (12in) in rows 60cm (24in) apart; for second-earlies, every 35cm (14in) in rows 70cm (30in) apart; and for maincrops, every 40cm (16in) in rows 75cm (30in) apart.

When frosts threaten, draw soil over the young shoots to barely cover them. In frosty gardens, cover with fleece in cold periods. As plants grow, draw up soil, every week or two, to the base of the lower leaves.

Instead of earthing up, you can use black plastic bags. Here, the 'seed' potatoes are planted as above but a slight ridge of soil – no more than 8cm (3in) – is made over the tubers and the bed is covered with black sheeting.

Potatoes can also be grown in pots, allowing one 'seed' tuber per 45cm (18in) diameter pot, or three tubers per 60cm (24in) tub. Fill the pot with multipurpose potting media to within

SWEET POTATOES

Sweet potatoes are a vigorous spreading tropical perennial grown for their sweet starchy roots, and for their tips and young leaves that can be used as 'greens'.

Any fertile garden soil, or potting medium in containers, will support sweet potatoes, as long as the site is sheltered but in full sun. Prepare the soil with one bucket of organic matter, such as garden compost, per square metre (yard). Before planting, rake in growmore, at 70g (2oz) per square metre (yard), or use twice that quantity of chicken manure pellets.

In late summer, take cuttings from disease-free plants, then in spring take soft green cuttings from the young plants. These cuttings (slips) can also be bought. Set each cutting in a 7–9cm (2½–3½in) pot. Cover with a plastic bag until rooted and then grow in a warm, sunny place until planting out in early summer.

Space plants 40cm (16in) apart, with 75cm (30in) between rows. If the soil is not well drained, plant in low ridges 20cm (8in) high and 30cm (12in) wide. Fleece or cloches greatly improve yields.

Sweet potatoes do not suffer from any significant pests or diseases.

25cm (10in) of the rim and plant so the tuber is barely covered. As the shoots grow, add more compost to within 5cm (2in) of the rim. Water so the soil does not dry out but is never soggy. Add general-purpose liquid fertiliser every week and gather tubers as soon as large enough.

When the foliage of second-earlies and maincrop potatoes dies back, lift and store the tubers after a two-week gap, to let their skins set firm and so resist damage and allow long storage. Dry tubers for two hours before storing in hessian or paper sacks, in a dark, dry and frost-free place.

RECOMMENDED CULTIVARS

Earlies

'Lady Christl': oval, waxy, pale yellow tubers, nematode-resistant

'Vales Emerald': oval, waxy, pale yellow tubers

Second-earlies

'Cosmos': drought-resistant, white, round tubers, good flavour

'Kestrel': drought-, nematode- and slug-resistant; white with pink eye

'Charlotte': small, medium tubers, firm texture, good flavour

Early maincrop

'Ambo': good flavour, large tubers, white with pink eye

'Picasso': nematode- and drought-resistant, white with pink eye

Maincrop

'Robinta': red; good drought, pest and disease resistance

'Sarpo Mira': strong blight resistance, dry, nutty texture

Salad

'Anya': small second-early tubers with firm texture and good flavour

Sweet potatoes

'Beauregard Improved': red skin, orange flesh, sweet flavour

'T65': red skin, pale flesh, vigorous and tolerant of poor conditions

Potato blight is potentially devastating and, although available fungicides may protect for a few weeks, the crop is best lifted before the blight destroys all the foliage. The haulm (stems and leaves) is severed and burnt or buried deeply, and, after a two-week gap to allow any spores in the soil to die out, the crop is lifted and stored. During storage, any rotting tubers are eliminated before the rot can spread. Some blight-resistant cultivars are highly effective.

Potato cyst nematode is the most damaging pest, as the yellow cysts suck nutrients from the plant's roots and then fall off to infest the soil for years. Resistant cultivars are available and crop rotation helps.

Slugs often ruin many tubers, especially in wet summers and ill-drained soils.

• TOMATOES •

Tomatoes are one of the most rewarding crops with heavy yields of tasty fruits. In warm, mild, sheltered southern areas, they can be grown outdoors in sheltered warm spots in the garden.

Tomatoes are usually either vine types or bushes. Bushes are very easy – each shoot ends up with a string of flowers (a truss). Bush tomatoes need little or no staking and are easy to grow under cloches or in cold frames, and some make good hanging basket plants.

With vine tomatoes, the truss comes out from the stem, and the stem has a growing point that grows more or less indefinitely. In addition, between each leaf and the stem (axil) another shoot arises and a major tangle can soon develop. To overcome this, each vine tomato is grown up and tied to a string or stake, and the shoots from the axil scrupulously removed. Vine tomatoes are more work than bush tomatoes but give a heavier crop and use space more efficiently, especially in glasshouses, and are also much easier to spray against blight disease.

Tomatoes are widely and usually cheaply sold as plants. However, for a wider choice of cultivars, and because it is easy, it is still worth raising tomatoes from seed.

FROM SOWING TO TRANSPLANTING TOMATO PLANTS

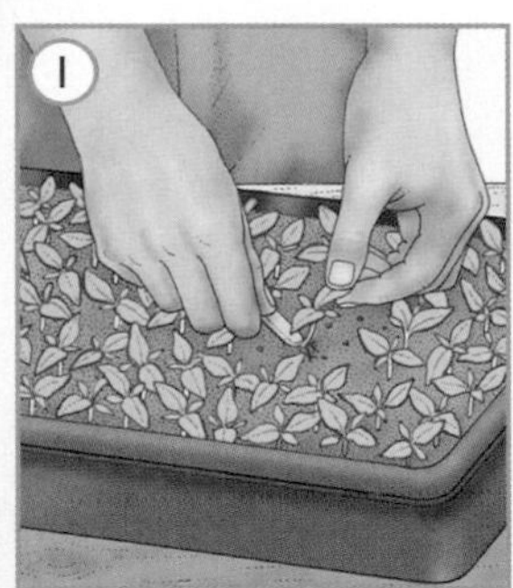

Plant up seedlings when they have 4–5 leaves in small pots. Grow on in bright light, at 12–18°C (54–64°F).

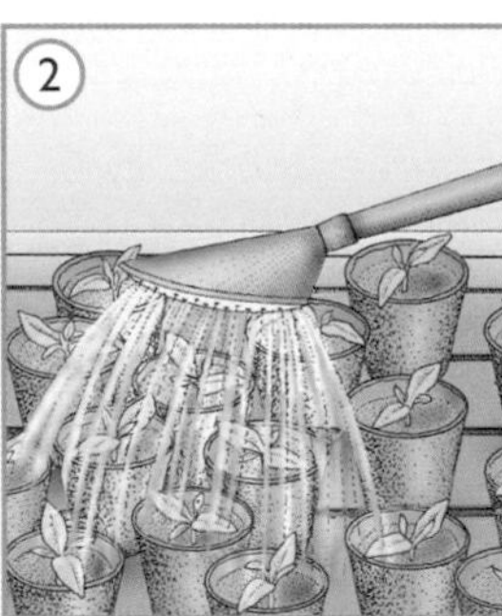

Water plants, keeping soil moist but never soggy. Liquid-feed weekly once roots appear from the pot base.

Plant in final site once the first flowers begin to show or when the plants are 15–23cm (6–9in) high.

Seeds for different colours, shapes and flavours can be kept for several years.

In late winter or early spring, start off tomatoes destined for glasshouses, and from early to mid-spring, sow outdoor tomatoes.

Use seedtrays or pans (shallow, wide pots) filled with any good-quality sowing or multipurpose potting compost. Sow thinly (a finger width apart) and barely cover the seed with sieved potting compost or fine vermiculite. Water with dilute copper fungicide to prevent damping off disease, and place in the light at 18–25°C (64–77°F). The ideal environment is a heated propagator in a frost-free glasshouse. Germination normally takes place within 14 days.

Pot on the young seedlings in individual 7–9cm (2½–3½in) pots of multipurpose potting media. Space the pots so that the foliage never touches, to avoid drawn, leggy plants. Windowsill-grown plants will be leggy, but in good light they will be usable.

GLASSHOUSE CULTURE

In mid-spring, plant glasshouse tomatoes in their final position, either in 45cm (18in) pots, growbags or straw bales, or in borders of soil fortified with a bucketful of well-rotted compost every square metre (yard), plus a general-purpose balanced fertiliser, at a rate of 100g per sq. m (3oz per sq. yd). Allow 45cm (18in) between plants, with 60cm (24in) between rows. Plant at the same depth as they were in the pot. Allow leggy tomatoes to trail a little initially before leading them up the string or support. The first flowers should then be only 30cm (12in) above the ground; if higher, the plant will reach the roof before it is bearing a good crop. Strong string or wooden stakes are needed to bear the 5kg (11lb) of fruit carried on a well-grown tomato.

GROWING GREENHOUSE TOMATOES

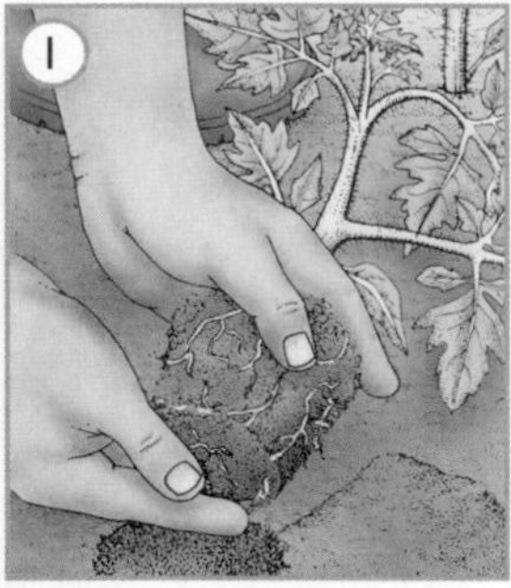

Set out plants with the rootball level with the soil. Keep plants moist to help the roots explore the soil.

Tie soft string around the stem of each plant and tie one end to a wire stretched above, or use canes.

Spray the flowers with a fine droplet spray or tap the canes on sunny days. This helps the flowers set fruit.

Remove lower leaves once the plants are 1.2–1.5m (4–5ft) high. Pinch out sideshoots in the leaf axils.

Remove the growing tip once the plants reach the roof of the glasshouse.

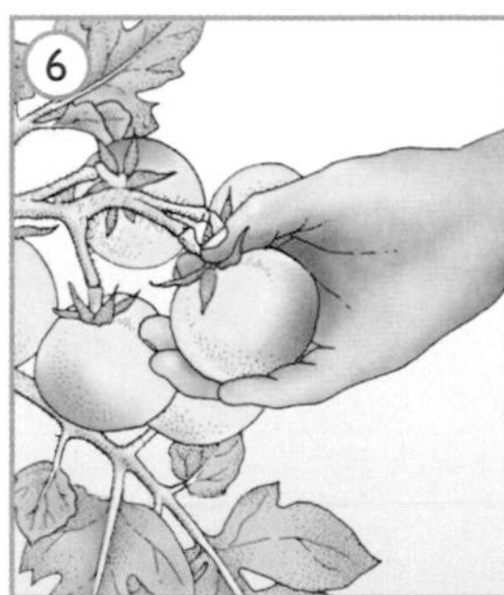

Pick the fruit as it develops full colour, keeping each stalk intact. At the end of the season, ripen fruit indoors.

Container plants may need watering twice or even three times a day compared with the no more than daily watering needed by border tomatoes. Tomatoes must never be dry or soggy. Feed containers weekly with tomato fertiliser once the plant roots have filled the container.

Tie in plants to the support every 25cm (10in). When they reach the roof, pinch out the tips two leaves beyond the last fruit cluster (truss).

Glasshouses often get too hot and bright, so use shade netting or paints and ventilate to keep temperatures lower than 25°C (77°F) and above 15°C (60°C).

Although draughts and insects from outside the greenhouse usually affect pollination, it is worth shaking flowering indoor plants every day to ensure pollen transfers within flowers. Fruits begin to ripen from the bottom and are gathered when they are fully coloured and beginning to soften.

At the end of the season, pick all green fruits still on the plants and leave to ripe in a warm place indoors. Alternatively, whole plants can be uprooted and hung in sheds to ripen, or plants can be laid on straw and covered with cloches to ripen in place. Green fruits can, of course, be used in pickles and chutneys.

OUTDOOR CULTURE

Outdoor cultivation of tomatoes is much the same as for indoor vine-type tomatoes, except that the growing tip is pinched out as soon as four or five trusses have formed – plants seldom ripen more outdoors and it is better for the plant to concentrate on ripening a limited number of fruit. The best crops usually come from garden soil but containers, growbags and other pots can be used on patios and where suitable soil for growing tomatoes is unavailable. However, the essential stout stake may be more difficult to arrange in outdoor containers.

Prepare soil with a bucketful of well-rotted manure or compost every square metre (yard) plus a general purpose balanced fertiliser, at 100g per sq. m (3oz per sq. yd).

Plant young bush tomato plants 45cm (18in) apart, with 75cm (30in) between rows. Mulch with straw or black plastic to keep the fruits from soiling.

Water every 10 days in dry spells in midsummer. If growth flags, topdress with a general purpose fertiliser such as growmore, at 70g per sq. m (2oz per sq. yd), and water in. Alternatively, liquid tomato fertiliser can be added during watering.

TOMATO PROBLEMS

Weeds can be troublesome in soil, although growing through black plastic can help deter their growth.

GROWING BUSH OR VINE TOMATOES OUTDOORS

Plant tomatoes out into well-cultivated soil. Water well before and after planting.

Support tomatoes with a short cane or stake to promote air flow through the plant.

Pinch out sideshoots on vine tomatoes. Early morning is the best time. Avoid leaving untidy wounds.

Remove the growing tip when four clusters of flowers (trusses) start to form fruit.

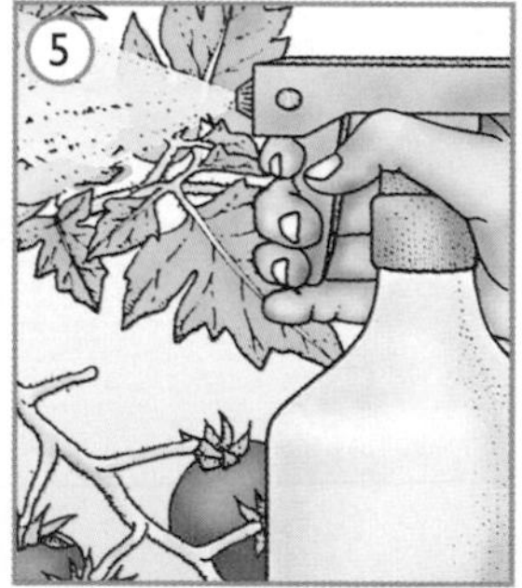

Spray with fungicide to protect from blight. Continue to snap out any new sideshoots that develop.

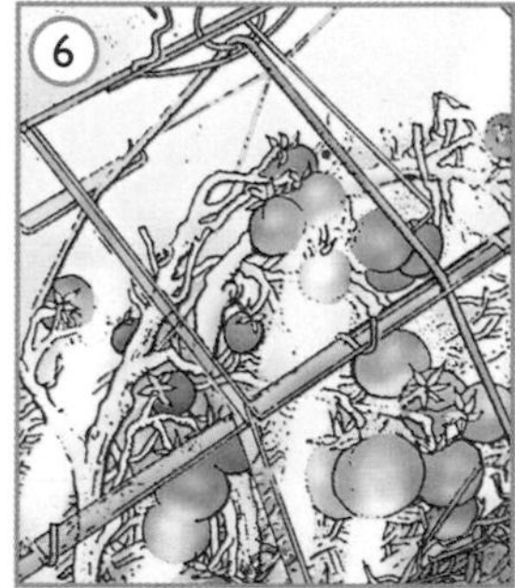

Cover bush tomatoes with cloches for earlier crops. Untie and lay down late-developing fruit on vines.

RECOMMENDED CULTIVARS

'Costoluto Fiorentino': beefsteak, large ribbed juicy fruits, cordon, good outdoors
'Floridity': hybrid, cordon, small plum fruits of excellent flavour and quality
'Gardener's Delight': hybrid, small very sweet fruits, cordon, good for greenhouse or outdoors
'Legend': hybrid, bold red fruits of medium-size, some tolerance of blight, cordon, good outdoors
'Outdoor Girl': robust outdoor-type with heavy crops of moderately large fruits, cordon
'Shirley': hybrid, reliable greenhouse-type, cordon, medium flavour
'Sungold': cordon, cherry with abundance of orange, very sweet fruits, good outdoors
'Sweet Million': hybrid, prolific trusses of tiny red fruits of superb flavour, cordon, good outdoors
'Tornado': hybrid, robust and reliable bush type with medium juicy fruits, good outdoors
'Vanessa': hybrid, greenhouse-type with bold red medium-size fruits that last well on the vine and have good flavour, cordon
'Yellow Perfection': sweet yellow fruits, heavy cropping early, cordon, good outdoors

Tomatoes are very susceptible to potato blight, which quickly destroys both plant and crop. There is no cure but copper fungicides applied at least every 14 days can limit the disease. No resistant cultivars are yet offered but some have a degree of tolerance. Indoor plants are often uninfected as long as their foliage remains dry. Diseases are favoured by wet conditions, which can largely be eliminated indoors, but outdoors they can only be addressed by removing diseased material promptly.

Other problems are much less damaging: aphids or greenfly can be eliminated with insecticides or, in glasshouses, with biological controls, as can glasshouse red spider mites and thrips. Foliage can sometimes be devoured by nocturnal caterpillars, which, like slugs, can be hunted down at night with a torch.

• CUCUMBERS •

Cucumbers are a popular crop among gardeners and come in a baffling range of types, most of which trail.

- Glasshouse, all-female cucumbers set no seed. Remove the occasional male flower.

- Glasshouse male and female cucumbers are old-fashioned types, seldom grown now, as the all-female forms are more productive.

- Ridge, or outdoor, cucumbers need to be fertilised and set seeds. They range from small, spiny ridge cucumbers to longer, smooth Japanese outdoor cucumbers. They have a robust flavour.

- Gherkins are small, spiny and prolific cucumbers that usually need to be fertilised to set fruit; used for pickling.

In mid-spring sow in 8–9cm (3–3½in) pots indoors; 20–25°C (68–77°F) is needed for germination. Plant out seedlings for indoor cucumbers as soon as the roots have bound the potting medium. Set out outdoor ones from mid-spring under fleece or cloches or, without protection, in early summer when frosts have passed.

Indoors, use a fertile border soil enriched with organic matter and fertiliser, or raise plants in growbags or pots at least 45cm (18in) wide and deep. Allow 75cm

FROM PLANTING TO HARVESTING GLASSHOUSE CUCUMBERS

Plant 2 plants in a standard growbag in mid-spring. Large pots or border soil can also be used, with 1 plant per pot or 45cm (18in) between border plants. Shade the plants in hot weather and liquid-feed.

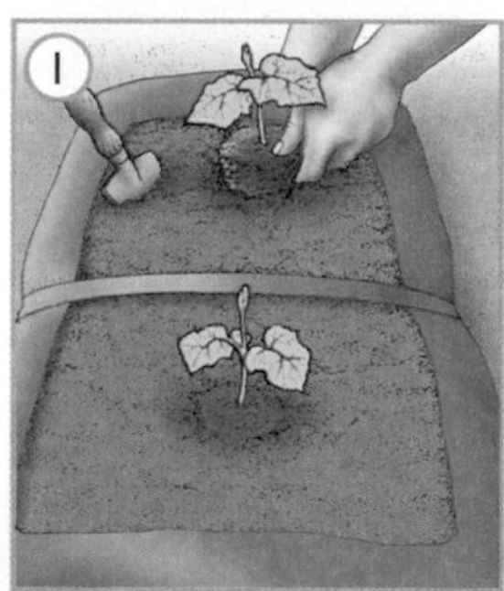

Support the plants by tying them to canes as they grow. Remove the growing points when the main stems reach the greenhouse roof. Maintain a temperature of 18–25°C (64–77°F).

(30in) in all directions between plants. Keep the rooting medium damp.

Outdoors, any well-drained garden soil in full sun will produce good crops, but on wet, cold clays, gather soil into flat-topped ridges 20cm (8in) high and 1m (3ft) wide. Dig in two buckets of organic matter, such as garden compost. Before planting, rake in growmore or another general-purpose fertiliser, at 100g per sq. m (3oz per sq. yd), or use twice as much organic fertiliser, such as chicken manure pellets. If organic matter is not available, increase the fertiliser by half. Set plants out at 1m (3ft) intervals. Water every 10 days in dry spells.

The usual glasshouse pests – aphids, red spider mite, thrips and whitefly – can be troublesome, especially if the vital heavy summer shading is insufficient. Biological controls are ideal or use insecticides such as oils or fatty acids. Use resistant cultivars to limit powdery mildew, and dust with sulphur.

RECOMMENDED CULTIVARS

Glasshouse cucumbers

'Carmen': high-quality female

'Zeina': mini cucumber for greenhouse, female

Ridge, or outdoor, cucumbers

'Masterpiece': robust; small, spiny but tasty fruits

'Tokyo Slicer': smooth skin

Allow side branches to develop, but pinch out their growing tips once they have 2 leaves. The first fruits will develop on the main stem, followed by fruits on the sideshoots.

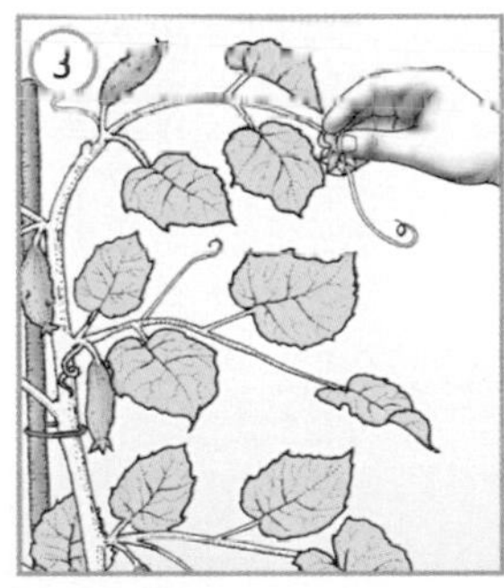

Cut cucumbers with a sharp knife once the fruits have parallel sides and the tip is rounded and no longer pointed. Delay will harm quality as well as hold up and reduce subsequent cropping.

• COURGETTES, MARROWS, SQUASHES & PUMPKINS •

Courgettes, marrows, squashes and pumpkins are all members of the cucumber family. They may be bushy in habit but they usually trail, and are all cultivated in a similar way. They are easy and very rewarding to grow in warm regions, often producing gluts, but in cold areas, protection with cloches, cold frames or greenhouses may be required.

- Marrows have large, elongated or round fruits filled with watery flesh. Use when mature or store until midwinter.

- Courgettes are usually green or yellow marrow fruits. Use when small, soft and immature, typically around the time the flower falls off after fertilisation.

- Summer squash has elongated, scalloped or round fruits, often yellow or white, filled with watery flesh. Best used when immature.

- Winter squash requires lots of warmth and light. Small to large, yellow, blue-grey, cream and other coloured

FROM PLANTING TO HARVESTING COURGETTES, MARROWS, SQUASHES & PUMPKINS

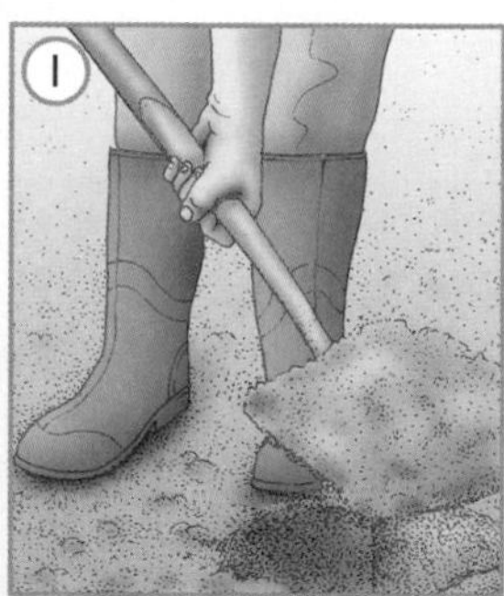

Dig holes at a spade's width and depth at the desired spacings for either bush or trailing varieties.

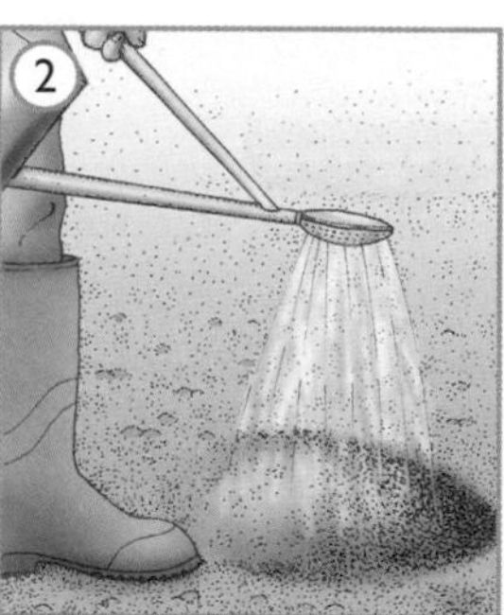

Water the soil once the holes have been filled with organic matter. Create a ridge around the planting hole.

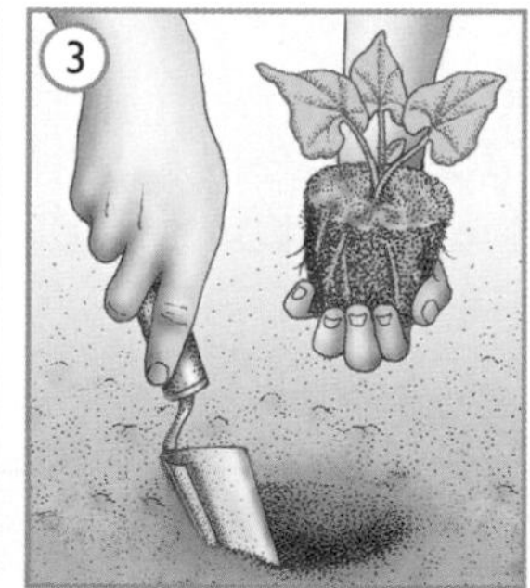

Transplant young plants into the prepared soil, or sow 3 seeds and thin to the strongest.

fruit may be bulbous, cylindrical, flattened or elongated. Use when mature. Good storage potential, often lasting until the following spring, having thick rinds and hard dry flesh.

- Pumpkins are large fruits, usually orange, with thick rinds and rather watery flesh. They store until midwinter at the latest.

- Gourds come in an enormous range of unusual fruits, which are attractive, but often not edible and sometimes potentially harmful, so need treating with caution. They are mostly grown for ornament.

Grow in well-drained soil of more than pH6, in full sun. Dig in a bucketful of rotted manure or other organic matter to every square metre (yard), as well as a general fertiliser, at 70g per sq. m

Water developing plants regularly, and begin to feed regularly once fruits develop.

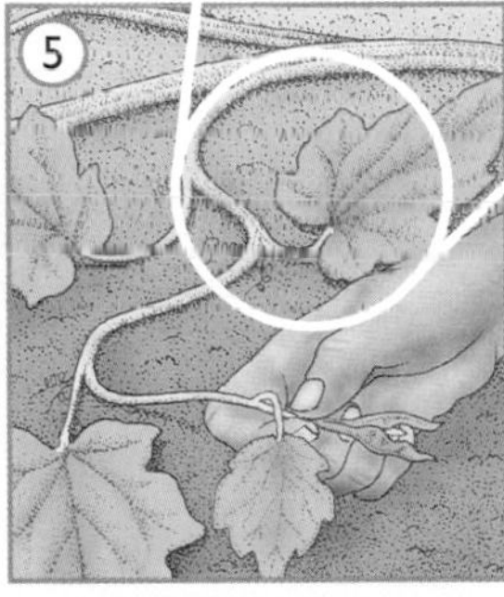

Pinch out the tips of all sideshoots of trailing varieties once they reach 60cm (24in) long.

Pick courgettes regularly when young and tender, and harvest marrows as required.

Female flowers have fruits below the flower, and often only appear several weeks after male flowers.

(2oz per sq. yd). If organic matter is unavailable, or you are using organic fertiliser, double the quantities.

In mid-spring, sow two seeds per 5–9cm (2–3½in) pot, setting each seed on its edge. Leave in good light to germinate, at 20–25°C (68–77°F). Liquid-feed and plant out from late spring until early summer – ideally under cloches or fleece – once strong bushy plants have four or five true leaves and strong roots.

In mild regions, in early summer, sow outdoors where the plants are to grow. Cover with cloches or fleece. Spacing depends on the plant habit: set bush cultivars 75cm (30in) apart, in rows 1m (3ft) apart, while trailing types do best at least 1m (3ft) apart, in rows 1.5m (5ft) apart. Train trailing types up arches, fences and wigwams or over hedges, sheds and compost bins.

In dry spells, water every 10–14 days to improve cropping and help limit mildew infection.. When growth is poor and female flowers seem slow in forming, topdress with nitrogen-rich fertiliser, at 35g per sq. m (1oz per sq. yd).

Cut summer squash and courgette fruits as soon as usable. Harvest marrows

To avoid a courgette glut, pick them very young, before the flower falls off and when most delicious and tender.

RECOMMENDED CULTIVARS

Courgettes

'Black Forest': F1 hybrid, trailing, dark fruits, for wigwams or fences

'Defender': F1 hybrid, bush, green fruits, virus-resistant

'Taxi': F1 hybrid, vigorous, quick-growing, yellow fruits

Marrows

'Minipak': bush marrow, with medium green fruits

'Tiger Cross': F1 hybrid, striped, bush, large fruits, virus-resistant

Summer squash

'Eight Ball': round, green fruits, bush

'Golden Early Crookneck': bush, yellow fruits, bent neck

'Sunburst': scalloped, bush, yellow

Winter squash

'Crown Prince': trailing, grey-blue, firm orange flesh, large fruits

'Harrier': butternut, early, bell-shaped fruits

'Hawk': butternut, early, pear shape

'Queensland Blue': trailing, grey, firm orange flesh, large barrel-shaped fruits

Pumpkins

'Atlantic Giant': trailing, giant, yellow

'Jack Of All Trades': Halloween-type trailing for carving or eating

'Munchkin': mini flat fruits, trailing, highly ornamental

'Rouge Vif D'Etampes': large, flat, slightly scalloped, orange fruits

when they reach their normal size for the cultivar, or leave to mature and store. Rest winter squash and pumpkin on a tile or piece of timber to avoid soiling, in order to develop the hard skin, full colour and ringing sound when tapped, characteristic of mature fruits. These can mature late. If frost threatens, cover the fruits with straw. Once the vines die, the fruits will not swell further and ripe fruits can be gathered.

Powdery mildew is the only significant problem. Using soil rich in organic matter and watering to avoid drought help reduce damage. Few effective fungicides are available to amateur gardeners.

• PEPPERS & AUBERGINES •

Peppers are annuals or short-lived perennials from tropical South America. The brightly coloured fruits are astonishingly variable; sweet peppers and chilli peppers may change from unripe green to ripened red, purple, black, yellow and orange, and may take many shapes, including round, barrel, pointed and flat.

In late winter or early spring, sow seeds thinly (a finger width apart) in shallow trays or pans (shallow but wide pots) filled with good-quality sowing or multipurpose potting compost. Just cover with sieved compost or fine vermiculite, and water with dilute copper fungicide to prevent damping off. Set in the light at 18–25°C (64–77°F). The ideal

FROM PLANTING TO HARVESTING PEPPERS

Pot up young plants, whether grown from seeds or bought, into pots at least 45cm (18in) deep, in a bright, warm place. Space them 45cm (18in) apart each way. Water the plants regularly.

Pinch out the main growing point on each plant once it has reached 30cm (12in), leaving 3–4 branches to make a bushy plant. Provide canes to support the branches if necessary.

Combat pests such as aphids or red spider mite in the glasshouse with biological or chemical controls. Pick off caterpillars by hand. Continue to water, keeping plants moist but never soggy.

Harvest the fruits as required from mid- to late summer. Fruits left to ripen to red become richly flavoured but will suppress the formation of more fruit, so for the maximum crop, harvest the immature green fruit.

RECOMMENDED CULTIVARS

Peppers

'Bell Boy': F1 hybrid, cylindrical, good in cool conditions
'Gypsy': F1 hybrid, long, pointed, greenhouse, red fruits
'Jalapeno': stubby hot red chillies
'Redskin': as 'Bell Boy', F1 hybrid, ideal for patios and cloches
'Scotch Bonnet': yellow pungent chillies ripen yellow from green

Aubergines

'Bonica': F1 hybrid, early maturing
'Fairy Tale': F1 hybrid, purple and white, sausage-shaped fruits
'Moneymaker': F1 hybrid, black, elongated fruit, unusually tolerant of cool conditions
'Thai Yellow Egg': tiny, yellow, egg-shaped fruits

environment is a heated propagator in a frost-free glasshouse. Germination should occur within 14 days.

Pot on seedlings into individual 7–9cm (2½–3½in) pots filled with good-quality multipurpose potting media. Keep the soil moist – never soggy – and feed with liquid fertiliser once roots appear from the bottom of the pot.

Prepare the soil with a bucketful of well-rotted manure or compost every square metre (yard), plus a general purpose balanced fertiliser, at 100g per sq. m (3oz per sq. yd).

In the glasshouse, set peppers in their final position in mid-spring, either in containers or in borders of soil fortified with a bucketful of well-rotted compost every square metre (yard), plus a general-purpose balanced fertiliser, at 100g per sq. m (3oz per sq. yd). Space plants 45cm (18in) apart and allow 60cm (24in) between rows.

Growbags and large pots filled with potting media will need watering daily and feeding weekly with tomato fertiliser once the plant roots have filled the container.

Outdoors plants are grown in the same way, but benefit from tall cloches or tunnels of fleece for extra protection.

AUBERGINES

Aubergines (also called eggplants or brinjal) are grown in the same way as peppers and tomatoes. But because the plants grow slowly, it is essential to sow them early and this can be difficult if a good warm, bright place for seed-raising

FROM PLANTING TO HARVESTING AUBERGINES

Plant up when flowers form. Allow 1 plant per 30cm (12in) pot, 2 to a growing bag, or space 60cm (24in) apart in the ground.

Pinch out growing tips when they reach 30cm (12in) tall to make a bushy, freely cropping plant. Support plants with canes.

Remove excess fruits to leave only 5–6 on each plant, evenly spaced for good growth. Pinch out any further flowers.

Gather fruits by cutting the stem with a sharp knife when they are large enough to harvest and showing full colour.

is unavailable. Without such facilities it may be best to buy plants.

Aubergines need a fairly fertile soil, obtained by adding a bucket of well-rotted manure every square metre (yard), plusa general-purpose balanced fertiliser, at 70g per sq. m (2oz per sq. yd). Plants can be set in their final position as recommended for peppers but they appreciate more light and warmth and about two thirds of the fertiliser.

Plants growing in large pots are often 'shy fruiting', so keeping plants in smaller, 30cm (12in) pots is better. Support fruits with canes and strings and pick when each fruit stops enlarging and before it becomes coarse and dull.

Whitefly and red spider mite can be a problem. When growing in border soil, verticillium wilt can be troublesome; plants grafted onto tomato rootstock will resist this disease and perform better.

• HAMBURG PARSLEY, SALSIFY & SCORZONERA •

HAMBURG PARSLEY

The hardy stumpy roots of Hamburg parsley have a mild parsley flavour with a carrot texture. The roots are raised like carrots, while the foliage lasts all winter and is used like parsley in stews, stocks and soups.

Choose any sunny, fertile, well-drained soil that is no less than pH6. Prepare and enrich the soil as for carrots (see p124). Sow in mid-spring with a finger width between seeds. Hoe weeds carefully and protect plants against carrot fly with insect-proof netting.

SALSIFY & SCORZONERA

These unusual roots – pale in salsify and black-skinned for scorzonera – are long and thin, and are raised (and eaten) like parsnips (see p132).

Very hardy and easy to grow, salsify and scorzonera have a delicate taste that is not as strongly flavoured as parsnips. In mid-spring, sow in the same way as parsnips with 30cm (12in) between rows, thinning to 15cm (6in) between plants. Plants seldom need watering or suffer from pests and diseases. Dig up the roots in winter as required.

FROM PLANTING TO HARVESTING HAMBURG PARSLEY

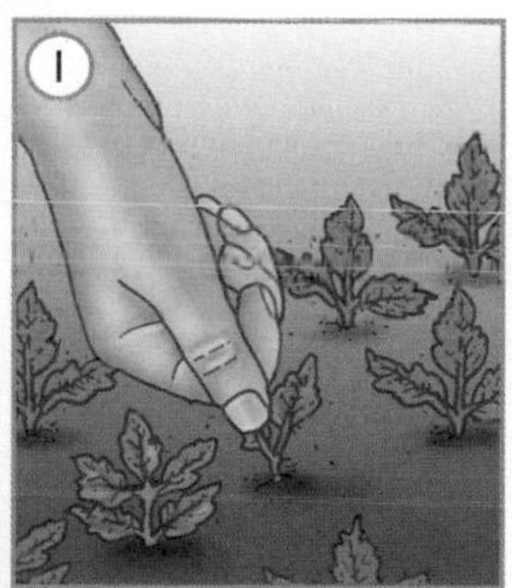

Sow the seeds in 2cm (¾in) drills, 30cm (12in) apart. Thin seedlings until they are 23cm (9in) apart.

Throughout summer, water the plants generously. Feed by topdressing with nitro-chalk.

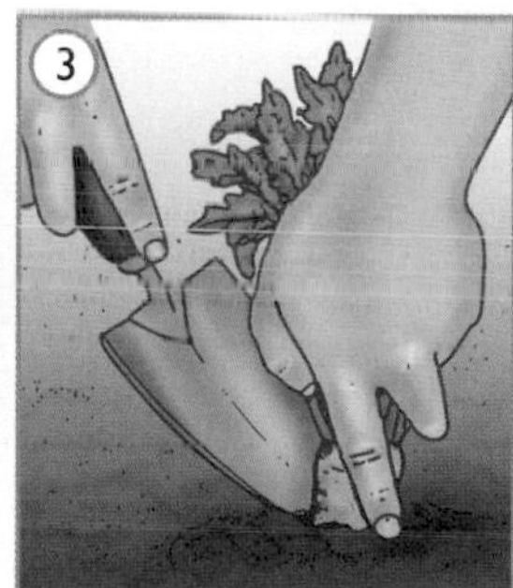

In early winter, lift the roots as required. Straw over any remaining in the ground.

• LAMBS LETTUCE •

Lambs lettuce, or corn salad, has dark green, boat-shaped, mild, earthy-flavoured leaves and is used for salads and as a cooked vegetable.

Any garden soil in full sun or light shade is suitable, as long as it was manured for a previous crop. If in doubt, rake in a general-purpose fertiliser, at 70g per sq. m (2oz per sq. yd).

Sowings, with a finger width between seeds, are made fortnightly from early spring until early autumn, to collect from mid-spring until midwinter. After early autumn, the leaves are more palatable if covered with a cloche or cold frame. Gather them as soon as they are usable, first by pulling up every other plant and then by picking individual leaves. Lambs lettuce suffers from no significant pests or diseases.

CRESS

Cress is a similarly robust salad that is undemanding and yields surprising numbers of leaves even in small spaces. Land cress is sown at the same time and in the same way as lambs lettuce but will be very fiery in flavour if the soil is infertile or allowed to dry. In fact, it is best when slightly shaded in summer. Protect winter crops with a cloche or fleece, or grow in tubs in an unheated glasshouse.

FROM SOWING TO HARVESTING LAMBS LETTUCE

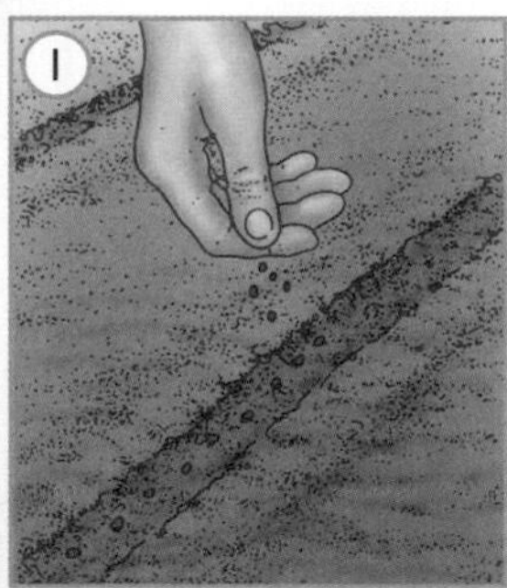

In late summer sow seeds thinly in 2cm (¾in) deep drills, which are 15cm (6in) apart.

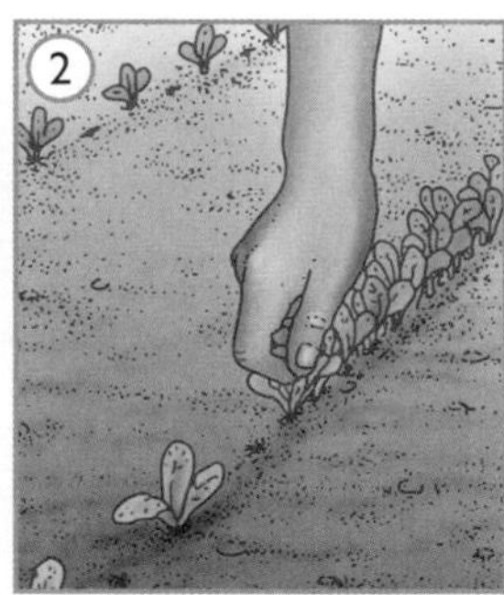

Thin the seedlings to 10cm (4in) apart. Remove weeds, and water in dry spells. Protect against frost.

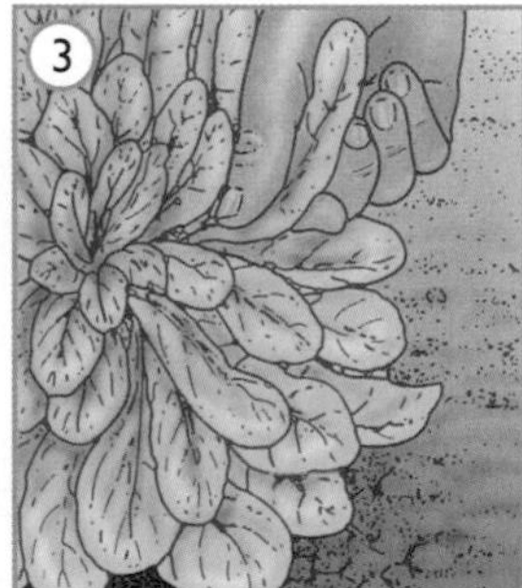

Pick the leaves as required, but never remove more than 3 leaves at a time from each plant.

• ROCKET •

Rocket is grown for its tangy, dark green leaves. A wide range is available, including wild species and crosses between different types. All are grown in the same way.

Grow in sunny, fertile, well-drained soil that is no less than pH6. Rake in growmore, at 50g per sq. m (1½oz per sq. yd), or twice as much organic fertiliser, such as chicken manure pellets. If the soil has not been improved for previous crops, use up to twice as much fertiliser if the soil is very poor.

In rows 15cm (6in) apart, make fortnightly sowings from early spring until early autumn, to crop from mid-spring until midwinter. Water in dry spells as drought stress leads to coarse textures. After early autumn, cover the leaves with a cloche or cold frame.

Flea beetles can perforate rocket foliage rendering it unappetising, so protect plants with fleece.

RECOMMENDED CULTIVARS

'Plain Rocket': peppery flavour, long, serrated, dark green leaves

'Skyrocket': as fast-growing as 'Plain Rocket', but with flavour similar to 'Wild Rocket'

'Wild Rocket': narrow, very strongly flavoured leaves

FROM PLANTING TO HARVESTING ROCKET

After watering the soil if dry and allowing it to drain, cut seed tape (see p42) into the desired length and place in a drill 1cm (½ in) deep, made with the corner of a hoe. Cover with soil and firm lightly.

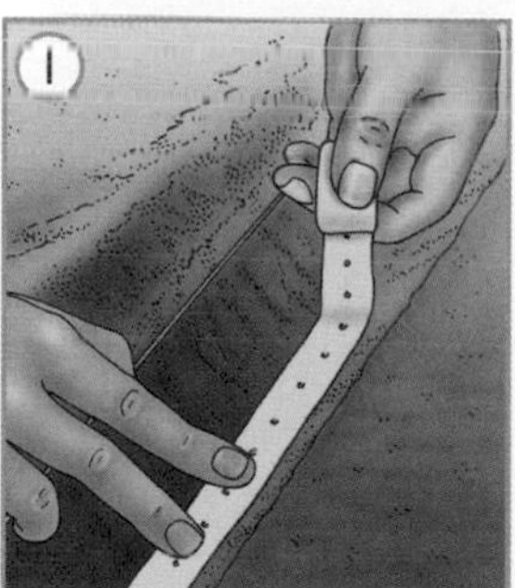

Cut or pick leaves as soon as they are large enough. Before the plant bolts (flowers), gather the whole plant. Older leaves can be too hot and coarse, so picking (and sowing) little and often is best.

• CHINESE BROCCOLI •

Chinese broccoli, sometimes called Chinese kale or kailaan, is one of the best oriental brassicas. It is grown for its flowering shoots borne on thick succulent stems, which are a bit narrower than ordinary broccoli. Its leaves are used in stir-fries and salads.

Sow in summer at monthly intervals, for gathering from late spring until winter. Late sowings may survive the winter, to flower in spring. Earlier sowings can bolt, unless raised in celltrays indoors. Plants can be grown in greenhouses for later supplies. Allow 45cm (18in) between rows and 15cm (6in) between plants.

The flower stalk is cut just before the buds open – a few open flowers do not matter – taking 10–15cm (4–6in) of stem, which can be split or sliced , then consumed. Follow-on shoots and leaves grow on to be gathered in turn, to provide a longer period of harvest, but the plants can quickly become woody, so sowing little and often is advisable. Whole young plants can also be gathered, although the waxy leaves soon become unrewarding.

Although susceptible to the usual cabbage family maladies (see p75), Chinese broccoli is easy to grow, as the plants are tough and outgrow problems.

FROM SOWING TO HARVESTING CHINESE BROCCOLI

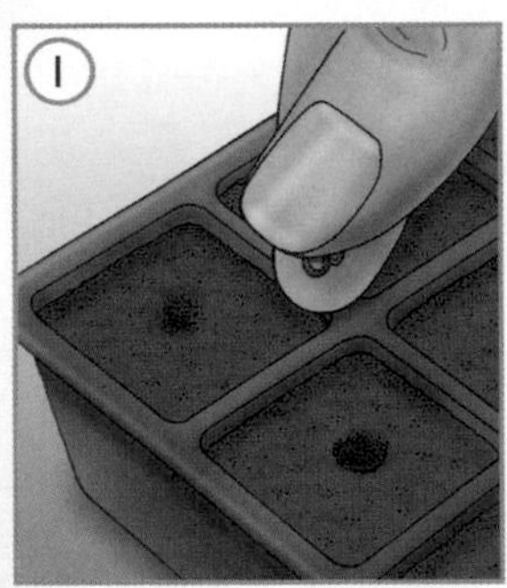

In each cell insert a seed into a shallow depression. Cover with sand or potting media, and water.

As soon as the roots bind the media in the cell firmly, water the seedling and plant in moist fertile soil.

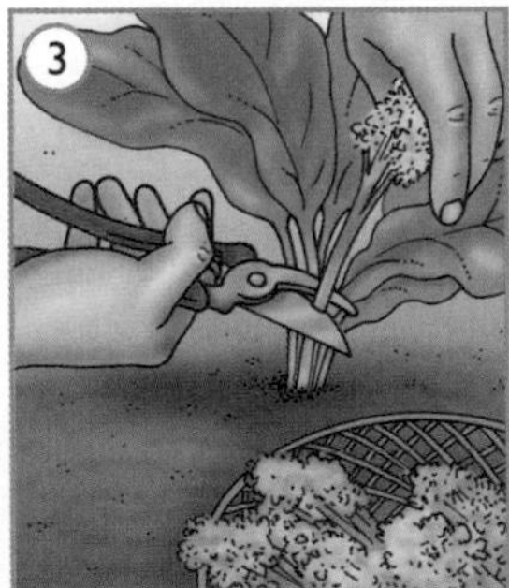

Harvest the leafy sprouts as soon as large enough to use. Eat promptly, as they quickly lose their flavour.

• PAK CHOI •

Pak choi (often called bok choi and Peking cabbage) are leafy plants of the turnip family. Their foliage is green or red, often with interesting veining; the stems can be green or white. The plants can be eaten as leaves for 'baby leaves' or whole plants can be used.

Dig in two buckets of well-rotted organic matter, such as manure, every square metre (yard) before sowing. Set rows 30cm (12in) apart, spacing plants at 25cm (10in) intervals if mature heads are being grown, and at 20cm (8in) for baby heads. Water in dry periods to avoid bolting. After about 10 weeks you can gather heads as required.

RECOMMENDED CULTIVARS

'Ivory': F1 hybrid, white-stemmed upright form, slow to bolt

'Summer Breeze': F1 hybrid, green-stemmed upright form that resists bolting in hot weather

'Yukina Savoy': rosette form, with savoy cabbage-like leaves

Pak choi is vulnerable to caterpillars, turnip sawfly, cabbage root fly, club root and flea beetles, so grow under fleece.

FROM SOWING TO HARVESTING PAK CHOI

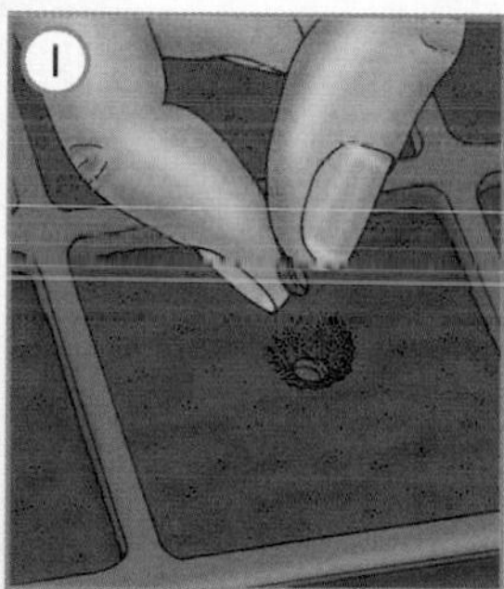

Make a shallow depression with a pencil or finger and insert 2–3 seeds. Cover and water. Thin to 1 plant.

As soon as the roots bind the media in the cell, extract each rootball intact and plant in moist fertile soil.

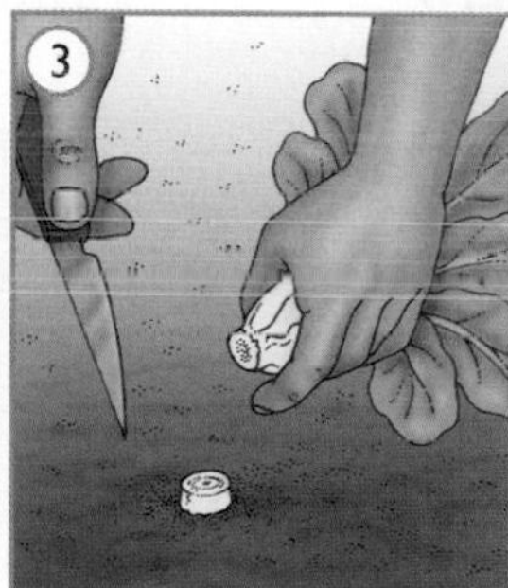

Cut the delicate, neat plants as soon as big enough to use and while still fresh and tender.

• EDAMAME BEANS •

Edamame, or soya beans, are not only the world's most important source of protein and edible oil but their immature pods are also a delicious vegetable when steamed and salted.

Prepare the soil by digging in one bucket of organic matter, such as garden compost, per square metre (yard). Before sowing, rake in growmore or other general-purpose fertiliser, at 70g per sq. m (2oz per sq. yd).

In mid-spring, raise seeds indoors at 18–25°C (64–77°F) in celltrays or 7cm (2½in) pots filled with good-quality multipurpose potting media. Plant out seedlings in early summer.

From late spring until midsummer, sow direct in the ground, 5cm (2in) deep, placing a seed every 8cm (3in), in rows 60cm (24in) apart. Cover with fleece or cloches to enhance growth.

The pods become ready for harvesting after about 12 weeks.

Edamame beans have no significant pests or diseases in the UK.

Specialist edamame beans suitable for Britain are hard to find, but robust grain types such as 'Elena' can be used as substitutes. Although not entirely satisfactory, they resist the cold and are not inhibited from flowering by the long days of British summers.

FROM SOWING TO HARVESTING EDAMAME BEANS

Place a large seed in each cell and cover and water lightly. Germinate in a warm place.

Once the roots bind the rooting media, plant in moist fertile soil. If cold, cover with fleece or cloches.

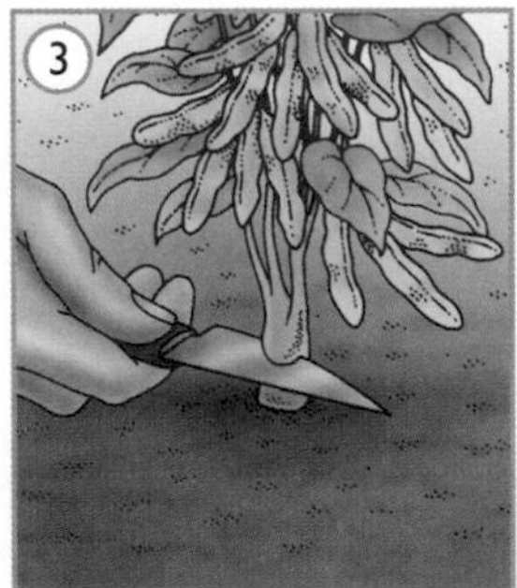

The pods reach the edible stage in a rush rather than in succession. Harvest the whole plant.

• MIZUNA GREENS & OTHER ORIENTAL LEAVES •

Mizuna greens (also kyona and Japanese greens) are one of the many mustard-like oriental greens useful, as mature plants, in oriental cuisine. They are also grown for their immature leaves used in salads. Easy to grow, they produce a high yield from a relatively small area. Early to late summer, at fortnightly intervals, are the best times to sow. In mild regions, sowings in early autumn can survive winter to provide a spring crop, especially with cloche protection.

In fertile soil, sow into drills 1cm (½in) deep, allowing a finger width between seeds, and set rows 30cm (12in) apart. Thin to 25cm (10in). Plants can also be raised in celltrays of multipurpose potting media; just cover the seeds with sieved potting media or fine vermiculite.

Ensure plants never run short of water, to prevent fiery tastes and woody textures developing.

RECOMMENDED CULTIVARS

'Leaf Radish': fast-growing; hairless foliage with white or pink stems
'Mibuna': narrow leaves
'Mustard Flaming Frills': purple serrated leaves

FROM PLANTING TO HARVESTING MIZUNA GREENS

Water dry soils before sowing thinly in a shallow drill, about a finger width deep, and cover with soil lightly pressed down with the back of the rake.

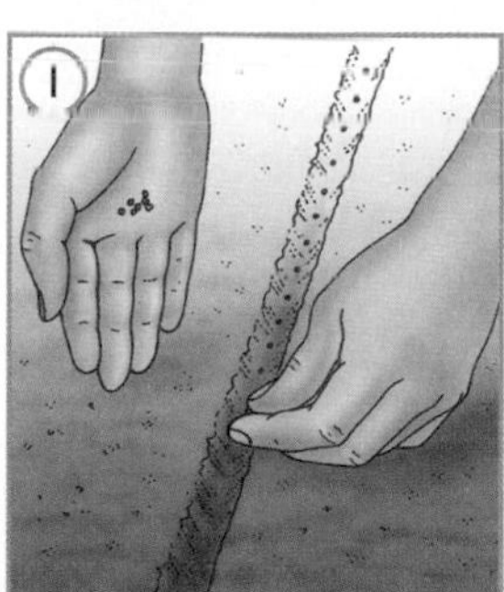

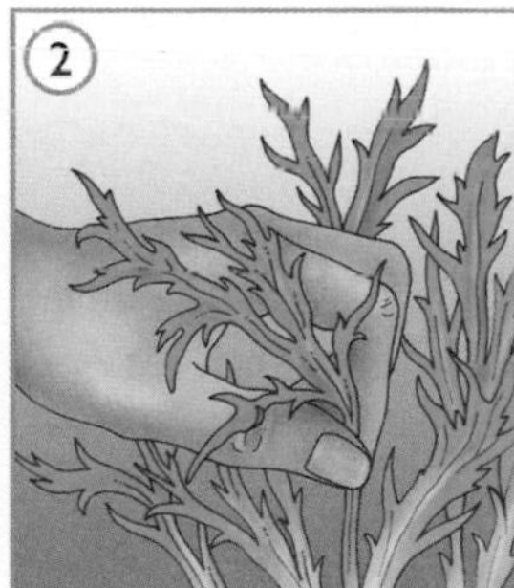

Gather leaves as soon as usable. These fast-growing leaves make good baby leaf salads as well as a nutritious green vegetable later, with good regrowth after cutting.

• TOMATILLOS •

This tomato relative is tender but more robust and easier to grow than tomatoes. Its green, yellow and purple fruits are attractive, too. Purple-fruited tomatillos are handsome plants for growing in patio containers. To achieve good pollination, grow at least two plants.

Plants should crop heavily in southern regions outdoors in a sunny site and soil fortified with a bucket of well-rotted manure every square metre (yard), plus a general-purpose balanced fertiliser, at 100g per sq. m (3oz per sq. yd).

In mid-spring, sow seeds a finger's width apart on the surface of firmed potting compost in shallow trays or pans. Seeds should germinate within 14 days if kept at a temperature of 18–25°C (64–77°F).

Pot on the young seedlings into individual 7–9cm (2½–3½in) pots filled with good-quality multipurpose potting media. Keep them moist – never soggy – and feed with liquid fertiliser once roots appear from the bottom of the pot. Allow 60cm (24in) between each plant, with 1m (3ft) between rows, and stake to avoid wind damage, as they can easily be 1m (3ft) or more high.

Tomatillos are not susceptible to potato blight, which seriously damages tomato plants.

FROM SOWING TO HARVESTING TOMATILLOS

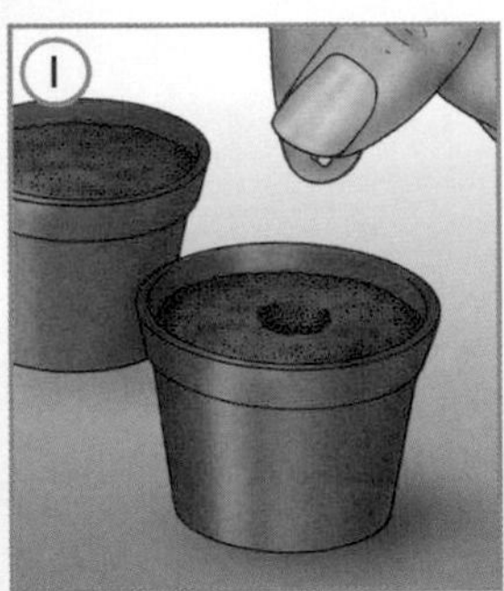

Sow in multipurpose potting media. Lightly cover with vermiculite or sieved compost, then water.

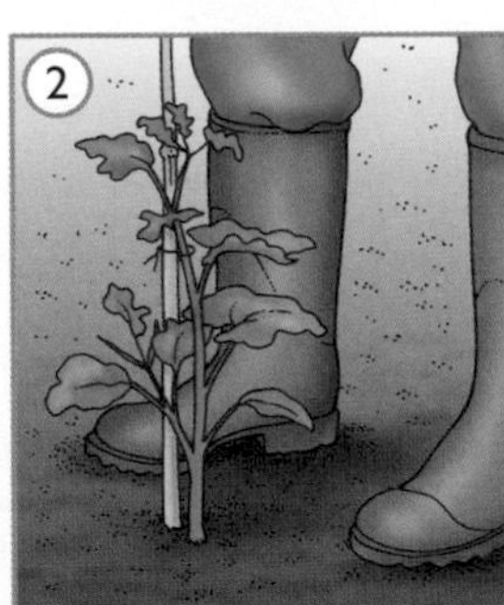

Using string in a figure-of-eight knot, tie each plant to a stake immediately after planting out.

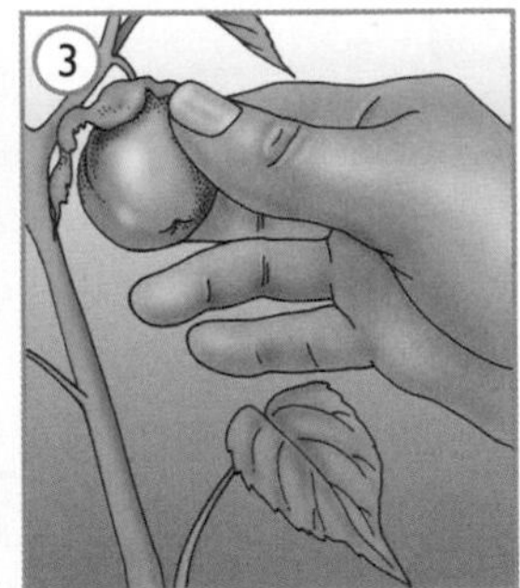

For the best flavour, gather fruits when they begin to change from green to yellow or purple.

• FLORENCE FENNEL •

Although a perennial, Florence fennel is grown as an annual for its crisp, aromatic, aniseed-flavoured bulbous stem base, which is used in salads or cooked in similar ways to celery. It needs to grow fast to avoid bolting.

In a sheltered but sunny site, dig in two buckets of organic matter per square metre (yard). Before sowing, rake in growmore, at 100g per sq. m (3oz per sq. yd), or use twice as much organic fertiliser, such as chicken manure pellets. If organic matter is not available, increase the fertiliser by half.

In midsummer, sow 1cm (½in) deep, allowing a thumb's width between seeds, and set rows 45cm (18in) apart, thinning to 30cm (12in) between plants. Alternatively, sow in celltrays and plant out immediately the roots bind the potting media. Use bolt resistant cultivars for earlier and later crops.

Keep plants weed-free and moist. Later crops benefit from cloche or fleece protection to enhance late season growth and shield from the cold. Bulbs can be cut as soon as they are big enough. Florence fennel suffers from no significant pests or diseases.

RECOMMENDED CULTIVARS

'Victorio': F1 hybrid, fast-growing and reliable with good bolting resistance

'Zefa Fino': fast-growing and good-quality bulbs

EARTHING UP FLORENCE FENNEL

The whitest bulbs come from drawing soil up around each swelling bulb. This also excludes some frost, extending the cropping period.

HERB DIRECTORY

• INTRODUCTION •

Herbs are the most useful part of any vegetable garden in terms of value for the area occupied. Bought herbs cannot match the freshness of home-grown ones. However, in winter, home-grown herbs are harder to provide, even if grown in greenhouses, and in any case flavour falls off as light levels dip. Since herbs crop abundantly, drying and freezing the summer surplus, just before they flower, are worthwhile.

Herbs are also some of the easiest plants to grow. Seeds tend to be inexpensive, and it is easy to save your own. Cuttings are usually easy to grow, and often are donated by other gardeners and neighbours.

Herbs make brilliant patio plants, whether in well-drained pots, troughs, raised beds or well-drained borders, where the warmth and light give a scented Mediterranean feel to your garden, and, in fact, these are the ideal growing conditions. Their robustness and reduced need for water mean herbs are low-maintenance.

There are an astonishing variety of herbs. In this book, only the most popular dozen or so can be covered but the catalogues and websites of seedsmen and herb nurseries offer great potential for building up a collection of fragrant, tasty plants, even if space is short.

Herbs are good subjects for gravel gardens, as they relish the dry soil and freedom from soil splash in rainy weather. Clay soils are not well suited to many herbs but raised beds will provide the sharp drainage needed. Shady gardens, too, will not raise good herbs, but a few like chives and mint will be fairly successful.

Some herbs, such as basil, coriander, dill and parsley, can be grown in rows in the vegetable plot, often as catch crops and intercrops (see pp24–25). They are easily raised from cheap seeds, and early crops can be produced from sowings in celltrays or pots indoors. Several sowings may be necessary for a continuous supply, but short, 1.5m (5ft) rows will prove sufficient. Not only can seeds be saved for sowing but some seeds – coriander seed, for example – can be used in cooking.

Herbs seldom need a rich soil, but a bucketful of well-rotted organic matter, such as garden compost, per square metre (yard) before planting will ensure good soil structure. Add composted bark to heavy soils. Lime to a pH of about 6.5 where soils are on the acid

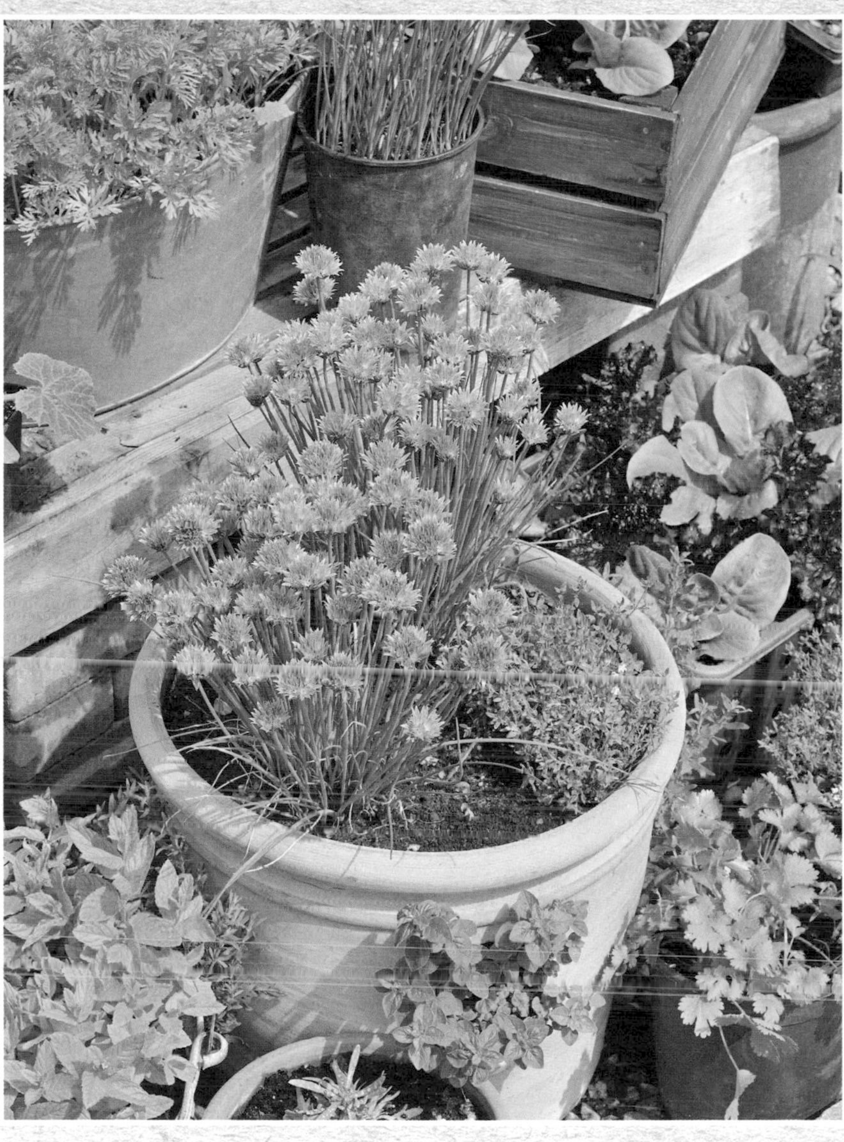

side (see p19). Rake in potassium-rich fertiliser, such as rose fertiliser, at 35g per sq. m (1oz per sq. yd).

Artfully arranged containers of herbs are appealing. On sunny days, they are fragrant, too.

Once planted, it is hard to clean up beds of perennial herbs, so the plot should be rid of perennial weeds such as bindweed before you start. Achieve this by leaving a summer fallow period, when any weeds can be dug out or treated with a glyphosate-based weedkiller. Covering the site with a black plastic sheet for a growing season is an easy way to clear soil of perennial weeds.

After planting, herbs will need watering until they are well established.

Herbs are usually free of pests, but any that occur are best dealt with by insecticides that leave no residues, such as ones based on fatty acids, oils or natural pyrethrum. Diseases can usually be checked by the prompt removal of affected foliage, but don't add it to the compost heap.

MAKING A HERB WHEEL

Mark a circle with pegs and string to the traditional size for a herb wheel, 0.6–1.2m (2–4ft) across. However, you can tailor the size and sections, or even the shape, to suit your own needs.

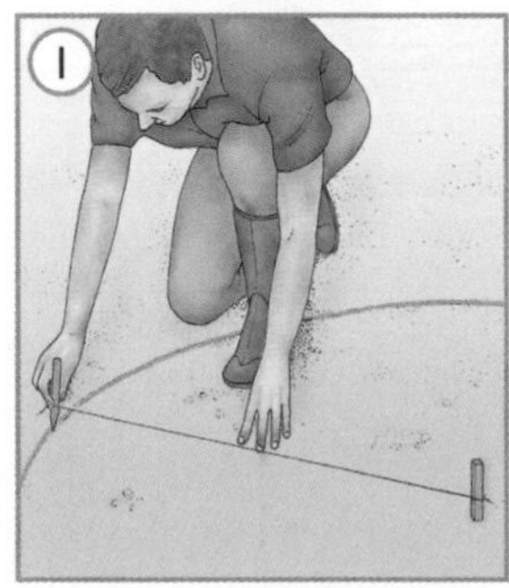

Dig out the circle to a depth of half a brick's length. Place the bricks on end around the edge. This forms a slightly raised bed, which provides the warmer and better-drained conditions that herbs enjoy.

Divide the bed into sections with double courses of bricks. Aim for no more than 6 divisions or the spaces will become fiddly. A ceramic pipe makes an ideal centre. Mortar the bricks and let set for a day.

Fill the sections with soil. Adjust the soil in each section to suit the herbs, but match your plants for size and vigour if the wheel is to look good. Line the mint section with weed-proof membrane to constrain the mint roots.

CHIVES

Chives (*Allium schoenoprasum*) are a mild-flavoured member of the onion family, which can be used instead of spring onions in salads, as well as replacing onions in many dishes. Chives can be bought potted or raised from seed. Alternatively, persuade a friend to split their clump in early spring to provide tufts of foliage with a few shoots and some roots. These are planted 15cm (6in) apart, in rows 25cm (10in) apart, in any fertile garden soil in full sun or light shade. Harvest foliage by cutting it at ground level. Lift and split plants when they become overcrowded.

DILL

Dill (*Anethum graveolens*), is a tall, 60cm (24in) annual member of the carrot family. Every four weeks from early spring to late summer, sow seeds 1cm (½in) deep, allowing a finger width between them, in rows 30cm (12in) apart, in sunny, well-drained soil. Thin plants to 15cm (6in). Plants can be used as soon as big enough until they form seeds.

FRENCH TARRAGON

French tarragon (*Artemisia dracunculus*) has a warm, aniseed-like flavour that is prized by cooks. This perennial grows to 1m (3ft) high and 50cm (20in) wide. It can be propagated only by division. To divide, lift the plant in spring and tease the roots out, selecting small leafy pieces and potting these up in any good multipurpose compost. French tarragon can continue to grow in containers or be planted into well-drained open ground, with 45cm (18in) between plants. Although hardy, it can suffer in cold wet weather, and potted ones benefit from a protective cloche in winter.

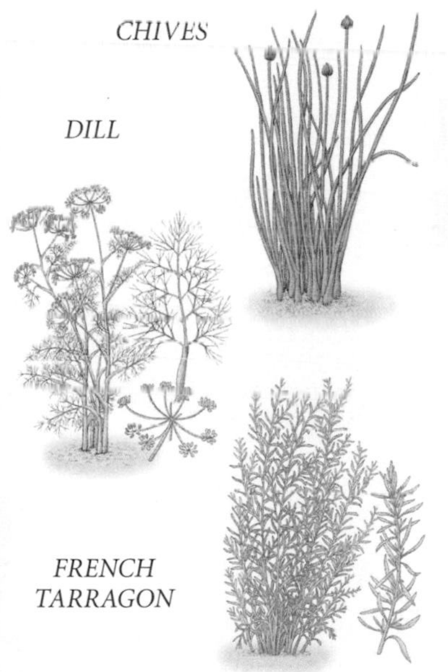

CORIANDER

Coriander (*Coriandrum sativum*) is a fast-growing annual reaching 60cm (24in) tall. It is grown from seeds sown every four weeks from early spring to late summer. Any sunny, well-drained soil is satisfactory. Sow seeds 1cm (½in) deep allowing a finger width between them, and in rows 30cm (12in) apart, thinning plants to 15cm (6in) gradually. Some especially leafy cultivars are available, including the slower-to-flower 'Santos' and 'Confetti'.

FENNEL

FENNEL

Fennel (*Foeniculum vulgare*) is a hardy perennial, reaching 1.5m (5ft) high and spreading 60cm (24in) in sunny, well-drained soil. Sow seeds 1cm (½in) deep, allowing a finger width between them, in rows 30cm (12in) apart, thinning plants to 15cm (6in) gradually.

CORIANDER

BAY

MINT

BAY

Bay (*Laurus nobilis*) is an evergreen tree. For herb use, it is restricted by frequent clipping and, often, container cultivation in a good potting medium. Propagate from semiripe cuttings. The flavour of dried leaves is less coarse. In cold winters, wrap plants in fleece.

MINT

Mints come in many forms, but the garden mint, or spearmint (*Mentha spicata*), is the essential one. It is a hardy perennial, 50cm (20in) high, spreading widely by its invasive roots. Curtail these by growing in pots or in bottomless containers in the garden. Grow in sunny, fertile sites that are not too prone to drought. In summer, cut back the foliage to promote fresh shoots.

BASIL

Basil (*Ocimum basilicum*) is a tender annual, growing 30cm (12in) high from seed sown indoors, ideally in celltrays, three to four seeds per cell, filled with multipurpose potting medium. Sow from early spring, and outdoors in early summer, singling seedlings as soon as they can be handled. Plant out in full sun after the risk of frost has passed in fertile garden soil or in containers. Leaves are gathered as required, and constant cutting will prevent flowering. 'Genovese' is the traditional richly flavoured Italian type of basil.

MARJORAM

Sweet marjoram (*Origanum majorana*) is a half-hardy perennial, which will persist from year to year in mild areas.

BASIL

MARJORAM

Grow from seed in sunny well-drained soil or potting media. Sow seed in celltrays and plant out in late spring. Cut back plants when they flower.

ROSEMARY

PARSLEY

Parsley (*Petroselinum crispum*) is a hardy biennial, sown from mid-spring and again in early and late summer for year-long supplies. Winter parsley comes from plants protected with cloches or potted and taken indoors. Sow seed 1cm (½in) deep, allowing a finger width between seeds, and in rows 30cm (12in) apart, thinning plants to 15cm (6in) gradually, using thinnings for the kitchen. Germination may take several weeks. Raising plants in celltrays is also possible. Many cultivars are offered but, in truth, there is little difference between them, except some have flat leaves, some curly. The former are said to be better flavoured.

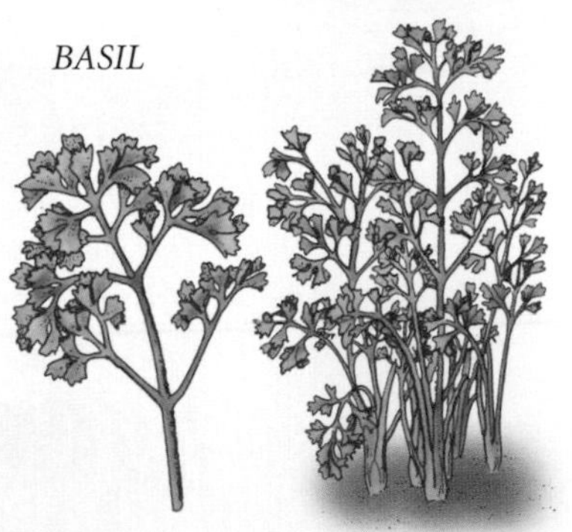

BASIL

SAGE

ROSEMARY

Rosemary (*Rosmarinus officinalis*) is an evergreen shrub that grows up to 1.5m (5ft) tall and is best raised from semiripe cuttings. It needs full sun and is not reliably hardy in very cold regions, unless grown in a sheltered site. A light prune in spring induces tender shoots and keeps the plant within bounds, prolonging its useful life.

SAGE

Sage (*Salvia officinalis*) is an evergreen subshrub, 60cm (24in) tall and best raised from semiripe cuttings, although seeds can be used. It needs full sun and is not reliably hardy in very cold regions. Cuttings taken in late summer and kept indoors are a useful insurance. Collect leaves as required in summer.

SUMMER SAVORY

Summer savory (*Satureja hortensis*) is a perennial best raised from seeds sown in pots in late spring. Pot on the seedlings and plant out when the roots bind the potting medium. Any well-drained sunny site will suit them. Two or three plants should be ample.

THYME

Thyme (*Thymus vulgaris*), a low-growing shrub, 45cm (18in) high and wide, is easily propagated from seeds sown in pots in spring, with the seedlings set out into individual pots as soon as they can be handled. Cuttings taken in summer are also effective. Thyme needs a well-drained soil or potting medium in a sunny, sheltered spot. Harvest leaves as required all year.

SUMMER SAVORY

THYME

• SOWING GUIDE •

Crop	Spring			Summer			Autumn			Winter		
	EARLY	MID	LATE	EARLY	MID	LATE	EARLY	MID	LATE	EARLY	MID	LATE
						VEGETABLES						
Artichokes, globe	S	P	H	H	H	H						
Artichokes, Jerusalem	P							H	H	H P	H P	H P
Artichokes, Chinese	P	P						H	H	H	H	H
Asparagus	S	P	H	H P	Sow in spring, plant in early summer, or as crowns in early spring harvest begins two years later							
Aubergines (greenhouse)	SI	P	P	P		H	H	H				S
Aubergines (cloches or fleece)	SI			P			H	H				
Beetroot (early)	SI		P	H	H	H	H					
Beetroot (maincrop)		S			H	H	H	H	H	H	S T	S T
Broccoli, Cape	H	H	H S	S P	P	P						
Broccoli, Chinese			S	S H	S H	S H	H	H	H	H		
Broccoli, sprouting	H	H	H S	S P	P	P						
Broad beans	S	S	S P	H	H	H				S		SI
Brussels sprouts	S		P			H	H	H	H	H	H	H SI
Cabbages, autumn		S	P	P			H	H	H			
Cabbages, Chinese				S	S	S H	H	H	S T	S T		
Cabbages, red	S	S	P	P		H	H	H	H	H	S T	S T
Cabbages, savoy	H S	S	S	P	P	H	H	H	H	H	H	H
Cabbages, spring	H	H	H	H	S	S	P	P				H
Cabbages, summer	S	P	P	H	H	H						SI
Cabbages, winter	H		S	P	P					H	H	H
Calabrese	S	S P	S P	S P	S P	P H	H	H	H	H		SI
Carrots	S	S	S	S H	S H	H	H	H	S T	S T	S T	S* S T
Cauliflowers (annual)	S	S P	S P	S P	S P	P H	H	H	H	H	H	H SI
Cauliflowers (biennial)	H	H	S H	S H	P	P						

KEY H = Harvest P = Plant S = Sow S* = Sow under cloches or fleece SI = Sow indoors T = Transplant TC = Take cuttings

Crop	Spring			Summer			Autumn			Winter		
Celeriac	S	S		P			H	H	H	H	S T	S T
Celery	S	S		P		H	H	H	H	H	H	SI
	EARLY	MID	LATE	EARLY	MID	LATE	EARLY	MID	LATE	EARLY	MID	LATE
Chard		S H	H	H	H	S H	H	H	H	H		
Chicory, witloof	H	S	S	S				H	H	H	H	H
Chicory, leaf					S	S	H	H	H	H	H	
Courgettes		S	S	S P	S P H	H	H					
Cucumbers (under glass)	S	P	P		H	H	H	H	H			S
Cucumbers, inc. gherkins (outdoor)		S	S	S P	S P H	H C						
Edamame		S		P		H	H	H				
Endives				S	S P	S P	H	H	H	H		
Fennel, Florence				S	S P	S P	H	H	H	H		
French beans, climbing (early)		SI		S P		H	H					
French beans, climbing (maincrop)			S			H	H	H				
French beans, dwarf (early)		SI		S P	H	H	H					
French beans, dwarf (maincrop)		S	S	S P	S H	H	H	H				
Kale	H	H	S		P		H	H	H	H	H	H
Kohlrabi	S	S P	S P	S P H	S P H	P H	H	H	H	H		SI
Leaf beets		S H	H	H	H	S H	H	H	H	H		
Leeks	S H	S	P	P	P	P	H	H	H	H	H	SI H
Lettuces (indoors)	P H	H	H				SI	SI P	P H	H		SI
Lettuces (outdoors)	S	S P	S P H	S P H	S P H	S P H	S H	H	H	H		SI
Marrows		S	S	S P	S P	H	H	H	S T	S T	S T	
Mizuna and oriental leaves		S	S	S H	S H	S H	H	H	H	H	H	

KEY H = Harvest P = Plant S = Sow S* = Sow under cloches or fleece SI = Sow indoors T = Transplant TC = Take cuttings

Crop	Spring			Summer			Autumn			Winter		
Onions, bulb	S T P	S T P	S T P	P		H	H	H	H	S T	S T	S T
	EARLY	MID	LATE	EARLY	MID	LATE	EARLY	MID	LATE	EARLY	MID	LATE
Onions, bulb (overwintered)				H	H	S T	S T	S T	S T			
Onions, salad	S H	S H	S H	S H	H	S H	H	H				SI
Onions sets	S T P	P		H	H	H	P H	H	S T	S T	S T	S T
Pak choi			S	S H	S H	S H	H	H	H	H		
Peppers (indoors)	SI	P	P	P		H	H	H				SI
Peppers (under cloche or fleece)	SI			P			H	H				
Parsley, Hamburg		S					H	H	H	H	H	H
Parsnips	S H	S				H	H	H	H	H	H	S H
Peas	S	S	S	S H	H	H	H					S*
Potatoes	S P	P			H	H	H	H	S T	S T	S T	S T
Potatoes, sweet				P		H	H	S T				
Pumpkins		S	S	S P	S P	H	H	H	S T	S T	S T	
Radishes (maincrop)	S	S	S H	S H	S H	S H	S H	H				S*
Radishes, winter					S	S	H	H	H	S T	S T	S T
Rocket	S	S	S H	S H	S H	S H	S H	H				S*
Runner beans		SI	S	S P	S H	H	H	H				
Salsify & scorzonera	H	S						H	H	H	H	H

KEY H = Harvest P = Plant S = Sow S* = Sow under cloches or fleece SI = Sow indoors T = Transplant TC = Take cuttings

Crop	Spring			Summer			Autumn			Winter		
Shallots	P (sets) S T	S T	S T	S T	H	H	S T	S T	S T	P (sets) S T	P (sets) S T	P (sets) S T
	EARLY	MID	LATE	EARLY	MID	LATE	EARLY	MID	LATE	EARLY	MID	LATE
Spinach		S H	S H	S H	S H	H	S H	H				
Squashes	S T	S	S	S P	S P	H	H	H	S T	S T	S T	S T
Swedes	H S T		S	S P	P		H	H	H	H	H S T	H S T
Sweet corn		S	S P	S P		H	H					
Tomatillos	S	S		P		H	H	H				
Tomatoes (indoors)	SI	P	P	P	H	H	H	H				SI
Tomatoes (outdoors)	SI			P		H	H	H				
Turnips	S	S	S	S H	S H	S H	H	H	H	H	S T	S*
HERBS												
Basil	SI	SI	S	S	S H	H	H	H				
Bay	P H	H	H	H	H	H	TC H	P H	P H	P H	P H	H
Chives	SI P	S P	P	H	H	H	H	S H				P
Coriander	SI	SI	S	S H	S H	S H	H	H				
Dill	SI	S P	S P	S P H	S H	S H	H	H				
Fennel	SI	S P	P H	P H	H	S H	H					
French tarragon	P	P		H	H	H	H	H				
Marjoram	SI	S	P	P H	S H	S H	H					

KEY H = Harvest P = Plant S = Sow S* = Sow under cloches or fleece SI = Sow indoors T = Transplant TC = Take cuttings

Crop	Spring			Summer			Autumn			Winter		
Mint	P		H	H	H	S H	H		P	P	P	P
	EARLY	MID	LATE	EARLY	MID	LATE	EARLY	MID	LATE	EARLY	MID	LATE
Parsley	S	S	S P H	P H	S H	S P H	P H	H	H	H		
Rosemary	SI P H	H	H	H	H	TC H	S TC H	P H	P H	P H	P H	P H
Sage	SI P H	S H	H	H	H	S TC H	TC H	P H	P H	P H	P H	P H
Summer savory	SI	S P	S P	P H	P H	H	H					SI
Thyme	SI P H	S H	H	H	H	TC H	S TC H	P H	P H	P H	P H	H

KEY H = Harvest P = Plant S = Sow S* = Sow under cloches or fleece SI = Sow indoors T = Transplant TC = Take cuttings

• GLOSSARY •

Allium Onion family, including leeks and garlic.

Base dressing Fertiliser applied before sowing and planting.

Blanching Practice of excluding light from vegetables – endive and celery, for example – to make them more palatable, paler, more tender and mild-flavoured.

Buffering Ability to absorb changes especially in acidity and nutrient levels, commonly found in soils.

Catch crop Crops grown on areas temporarily unoccupied before, after or between other longer-term crops.

Celltray Modular tray, each cell being a mini-pot in which plant(s) are grown.

Chitting Sprouting where shoots arise on seed potatoes and other tubers and where seeds sprout root tips.

Compost May be organic matter for feeding the soil (see Garden compost) or special growing media for use in pots.

Cultivate Any action to break up soil, but specifically using a pronged cultivator.

Dibber Sharp stake like hand-size tool for planting.

Drill Groove in soil in which seed is placed.

Earth up Draw soil into ridges around potatoes to exclude light or around other crops to steady them against wind.

Gap up Replace plant losses after thinning or planting.

Garden compost Composted garden waste, not suitable for potting.

Geotextile Very strong synthetic fabric sold in builders' merchants that filters out fine particles but allows water to pass through and is used to reinforce and protect areas such as paths from soil creeping in.

Green manure Plants grown to be dug into the soil to control fertility.

Hill/Hilling see Ridge.

Hoe Slice off weeds and uproot them with a hoe (blade mounted on a handle).

Intercrop Plants grown in temporarily vacant areas between other, slower-growing crops.

Leafmould Leaves of trees stacked and allowed to rot without any additional materials, resulting in an especially high-quality, low-nutrient form of organic matter that is ideal for use in home-made potting media or for improving the soil.

Liquid feed Fertiliser applied as liquid.

Legume Plants of the pea and bean family that can get some or all of their nitrogen needs from bacteria associated with their roots.

Manuring Adding nutrients and especially bulky organic matter to increase soil fertility.

Module see Celltray.

Mulch Cover soil around plants with organic matter or opaque sheets, to limit water loss and reduce weeds.

Organic Form of cultivation where the soil is managed and improved to support plant growth, as opposed to feeding plants with fertilisers. Pests, diseases and weeds are controlled by gardening practices (husbandry) rather than by intervention with pesticides, especially synthetic ones. Also a gardening method based on natural processes and also applied to materials not of synthetic origin.

Organic matter Bulky, well-rotted soil improvers such as manure, garden compost or leafmould.

Pan Hard, impermeable layer in the soil profile that often hinders drainage and root growth. May arise naturally or, more commonly, by repeated rotary cultivation to the same depth.

Peat-free Potting compost free of peat and, therefore, environmentally beneficial.

Peds Small lumps of soil formed when the soil fractures naturally.

Pesticide Material used to control insects (insecticide), slugs (molluscide), weeds (herbicide) or disease (fungicide).

Photosynthesis Chemical process within the leaves of green plants that uses light to power the synthesis of organic materials from water and carbon dioxide, to provide energy for plant activity, including growth.

Potting compost Growing medium with nutrients and structure optimised for plants in pots and trays.

Potting media see Potting compost.

Pre-germinated seed Seeds germinated on wet absorbent paper under ideal conditions, or by other means, before being sown in less hospitable soil.

Pricking out Moving seedlings from seedtray or pot to individual cells, pots or into seedtrays.

Primed seed Seeds allowed to take up water under controlled conditions to the point where they are about to germinate. More rapid and more even germination follows after sowing.

Puddle Water to saturate the soil.

Rhizome Specialised stem that lies on the soil surface or is buried and has the ability to send up shoots, roots and stems along its length, especially if broken. Often encountered in noxious weeds such as couch grass.

Ridge Dig into raised ridges (called hills in America) to improve drainage.

Rotation Sequence of cropping to control disease and fertility.

Seedbed Finely tilled soil made perfectly level so that seeds can be sown at the appropriate depth.

Seed tape Tape in which seeds are embedded at exact intervals. The tape dissolves, seeds germinate and the resulting plants need no further thinning out.

Set Bulb or other small piece of plant used to propagate crops.

Soil profile The layers of soil exposed when a soil inspection pit is dug.

Spit Depth of the spade blade.

Stale seedbed Seedbed left to grow weeds, which are removed before sowing so that subsequently fewer weeds arise.

Station sowing Sowing several seeds where one plant is finally allowed to grow.

Stomata Pores in leaves and stems that allow carbon dioxide and water vapour to be exchanged with the outside atmosphere and which are controlled by the plant to limit water loss.

Subsoil Lower layer of soil found below topsoil and much less rich in nutrients, organic matter and living organisms. If loosely structured and well drained, it can be explored by plant roots.

Thin Remove surplus plants.

Till Break up soil and make it level.

Tilth Even layer of well-broken crumbs of soil, ideal for germination.

Topdressing Adding extra fertiliser during the growing season to maintain growth.

Topsoil The dark, fertile upper layer of soil containing most organic matter, living organisms and nutrients, crucial to good plant growth.

Transpiration Water loss from plant tissues, especially via the stomata.

Transplant Move plants from seedbed, trays or pots into the open soil, or a plant suitable for transplanting.

Trench Area excavated so that organic matter can be lavishly placed beneath where crops are intended to grow. Also a very deep digging method.

• INDEX •

• PICTURE CREDITS •

Note The acknowledgements below appear in source order.

Alamy Anne Gilbert 132; John Glover 25, 43; Rob Walls 32

FLPA Nigel Cattlin 20 left

Fotolia Barbara Helgason 8

GAP Photos BIOS/Gilles Le Scanff and Joëlle-Caroline Mayer 112; Christina Bollen 2; Heather Edwards 108; Jenny Lilly 99; Jo Whitworth 90; Mark Bolton 95; Maxine Adcock 131; Pernilla Bergdahl 129

Garden World Images Anne Green-Armytage 46–7; Dave Bevan 35 above, 67; David Rose 147; Deni Bown 155; Gary Smith 10–11, 35 below, 64–5, 107, 150, 156 below, 173; Gilles Delacroix 170–1; Jacqui Dracup 52; John Swithinbank 30, 82, 156 above; Leonie Lambert 54; MAP/Arnaud Descat 72, /Noun 7; Martin Hughes-Jones 9, 78, 126; Mein Schöner Garten 28–9; Nicholas Appleby 103; Rita Coates 81; Rowan Isaac 86; Trevor Sims 16

Photolibrary AFLO RF/Toshihiko Watanabe 144; Garden Picture Library/Andrea Jones 13, /Anne Green-Armytage 104, /Christopher Fairweather 85

RHS Tim Sandall/The Garden 20 centre and right